AF292456

MICHELANGELO

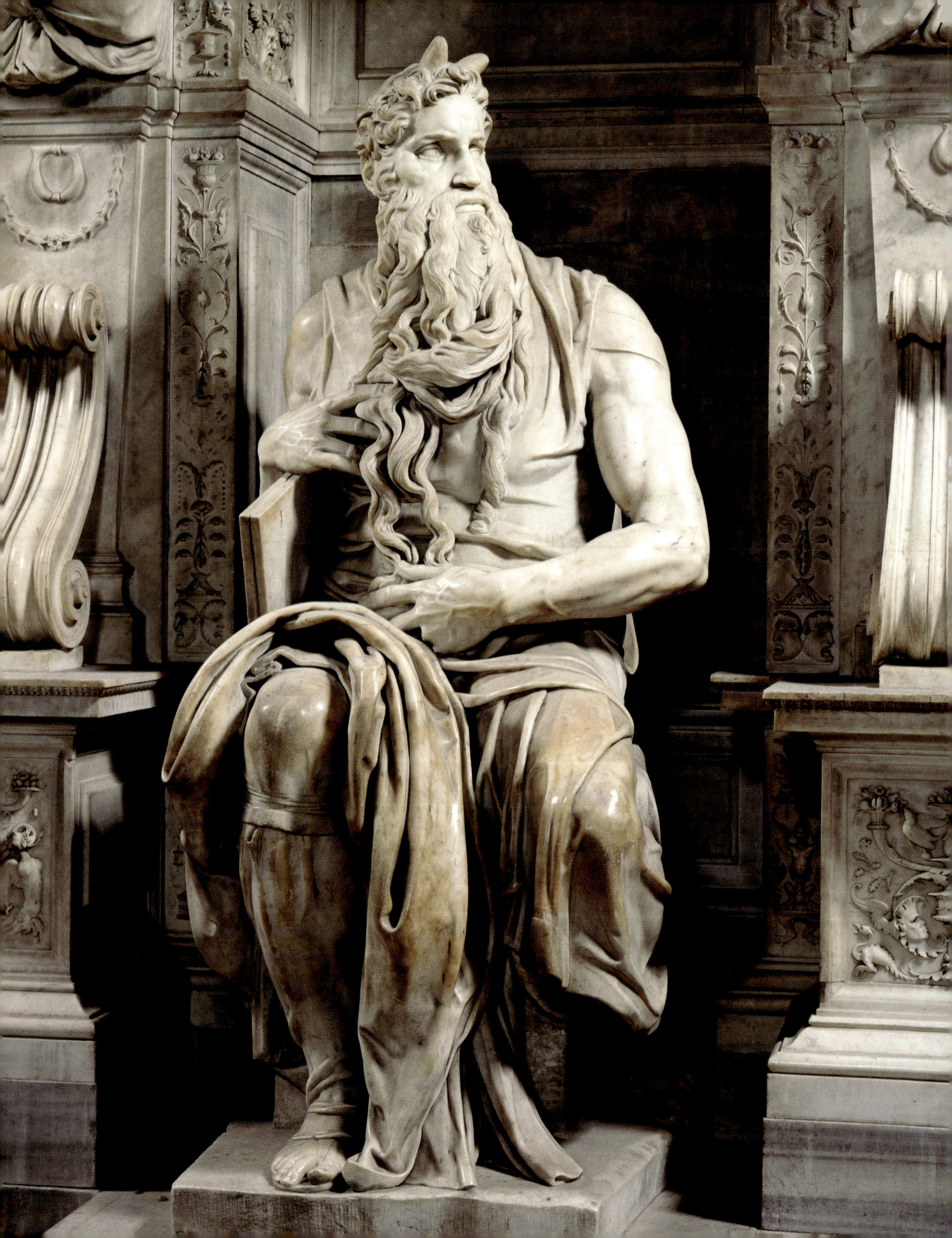

ART **MASTERS**

MICHELANGELO

SUSIE HODGE

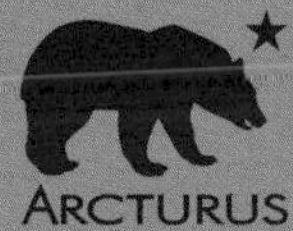

ARCTURUS

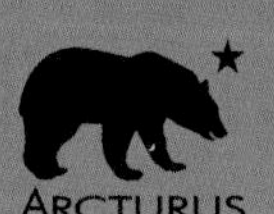

This edition published in 2024 by Arcturus Publishing Limited
26/27 Bickels Yard, 151–153 Bermondsey Street,
London SE1 3HA

ISBN: 978-1-3988-5041-5
AD007296UK

Printed in China

CONTENTS

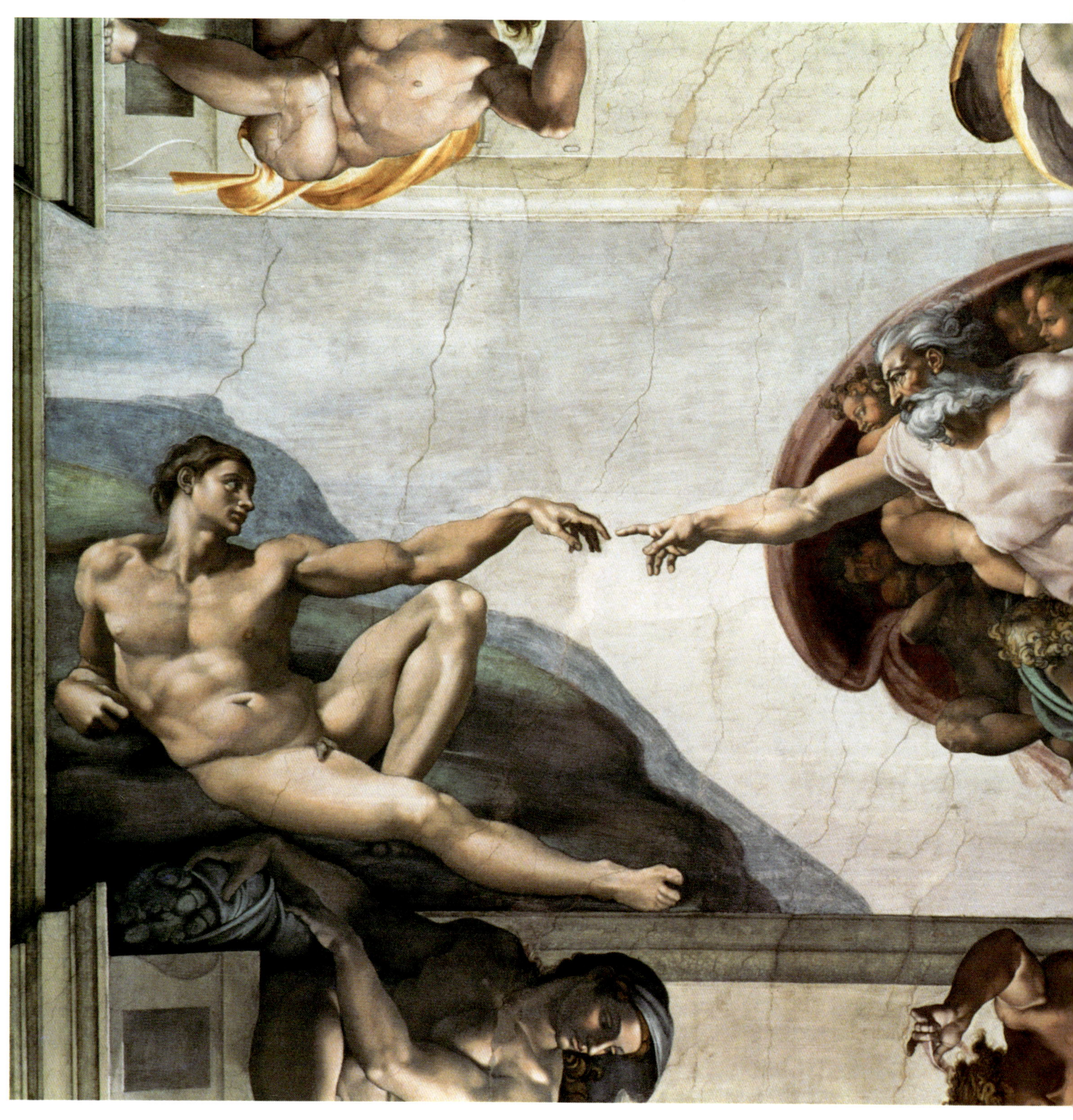

The Creation of Adam, 1511–12. Part of Michelangelo's vast Sistine Chapel ceiling, this depicts a story from the Old Testament Book of Genesis, when God creates Adam, the first man. It was the first time that God had been portrayed as a simple, elderly man rather than an imposing figure. Their hands that almost touch convey a sense of tension and dynamism as God creates human life. This image was revolutionary when first revealed and remains iconic to this day.

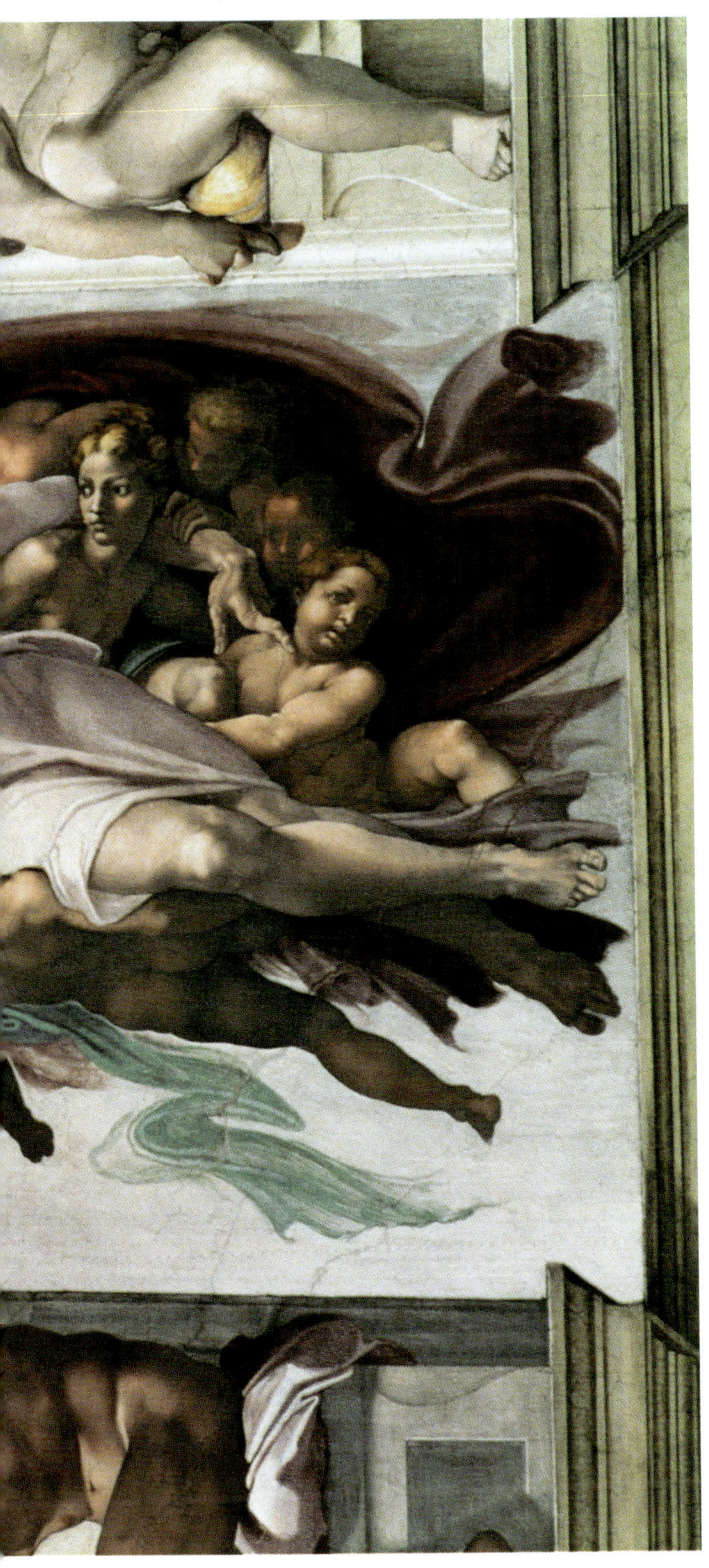

INTRODUCTION

One of the most celebrated figures of the Italian Renaissance, and considered by many to be the greatest artist of all time, Michelangelo di Lodovico Buonarroti Simoni (1475–1564) was a sculptor, painter, architect and poet. In recognition of his outstanding skills, he was often called *Il Divino* (the Divine One) during his lifetime, and he has exerted a huge influence on the development of Western art ever since. Born in the Republic of Florence during a period now known as the High Renaissance, Michelangelo produced some of the most famous works of art in the world, including the marble sculptures of the *Pietà* in Rome and *David* in Florence, and the Sistine Chapel frescoes. At the age of 74, he succeeded Antonio da Sangallo the Younger (1484–1546) as the chief architect of St Peter's Basilica. As a poet, he was influenced strongly by Dante Alighieri (*c.* 1265–1321) and over 300 of his poems survive, along with many letters he wrote to his family, friends and patrons, as well as sketches for his artworks. All are revealing – about himself, his life and his work. In 1506, when he was only 31, the Florentine government described him to the Pope as 'an excellent young man and in his profession unequalled in Italy, perhaps in the whole world'. Two biographies about him were written while he was alive, making him the first artist of the Western world to have a biography published during his lifetime. Ascanio Condivi (1525–74) wrote *The Life of Michelangelo Buonarroti*, published in 1553. Giorgio Vasari (1511–74) wrote *The Lives of the Most Eminent Painters, Sculptors and Architects*, published in 1550 and updated in 1568. Vasari stated that Michelangelo's work transcended that of any artist either living or dead, and he was 'supreme in not one art alone but in all three'. In that respect, Michelangelo was a true Renaissance man and his life, work and fame transformed forever our idea of what an artist can be.

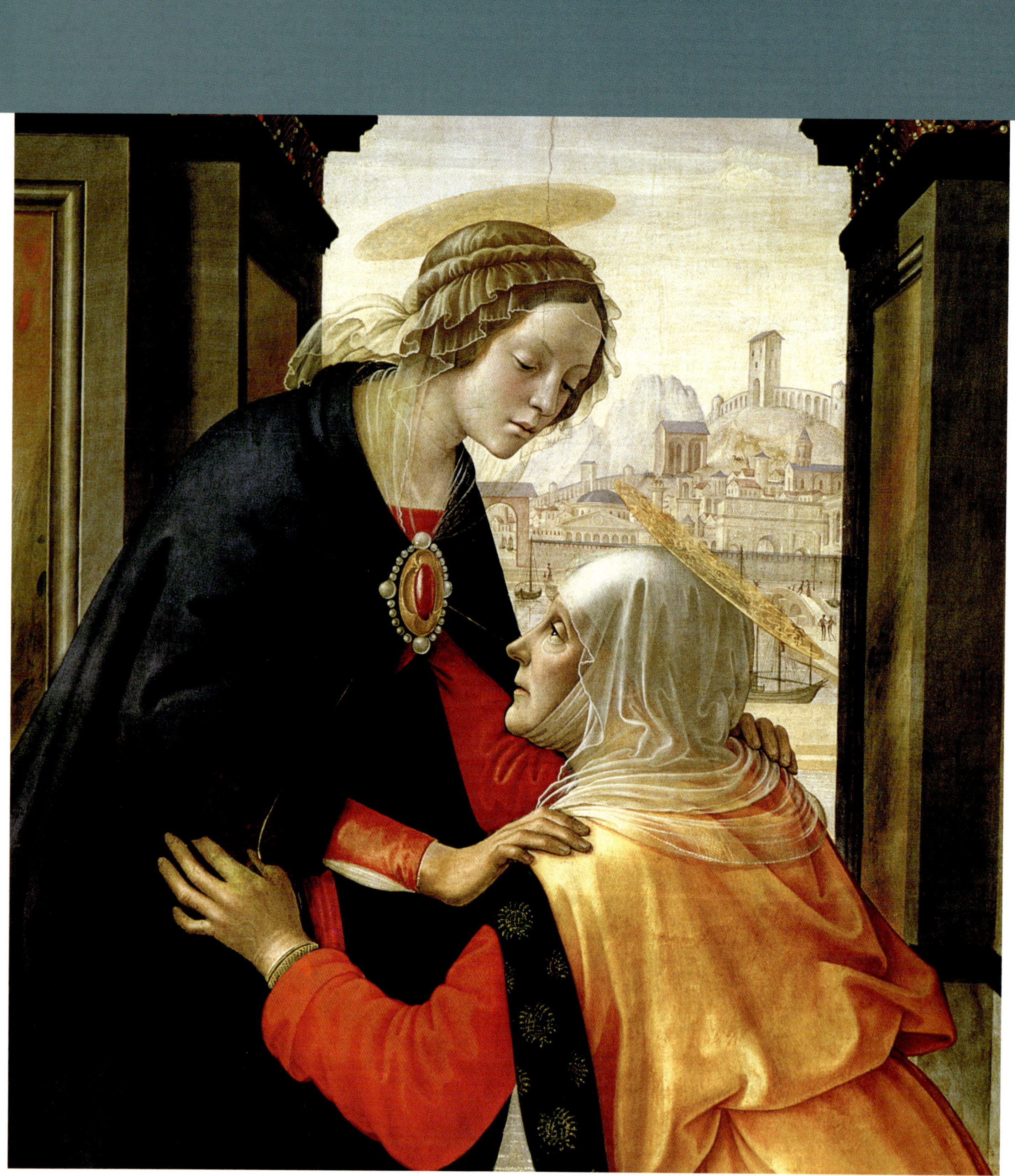

CHAPTER 1

A Renaissance Education

Michelangelo was born in Caprese, a small town near Arezzo in Tuscany, today known as Caprese Michelangelo, about 100 km (62 miles) from Florence. He was the second of five sons born to Ludovico di Leonardo Buonarroti Simoni (1444–1534) and Francesca di Neri del Miniato di Siena (1455–81). Ludovico had been a banker in Florence, but the bank failed and at the time of Michelangelo's birth he was working in a temporary government post in Caprese, acting as the town's judicial administrator and *podestà* (roughly equivalent to the mayor). So Michelangelo was born in the Casa del Podestà – the Mayor's House. The Buonarroti family claimed to descend from Countess Matilda of Canossa (1046–1115) which has since been proved incorrect, but Michelangelo believed it. He was baptized in Caprese in the thirteenth-century church of St John the Baptist, and a month after his birth, the family moved back to the house they shared with other relatives in the parish of Santa Croce in Florence. Soon after that they moved to a farmhouse owned by Ludovico and his brother in the hillside village of Settignano, about 8 km (5 miles) from Florence. In the hills surrounding Settignano were stone quarries, and the village was populated with stonecutters. As his mother was in poor health (she died at the age of 26 when Michelangelo was 6), the new baby was sent to a wet nurse in the village – a relatively common practice among the upper and middle classes. Often, babies remained with the wet nurse's family until childhood, which happened with Michelangelo. His wet nurse was married to a stonecutter, and Michelangelo later told his biographer Giorgio Vasari: 'Along with the milk of my nurse I received the knack of handling chisel and hammer, with which I make my figures.'

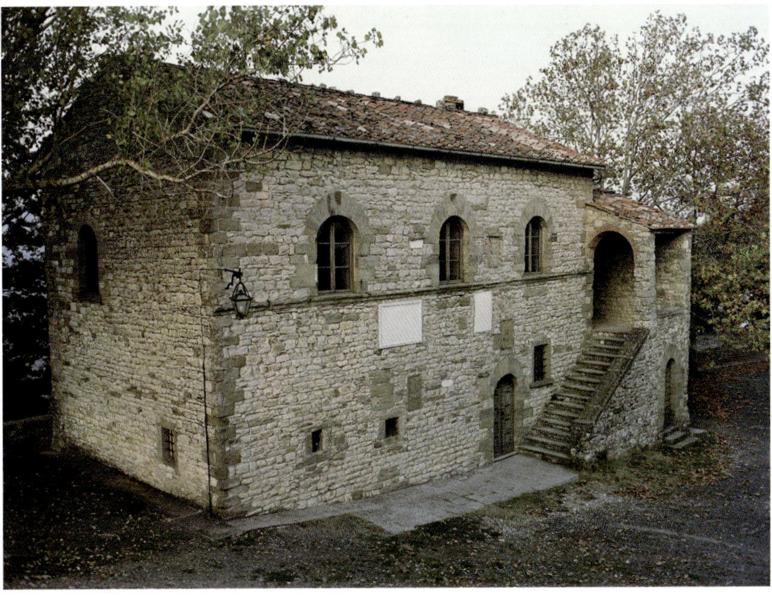

The Visitation, Domenico Ghirlandaio, 1491. Part of a series made by Ghirlandaio in the Tornabuoni family chapel in the church of Santa Maria Novella in Florence, this painting shows the meeting of Mary and Elizabeth. It was exceptional for the time, with its lifelike qualities, including the natural-looking positions of the figures, their faces and draping fabrics.

Michelangelo's house in Caprese. As his father held the post of podestà in Caprese when he was born, Michelangelo's first home was the House of the Podestà. The village subsequently became so renowned that it is now called Caprese Michelangelo.

THE RENAISSANCE

The Renaissance occurred because of multiple events and situations. Approximately 150 years before Michelangelo's birth, the Black Death or Bubonic Plague (1347–1351) devastated the populations of Europe and Asia. In Italy as elsewhere, it resulted in wide-ranging social, economic, cultural and religious changes. The Plague had spread to Italy from Russia through Genoese merchants who fled Crimea when attacked by Mongol warriors. Italian society was ravaged as the Plague spread rapidly through dirty, overcrowded, urbanized areas, killing huge swathes of people – and halving the population of Florence. Trade stopped, businesses failed and unemployment rose. As things recovered, there was a surge of rebuilding, and many survivors looked to the past as they rebuilt their world. Gradually Italy revived, and some places even became richer than before. Another consequence of the Plague was its contribution to the collapse of the feudal system that had structured Europe during the Middle Ages, and which gradually fell to a system of government based on independent city states led by powerful rulers.

In 1523, the artist Albrecht Dürer (1471–1528) first used the term *Wiedererwachsung* – German for 're-awakening' – to describe contemporary Italian painting that was reviving aspects of classical art. In 1550, in his book *The Lives of the Most Eminent Painters, Sculptors and Architects*, the artist, architect and art historian Giorgio Vasari described the revitalization of art and architecture in Italy which built on ideas from ancient Greece and Rome as *rinascita*, the Italian word for 'rebirth'. As Italy recovered from the Plague, cultural changes followed, beginning with the rise to power of the city of

Florence, initially through wool trading and banking, and aided by the emergence of writers such as Dante Alighieri, scholars such as Petrarch (1304–74) and artists such as Giotto di Bondone (*c.* 1266–1337). Plague survivors began to consider the here and now more than the hereafter, with a new emphasis on the importance of the individual rather than God's will. The wealthy and powerful commissioned new writing, painting, sculpture and architecture, and as a result there was a great surge in creativity, fresh thinking, new political and economic organization and greater explorations of the earth and the universe. Continents were discovered and commerce expanded as European merchants openly traded with Muslim, African and Hindu businessmen, regardless of religious and cultural differences. Among the new inventions, in 1438, Johannes Gutenberg (*c.* 1398–1468) created the printing press, which encouraged literacy and helped to spread ideas.

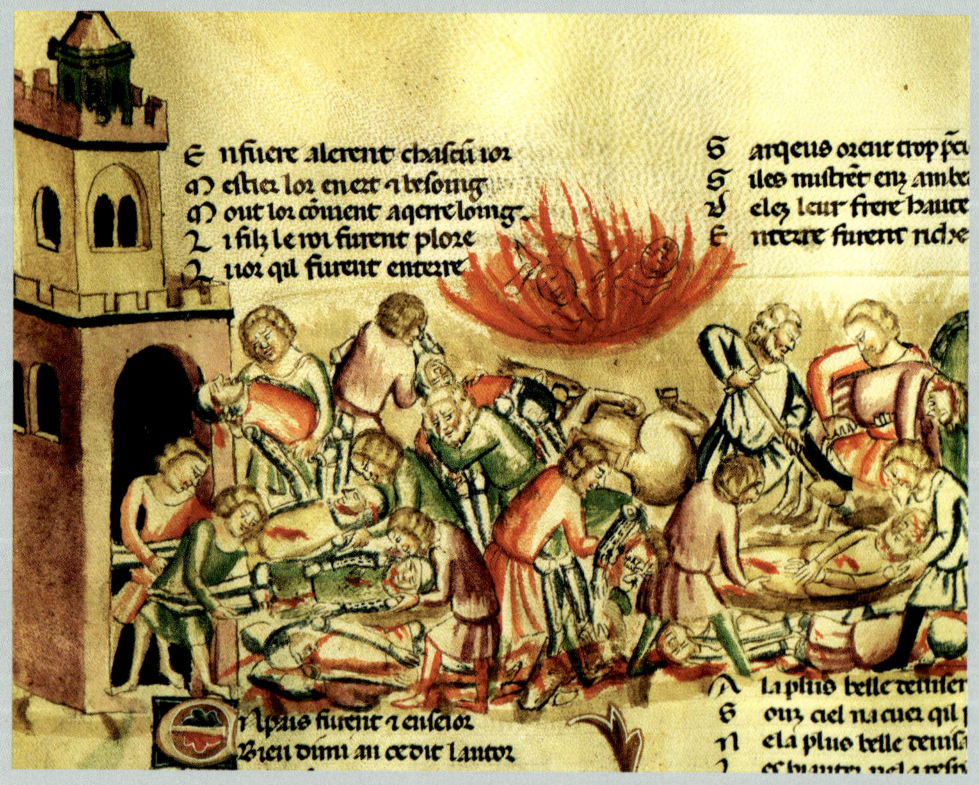

Black Death, *Venetian miniature, fourteenth century. Devastated by the Bubonic Plague, Italy experienced a massive loss of life. Consequently, the influence of the Catholic Church became less powerful.*

Baptistery doors, Lorenzo Ghiberti, 1425–52. Florentine sculptor, designer and goldsmith Lorenzo Ghiberti (1378–1455) won a competition to create heavy bronze doors for the Florence Baptistery. This is a detail of one of the panels, showing the detail and appearance of depth and distance. He also gilded the doors with a mixture of gold dust with mercury. Michelangelo is said to have described Ghiberti's doors as 'The Gates of Paradise'.

The Birth of Venus, *Sandro Botticelli, c. 1485. In Italy in the second half of the fifteenth century, the Florentine painter known as Sandro Botticelli (c. 1445–1510) was one of the most esteemed artists, whose work attracted some of the greatest patrons of the day. Mythology as opposed to Christianity in art was a Humanist idea, and this represents Venus, the mythological goddess of love, beauty and fertility, arriving at the island of Cyprus.*

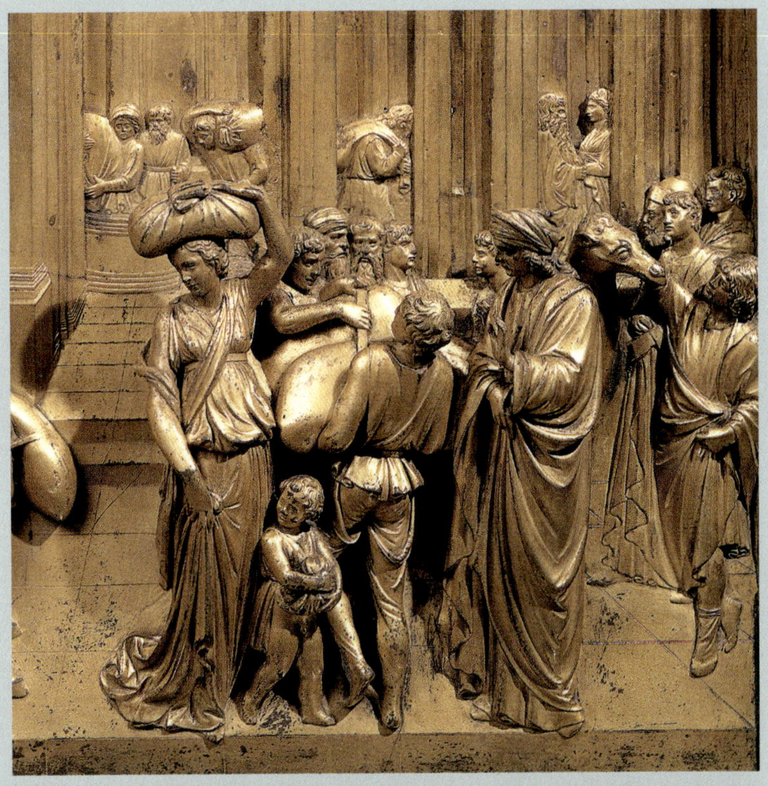

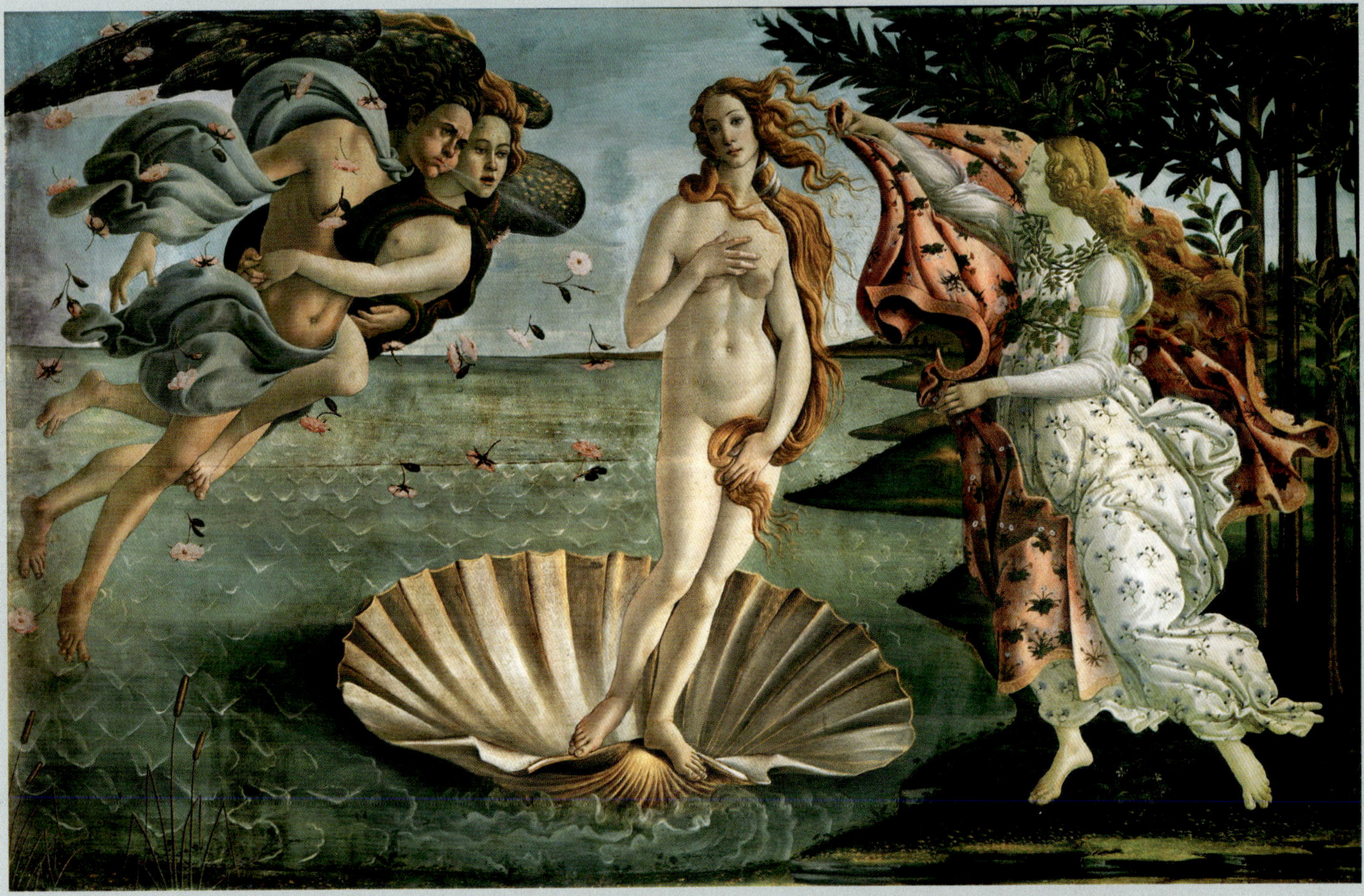

Below: The Crucifixion, Giotto, c. 1288–9. Working more than 150 years before Michelangelo was born, Giotto created imagery that had not been seen before. Rather than working to a format as previous painters had done, Giotto focused on realism. For instance, this crucifix emphasizes Christ's human aspects, such as his natural weight and gestures as his head falls forward and his body slumps. These ideas were inspirational to Michelangelo.

Right: David, Donatello, c. 1440. David was the biblical hero – a youth who killed the giant Goliath with stones. In this work by Donatello, one of the greatest sculptors of the early Renaissance, David is nude except for his helmet and boots, with his foot on Goliath's severed head. This was the first free-standing nude male sculpture made since antiquity.

ARTISTIC AMBITION

A year after the death of his mother, Michelangelo was sent by his father to a grammar school in Florence, where he studied a range of subjects, including the basics of reading and writing, and learning how to write legal letters and documents. Although the school provided him with a thorough education, he knew from an early age that he did not want to follow an academic or business career, but rather wanted to be an artist, and he spent a great deal of time drawing when he should have been studying. Furious at what he perceived as his son's unsuitable ambition, Ludovico

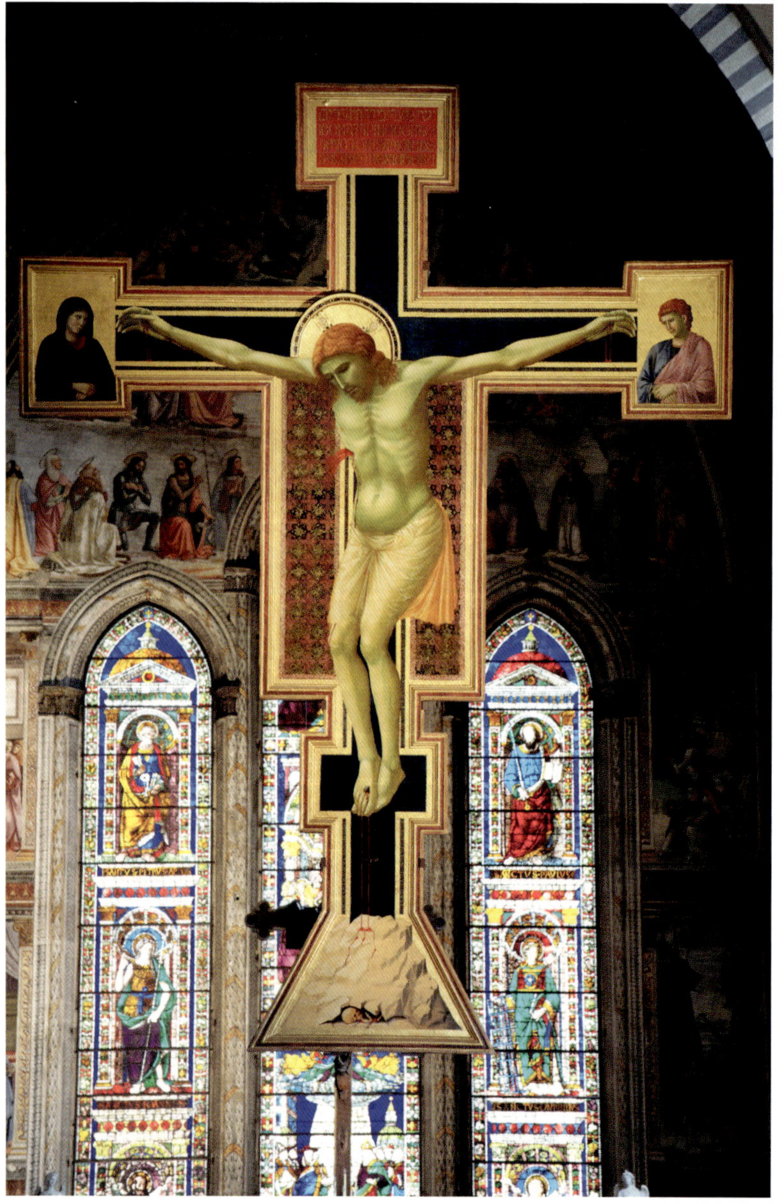

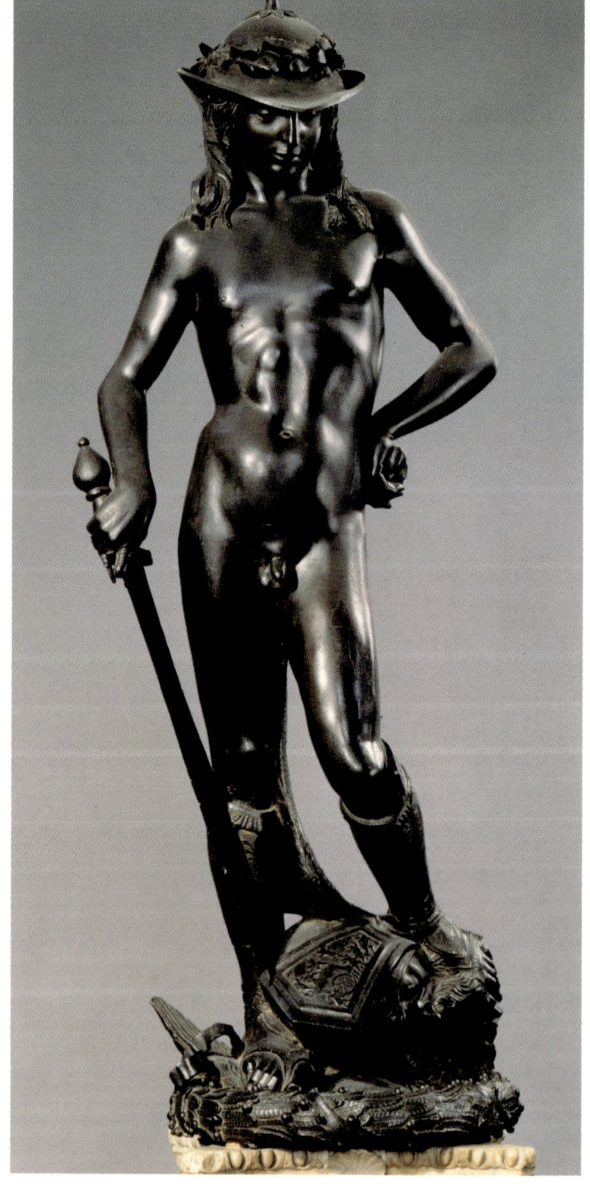

allegedly beat him in an attempt to make him concentrate on his studies. It had little effect: Michelangelo continued to draw and to study the artworks that were all around him in Florence, by such great artists as Giotto, Donatello (*c.* 1386–1466) and Masaccio (1401–28). He also spent time in artists' workshops in the city. From the age of 12, he worked as an odd-job boy in the busy Florentine workshop of Domenico Ghirlandaio (1448–94) and his brother Davide (1452–1525).

APPRENTICESHIP

When Michelangelo was 13, his father capitulated to his son's wishes and allowed him to become apprenticed to Domenico and Davide Ghirlandaio to train as an artist. An agreement was signed on 1 April 1488 for a three-year apprenticeship. In return for assisting the Ghirlandaio brothers, he would be taught to draw and paint and practise his art. For this, he would be paid 24 florins; six in the first year, eight in the second and ten in

the third. It was extremely unusual at the time for apprentices to be paid anything, and this is an indication of Michelangelo's promise. His responsibilities included grinding pigments and preparing other materials for the artists. He started learning his craft by copying engravings, such as detailed images by the German artist Martin Schongauer (*c.* 1450/53–91). Another of his duties was to study the art around him in Florence, which he had already started doing. However, after just a year, an opportunity to be part of the powerful Medici household arose. Lorenzo de' Medici (1449–92) was starting a school of sculpture. He employed sculptor Bertoldo di Giovanni (*c.* 1440–91), a former pupil of and assistant to Donatello, to guide the young sculptors, and he asked Domenico Ghirlandaio if he had any apprentices who would benefit from such an opportunity. Ghirlandaio recommended his two most able pupils: Francesco Granacci (1469–1543) and Michelangelo.

The Tribute Money, *Masaccio, c. 1426. Located in the Brancacci Chapel of the basilica of Santa Maria del Carmine in Florence, this fresco by Masaccio is part of a cycle on the life of St Peter from the Gospel of Matthew, in which Jesus directs Peter to find a coin in the mouth of a fish to pay the temple tax. Masaccio's use of perspective was pioneering.*

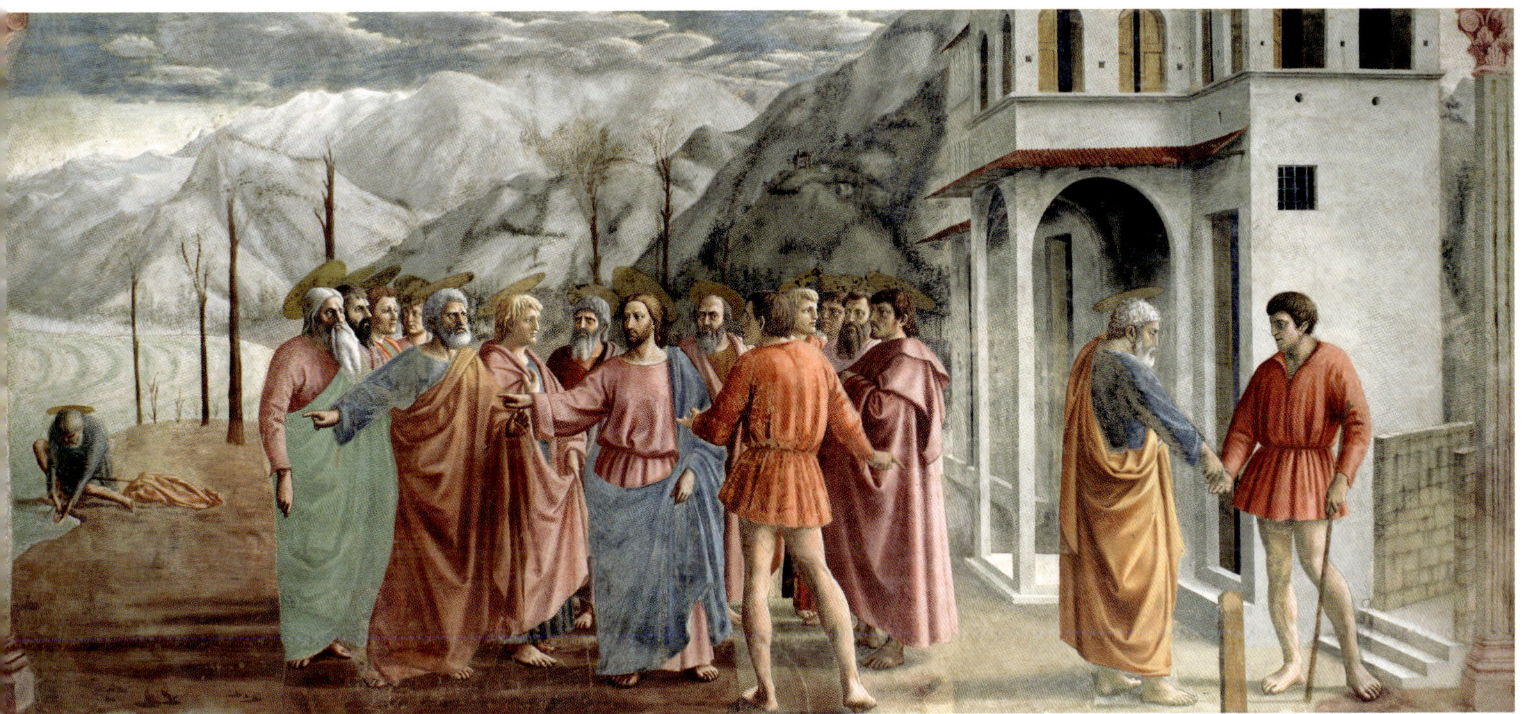

FLORENCE

Michelangelo was born at a time when Florence was becoming one of the wealthiest and most important economic, social, cultural, political and artistic centres in Italy. Because it is built on fertile land and situated on a major route between northern Italy and Rome, it quickly grew from a small Roman settlement to a bustling commercial centre. In 1252, it minted its own currency, the florin, which came to be used throughout Europe, and the city became a powerful banking hub, with many Florentine banks opening branches abroad. Economic strength stimulated the growth of merchant and arts guilds and attracted immigrants, adding to the city's expansion. Florence also exported vast amounts of high-quality wool and other textiles to other parts of Italy and Europe. As one of the consequences of its economic success, Florence became Italy's greatest centre of the arts and learning. Art was

Detail of the Carta della Catena, *a nineteenth-century reproduction of a 1490 map of Florence. In this panoramic view of fifteenth-century Florence, it can be seen how crowded the city was in Michelangelo's lifetime.*

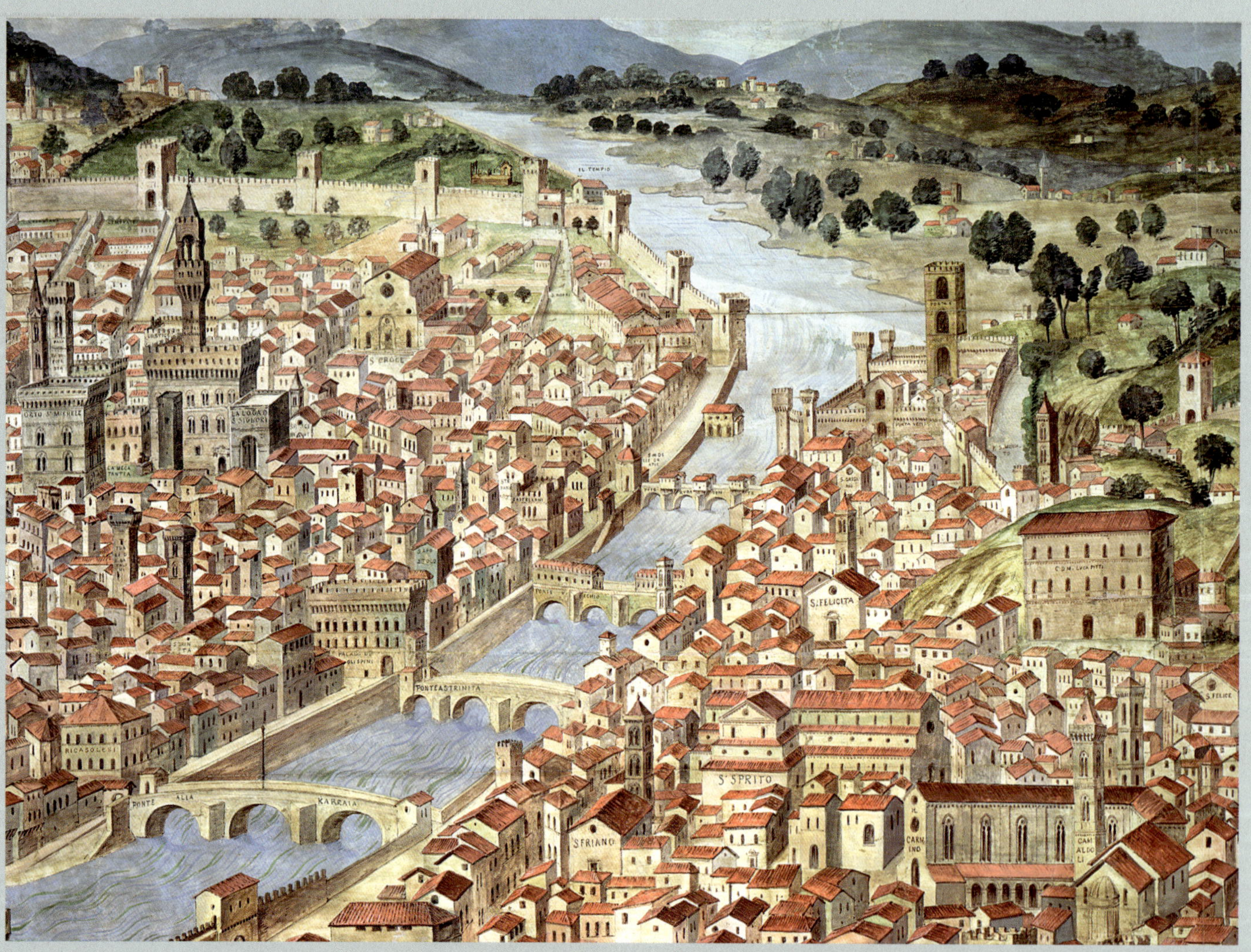

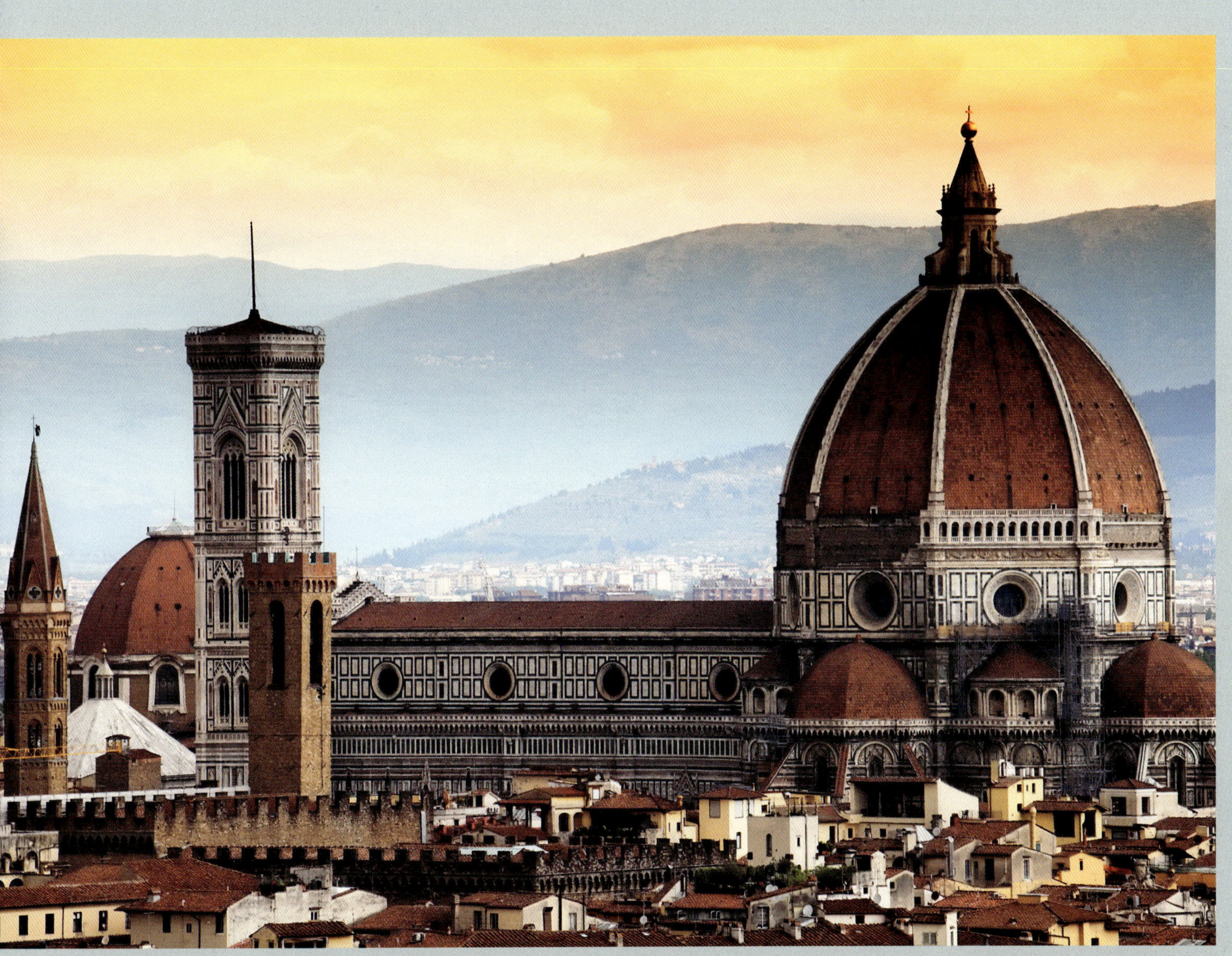

The Duomo, Florence. The Cattedrale di Santa Maria del Fiore (Cathedral of St Mary of the Flower), known more commonly as Florence Cathedral, was begun in 1296 in a Gothic design. It was completed in 1436, with the unique dome designed by Filippo Brunelleschi. The exterior is clad with polychrome marble panels in green and pink, bordered by white. It was the pride of Florence, and while he was an apprentice Michelangelo would have seen it almost every day.

sponsored by the *signoria* (the town council), the merchant guilds and wealthy patrons such as the Medici family. In the early fifteenth century, radical artists and architects created unprecedented works: for instance, the architect Filippo Brunelleschi (1377–1446) became especially famous for his feat of engineering in the design of the dome of Florence Cathedral and the development of the mathematical technique of linear perspective in art. Great churches and palaces were built and decorated with frescoes and statues. The exterior niches of the Church of Orsanmichele, for instance, feature statues by Donatello, Ghiberti, Andrea del Verrocchio (*c.* 1435–88) and Nanni di Banco (*c.* 1384–1421). Other outstanding artists whose work Michelangelo saw as he grew up include Giotto and Masaccio. Alongside all this was an exciting renewal of interest in learning and in the study of ancient Greek and Roman art, architecture and writing.

THE MEDICI

The House of Medici was an Italian banking family and political dynasty that ruled Florence for many years. Originating in the Mugello region of Tuscany, the family amassed wealth through banking and commerce and founded the Medici Bank in Florence in 1397. During the fifteenth century, the bank became the largest in Europe, and until its collapse in 1494 was one of the most prosperous and respected institutions in Europe, enabling the Medici to rise in power and ultimately rule Florence. During the time of their greatest influence, the Medici produced four popes and two queens of France. In 1532, the family acquired the hereditary title Duke of Florence, and within four decades, this became raised to the Grand Duchy of Tuscany. As Medici power increased, they dominated the Florentine government and created an environment in which art and Humanism flourished. They and other prosperous families of Italy, including the Visconti and Sforza in Milan, the Este in Ferrara, the Borgia in Rome and the Gonzaga in Mantua, helped to lay the foundations for the Italian Renaissance. Among other things, the Medici family financed the invention of the piano and the opera, funded the construction of St Peter's Basilica in Rome and Santa Maria del Fiore in Florence, and commissioned the greatest artists of the period, including Michelangelo. The first Medici family member to rule Florence was Cosimo de' Medici (1389–1464), who was succeeded by his son Piero di Cosimo de' Medici (1416–69), and grandson Lorenzo in 1469, a great patron of the arts. After Lorenzo's death in 1492, his son Piero (1472–1503) took charge, but only for two years. In 1494, Charles VIII of France entered Tuscany on his way to claim the Kingdom of Naples. Piero made a treaty with Charles, and the furious Florentines forced him into exile, restoring a republican government. Medici rule was restored in 1512, but by 1527 the family had been banished completely and the city re-established as a republic.

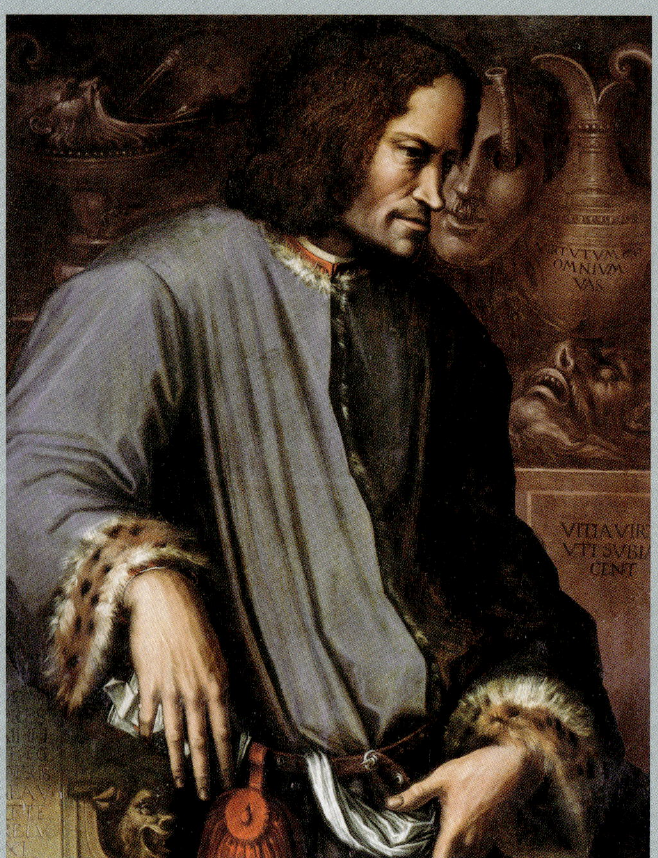

Lorenzo de' Medici, *Giorgio Vasari, 1533/4. Although Lorenzo de' Medici died before Vasari was born, this portrait commemorates him for his great patronage of the arts.*

The Medici coat of arms at the Palazzo Vecchio in Florence. There are many theories about the origin of the balls on the Medici family coat of arms, but nothing is conclusive. The family emblem of five red balls and one blue on a gold shield is prominently displayed on buildings that have connections with the Medici.

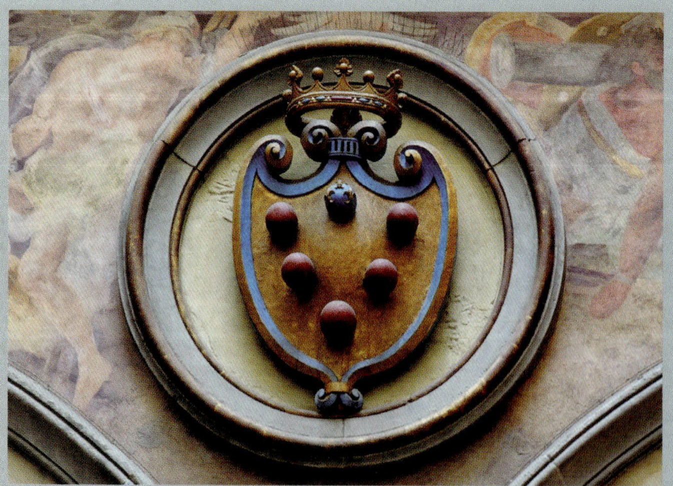

LIFE IN THE MEDICI HOUSEHOLD

After spending time with the Ghirlandaio brothers and learning about drawing, printmaking and fresco (he probably assisted in the frescoes in the Tornabuoni Chapel), Michelangelo was delighted to work in the gardens of the Palazzo Medici that had been built between 1444 and 1448 near the Basilica of San Lorenzo. He moved there from the Ghirlandaios' workshop in 1489, and was able to study and copy original ancient Greek and Roman sculpture; Lorenzo de' Medici had one of the finest collections of ancient Roman art then in existence. When Lorenzo noticed how advanced the boy was, he sent for Michelangelo's father and asked if Michelangelo could live in his household as a member of the family. It was a wonderful opportunity, and Michelangelo lived at the ducal palace for three years in the company of many learned individuals. Lorenzo also gave Ludovico a job, and so the connection between the Medici and Buonarroti families was established. Michelangelo stayed in the Medici household for three years, until Lorenzo's death in 1492. During that time, his sculptural skills progressed so rapidly that jealousies arose among the other students. On one occasion, he had an argument with fellow student Pietro Torrigiano (1472–1528) when they were drawing

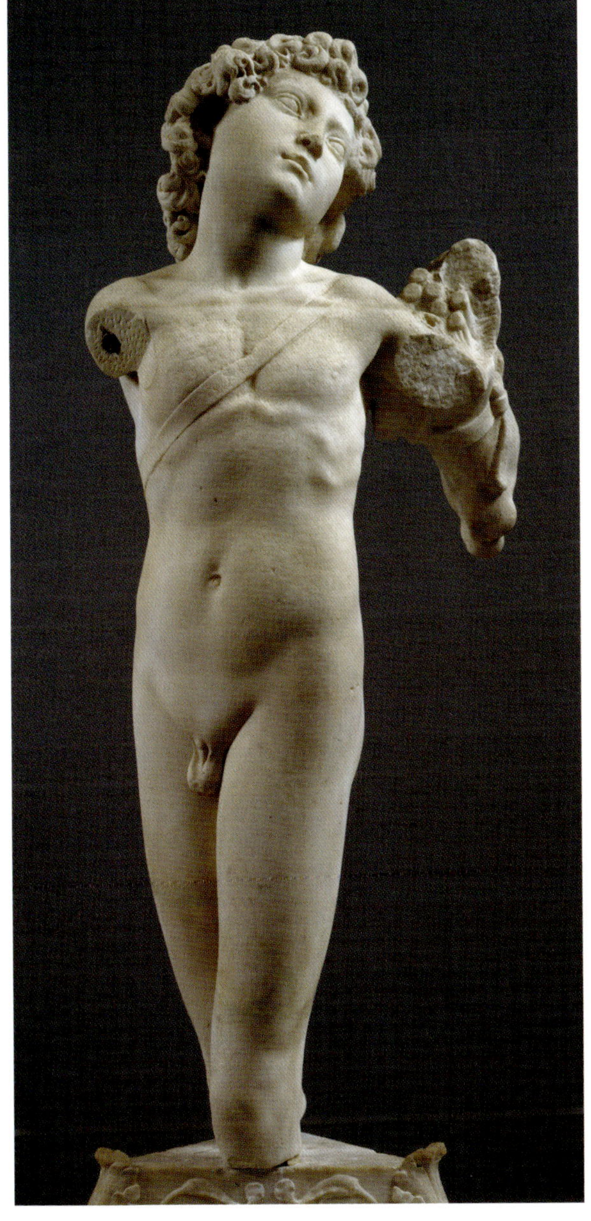

The Young Archer, c. 1490. Demonstrating his precocious skills at just 15 years old, Michelangelo created this marble figure of Cupid (now damaged), while he was working in the sculpture school of Lorenzo de' Medici.

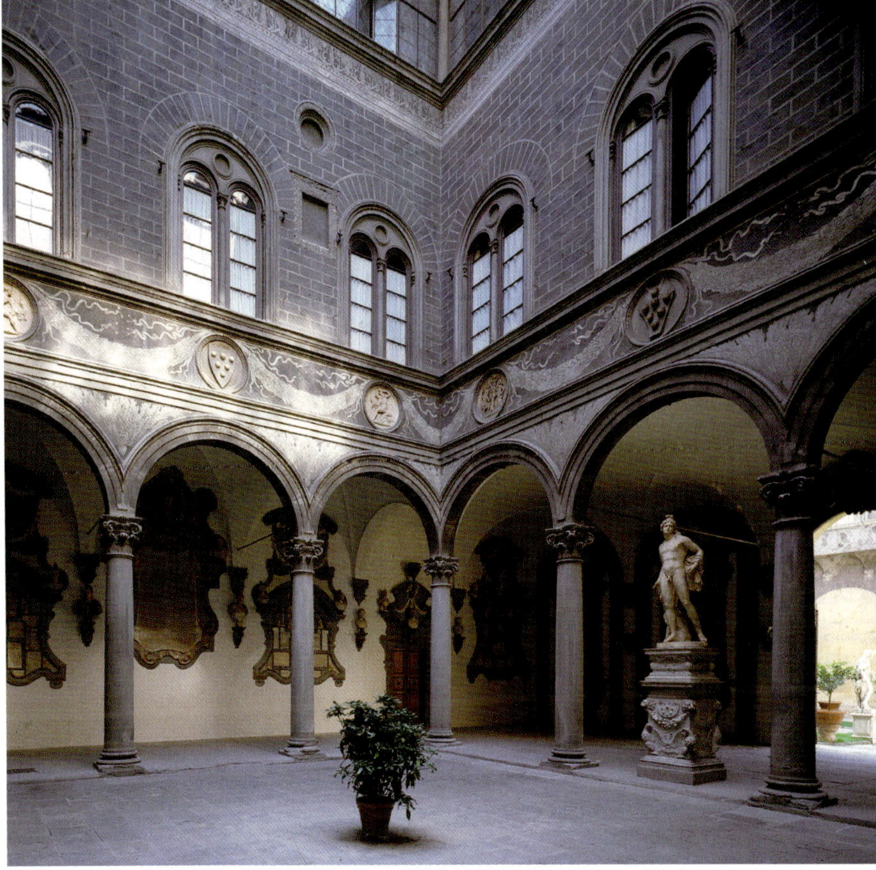

The interior courtyard of the Palazzo Medici. On the right is a view through to the sculpture garden where Michelangelo studied.

from Masaccio's frescoes in the Brancacci Chapel of Santa Maria del Carmine. Allegedly, Michelangelo made disparaging remarks about Torrigiano's sketches, so Torrigiano punched him, later recalling: 'Clenching my fist, I gave him so violent a blow upon the nose that I felt the bone and cartilage break.' For his violence, Torrigiano was banished from Florence, and Michelangelo had a crooked nose for the rest of his life.

HUMANISM

Growing up in Florence, Michelangelo was aware of the power struggles between the Church and Humanism. Humanism had been rising in popularity since the fourteenth century when writers such as Petrarch and Boccaccio (1313–75) had described the Roman age as a period of light and splendour, followed by a time of darkness and gloom. Petrarch in particular proposed studying ancient, classical literature

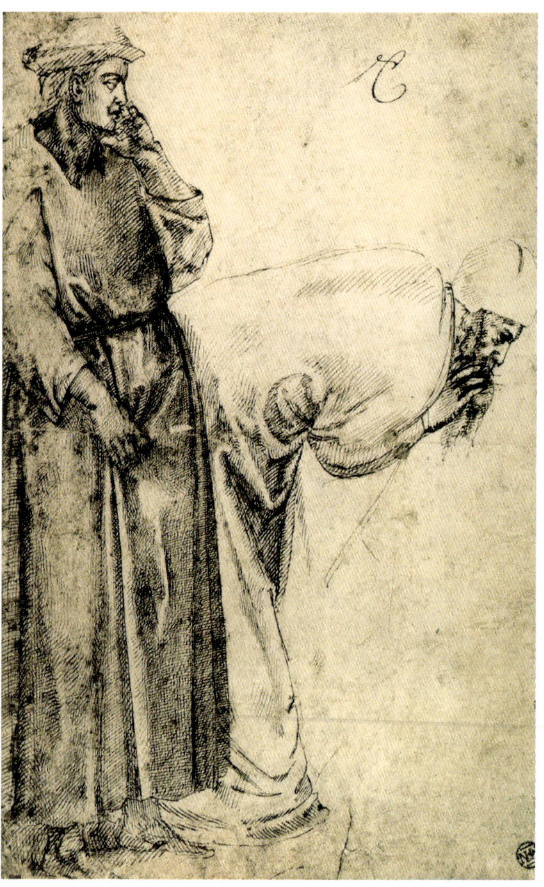

Two male figures after Giotto, 1490–2. This is the 16-year-old Michelangelo's figure study after the fresco of the Ascension of St John the Evangelist (below), part of a series of drawings he made from the works of Giotto and Masaccio.

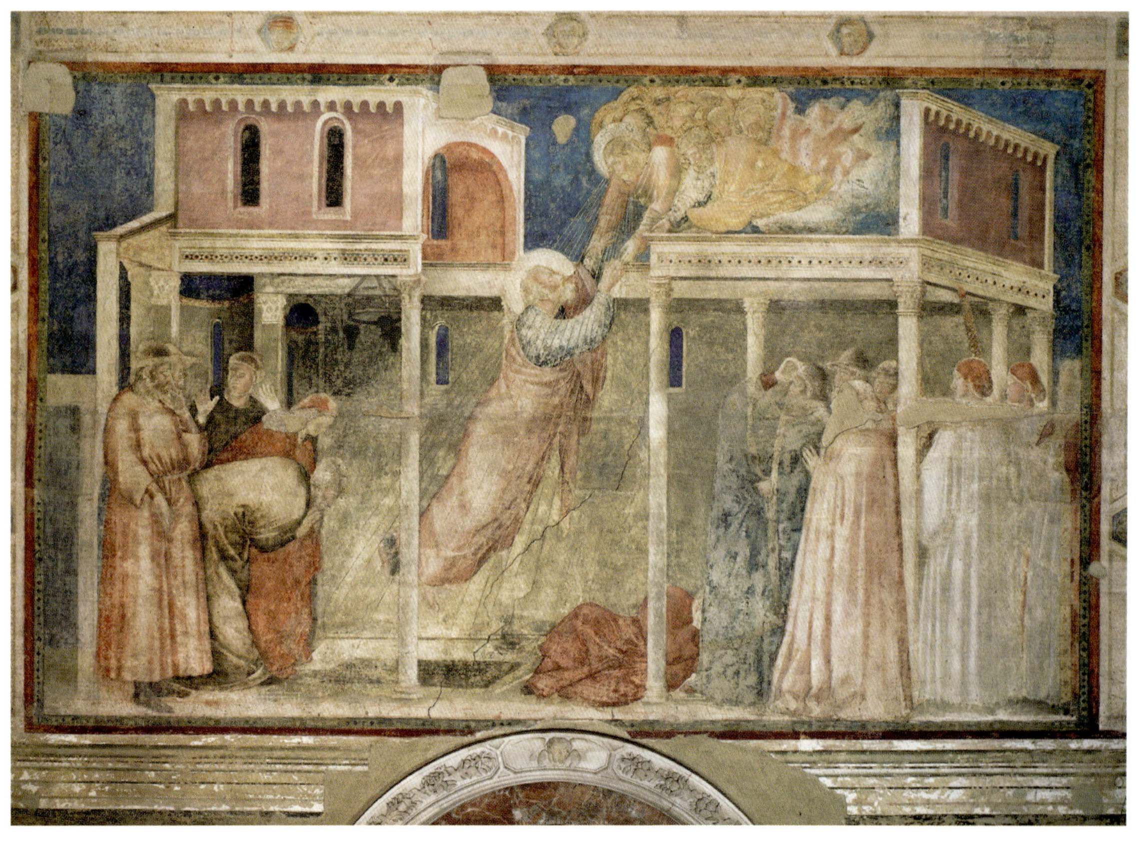

The Ascension of St John the Evangelist, Giotto, c. 1320. Giotto was recognized as a great pioneer and so young art students of Florence copied his work to learn from him. This fresco in the Peruzzi Chapel of Santa Croce depicts the ascension of John the Evangelist. Giotto's innovations include the naturally startled reactions of the people at the tomb and the sense of three-dimensionality.

to encourage a return to more intellectual and cultured lifestyles. After the Crusader sacking of Constantinople in 1204 and then later, when the city was conquered by the Ottoman Empire in 1453, many Byzantine scholars escaped to Italy where they spread knowledge of the ancient Greeks and Romans. The study of ancient Greek and Latin texts instigated concepts of individualism, moderation and reason, which contrasted with the focus on life after death that had prevailed throughout the Middle Ages. It became known as Humanism, and Humanists considered life in terms of the present and of the importance of thinking for oneself, encouraging interests and learning in poetry, drama, natural history, mathematics, architecture and art. Such subjects had been suppressed for centuries in favour of religious rules and dogmas. After this start in Italy, Humanist notions spread across Europe from the late fifteenth century, influencing Renaissance developments in particular in Germany, France, England and the Netherlands. Although Michelangelo was a devout Catholic, he became inspired by the Humanist movement and he helped to revive aspects of ancient Greek and Roman art. Particularly in his sculpture and paintings, he made humans the heroes rather than God, which makes him one of the greatest Humanists of the Renaissance period.

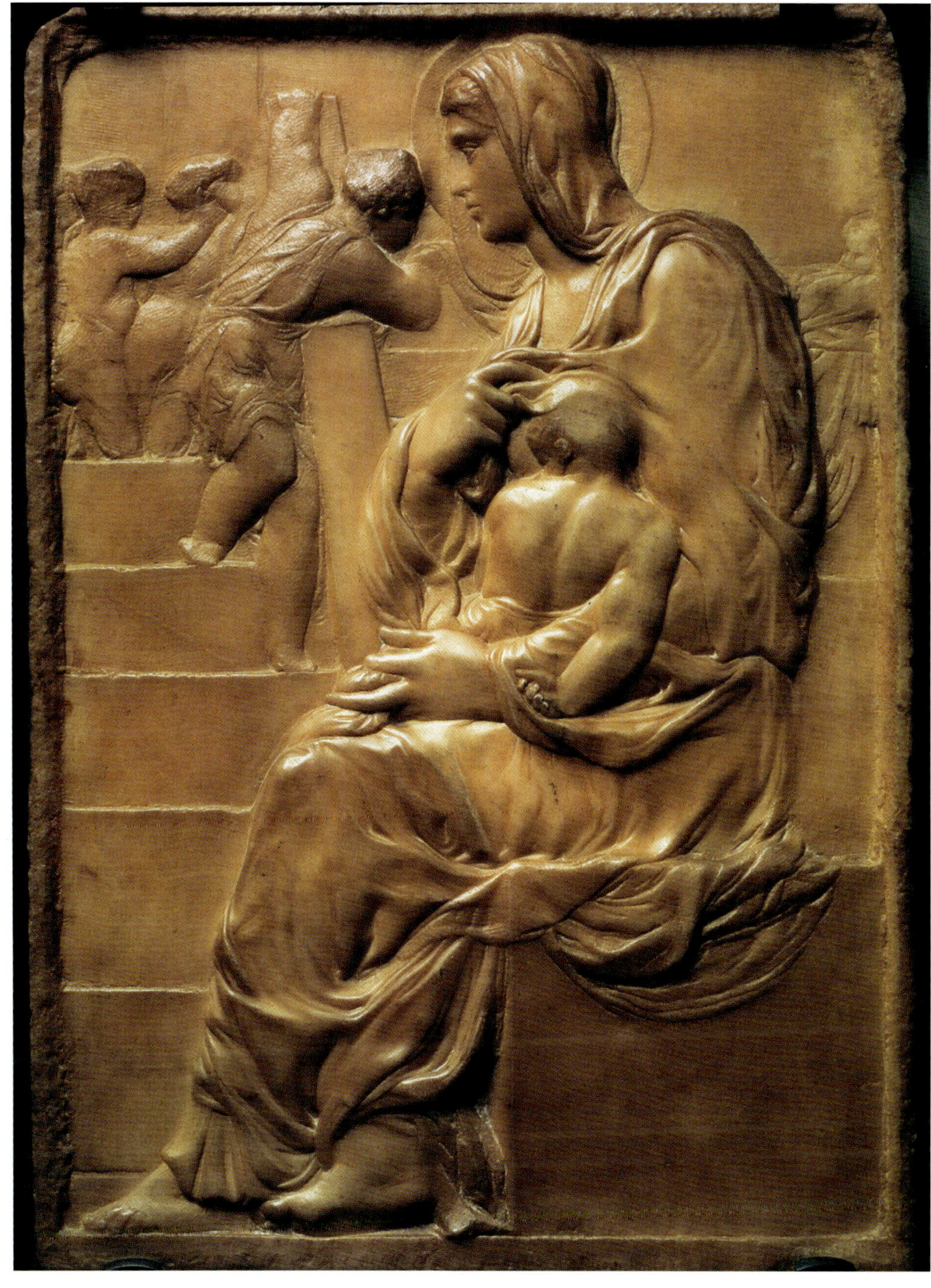

Madonna of the Stairs, c. 1490. Created when Michelangelo was about 15, this relief skilfully conveys depth and distance. On a square stone, seated and in profile is the Madonna with the Child on her lap. To her side in the distance are stairs with figures engaged in lifelike activities.

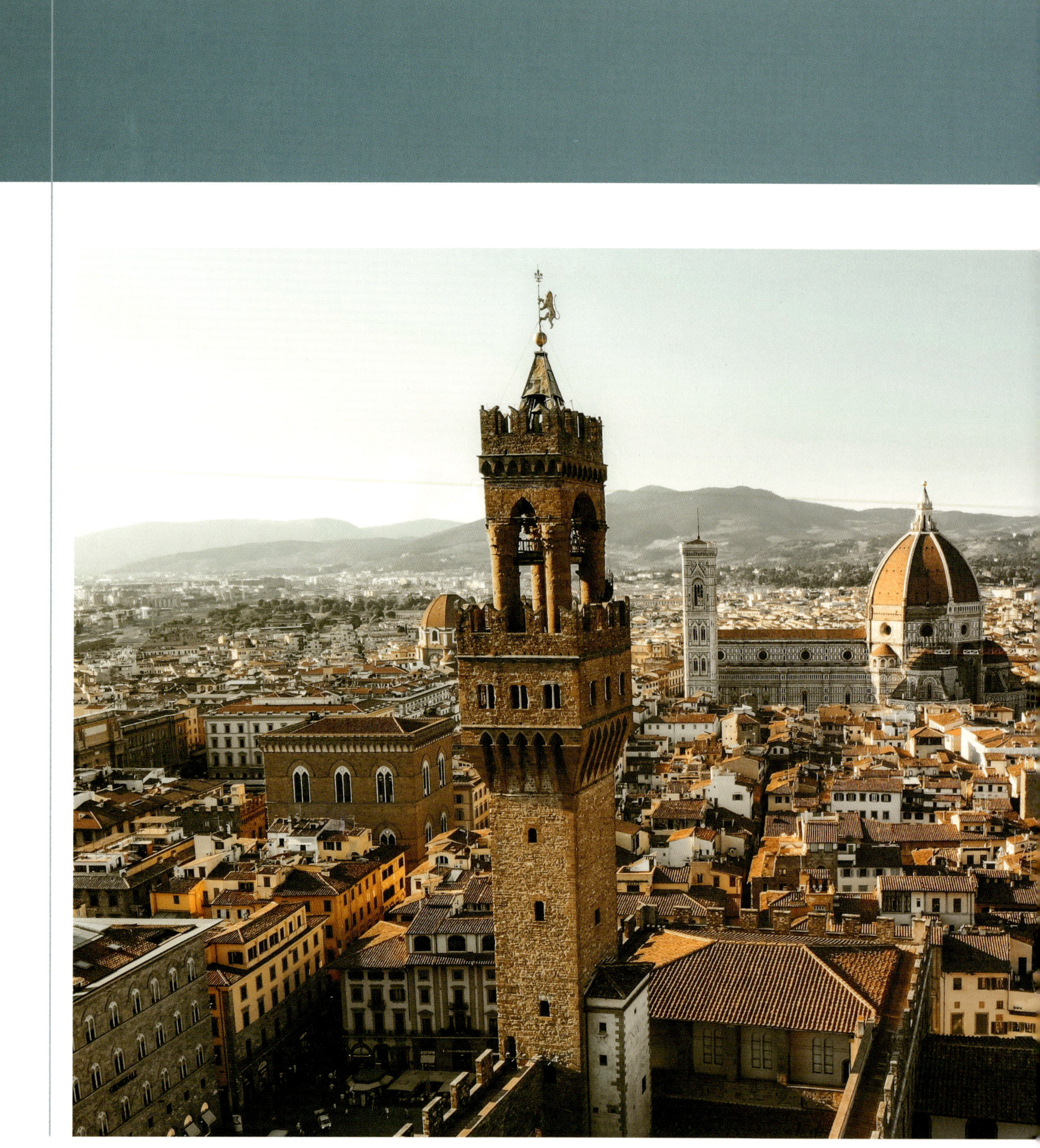

CHAPTER 2

Becoming a Master

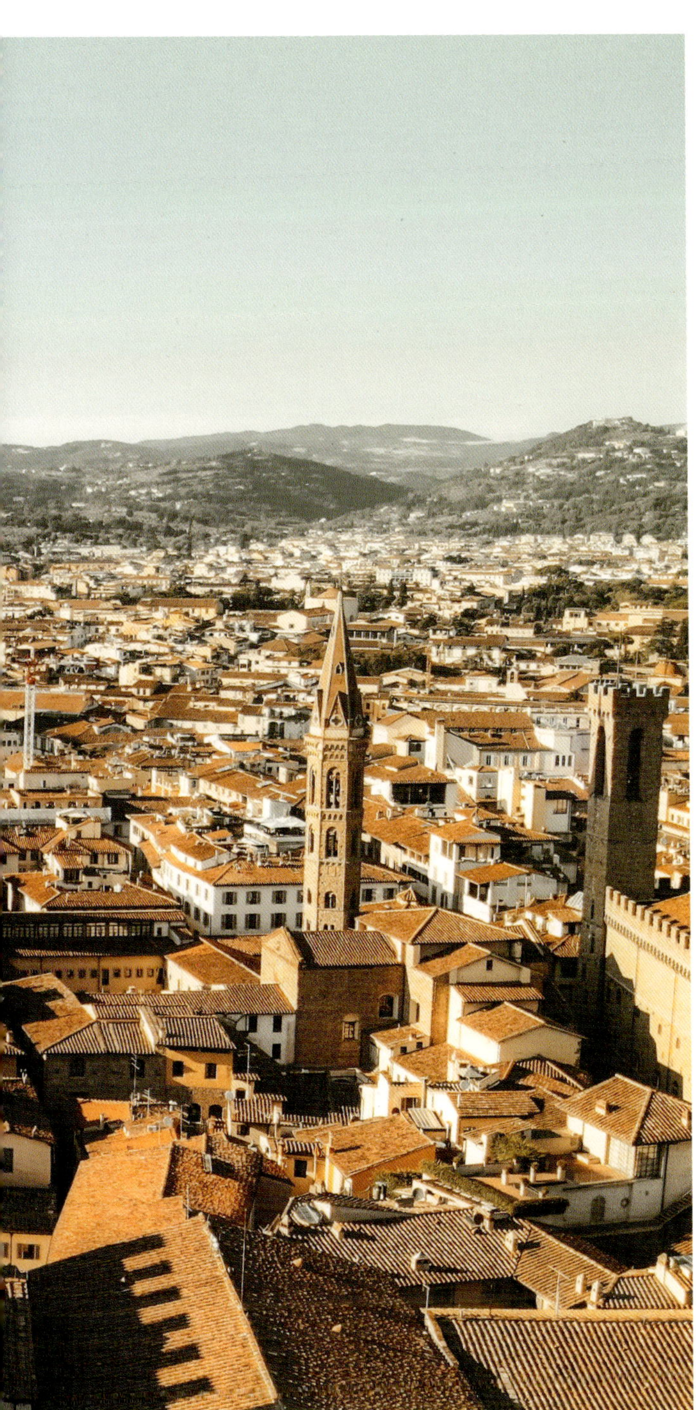

To be growing up in Florence amongst the artistic, scientific and literary developments, and surrounded by some of the most learned men of the time, was extremely exciting for an intelligent and ambitious young man like Michelangelo. He was in a rare and privileged position, able to discuss and learn about some of the innovative philosophical developments that were also occurring.

NEOPLATONISM

The Athenian philosopher Plato (428/7 or 424/3–348/7 BCE) is one of the most influential figures in Western philosophy. His ideas are wide-ranging, but it is his Theory of Forms that is the most influential and the foundation of Platonism. In it, he asserted that there are two worlds: the physical and the spiritual. The physical world – what we see and interact with each day – is changing and imperfect. It is not the 'real' world, but rather is only a shadow or image. True or ultimate reality exists beyond it, in the spiritual world, the Realm of Forms (sometimes called the Realm of Ideas or Realm of Ideals).

During the third century, some of his ideas were resurrected by the Hellenistic philosopher Plotinus (204/5–70). Combined with certain other ideas, these became known as Neoplatonism.

After Plotinus, other philosophers developed their own systems of thought that synthesized aspects of the theories of Plato, Aristotle (384–322 BCE) and the Stoics, broadening the remit of Neoplatonism. In 1484 in Florence, Marsilio Ficino (1433–99) published his translation in Latin of the complete works of Plato. He also translated many Neoplatonic works including everything written by Plotinus. Building on Ficino's work, starting in Florence and spreading far beyond, several other thinkers, including Pico della Mirandola (1463–94), sought to link ideas of Neoplatonism and Christianity, and to suggest a rationale for life. In this way, elements of Neoplatonism became one of the major underlying themes of Renaissance thought and art.

Photograph of Florence across the city centre with the Palazzo Vecchio in the foreground and the Cathedral of Santa Maria del Fiore (the Duomo) in the distance.

THE PLATONIC ACADEMY

The scholar and priest Marsilio Ficino was one of the most influential Humanists of the early Italian Renaissance. Sponsored by the Medici, he organized the Florentine Academy or the Platonic Academy, which was an attempt to revive Plato's Academy of ancient Greece. Between 1462 and 1494, a circle of scholars met regularly to study and discuss the works of Plato and his followers, considering especially the defence of the dignity and liberty of individuals. In 1462, Cosimo de' Medici placed a villa he owned in Careggi at Ficino's disposal, asking him in return to study and translate the manuscripts of several ancient Greek philosophers, including several by Plato which were in Cosimo's possession. To support this study and translation, Ficino began the Platonic Academy, but it was never official. However, its meetings became renowned and its intellectual influence spread far beyond Florence. Members were highly respected individuals, including the classical scholar and poet Poliziano (1454–94), the philosophers Cristoforo Landino (1424–98) and Pico della Mirandola, and the bishop, diplomat and writer Gentile de' Becchi (1420/30–97). It is clear that Michelangelo must have spent time with members of the Platonic Academy, as the poems he wrote later express many of the same beliefs and doctrines.

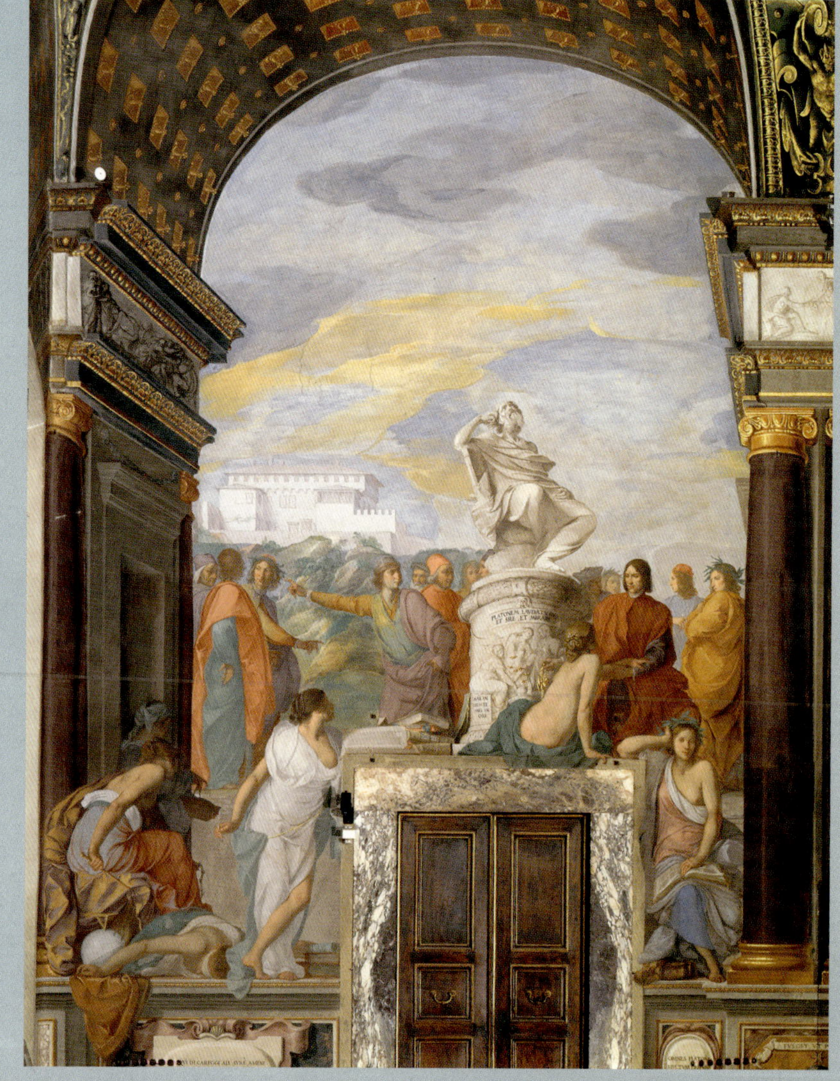

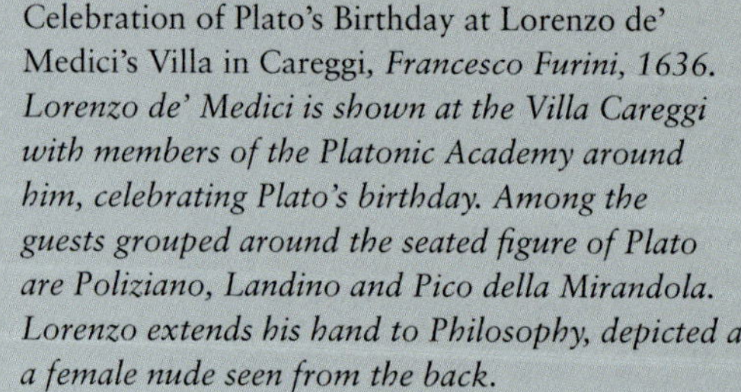

Celebration of Plato's Birthday at Lorenzo de' Medici's Villa in Careggi, Francesco Furini, 1636. Lorenzo de' Medici is shown at the Villa Careggi with members of the Platonic Academy around him, celebrating Plato's birthday. Among the guests grouped around the seated figure of Plato are Poliziano, Landino and Pico della Mirandola. Lorenzo extends his hand to Philosophy, depicted as a female nude seen from the back.

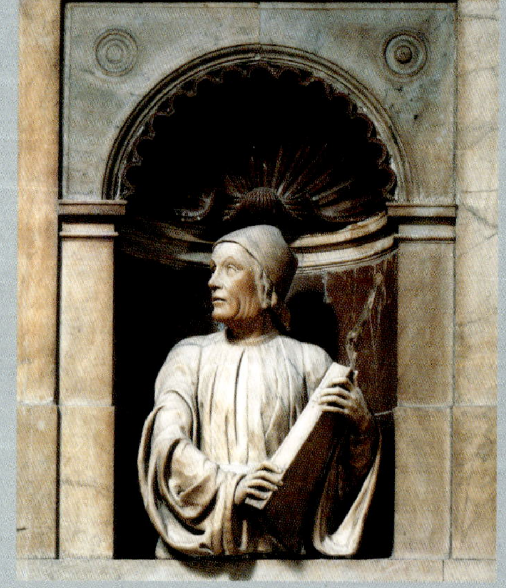

Marsilio Ficino, Andrea Ferrucci, 1521. Sculpted by Andrea Ferrucci (1465–1526) in the Santa Maria del Fiore, this is a bust of Ficino holding his translation of the works of Plato.

KNOWLEDGE OF ANATOMY

After Lorenzo de' Medici's death in April 1492, Michelangelo returned to his father's house, which contrasted with the luxury and stimulation he had experienced at the Medici court. In the following months, he carved a wooden crucifix as a gift to the prior of the church of Santo Spirito on the south side of the River Arno. The prior had allowed him to study corpses from the church's hospital for anatomical purposes. The study of anatomy was unusual and difficult, but as Italian Renaissance artists attempted to develop more lifelike portrayals of the human figure, several managed to organize this. Opportunities for direct anatomical dissection were restricted. Vasari wrote that the Florentine sculptor, painter and printmaker Antonio Pollaiuolo (*c.* 1432–98) was the 'first master to skin many human bodies in order to investigate

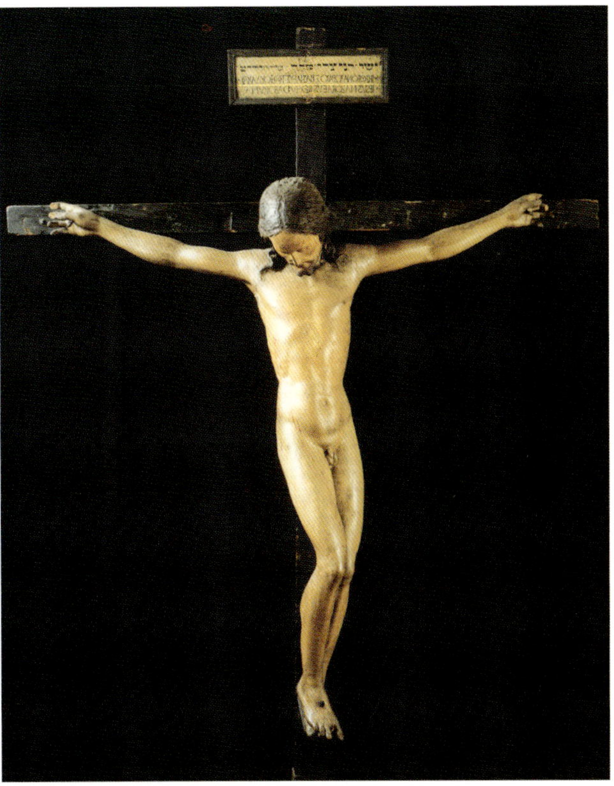

Crucifix, c. 1493. *After Lorenzo de' Medici's death, the 17-year-old Michelangelo was a guest of the convent of Santa Maria del Santo Spirito, where he sculpted this wooden crucifix, which was placed over the high altar.*

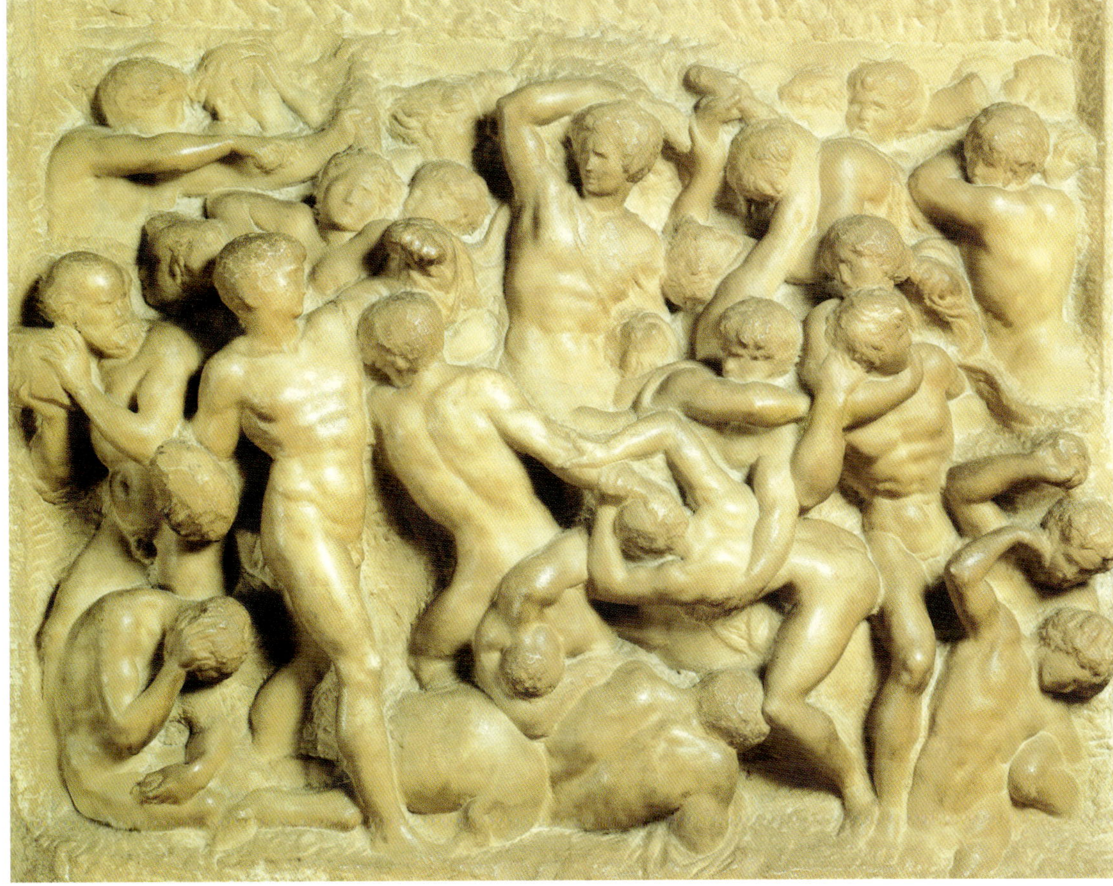

Battle of the Centaurs, c. 1492. *Inspired by a classical relief created by Bertoldo di Giovanni depicting a mythic battle between the Lapiths and the Centaurs, and suggested as a subject by Poliziano, this unfinished relief was the last work created by Michelangelo before Lorenzo de' Medici died.*

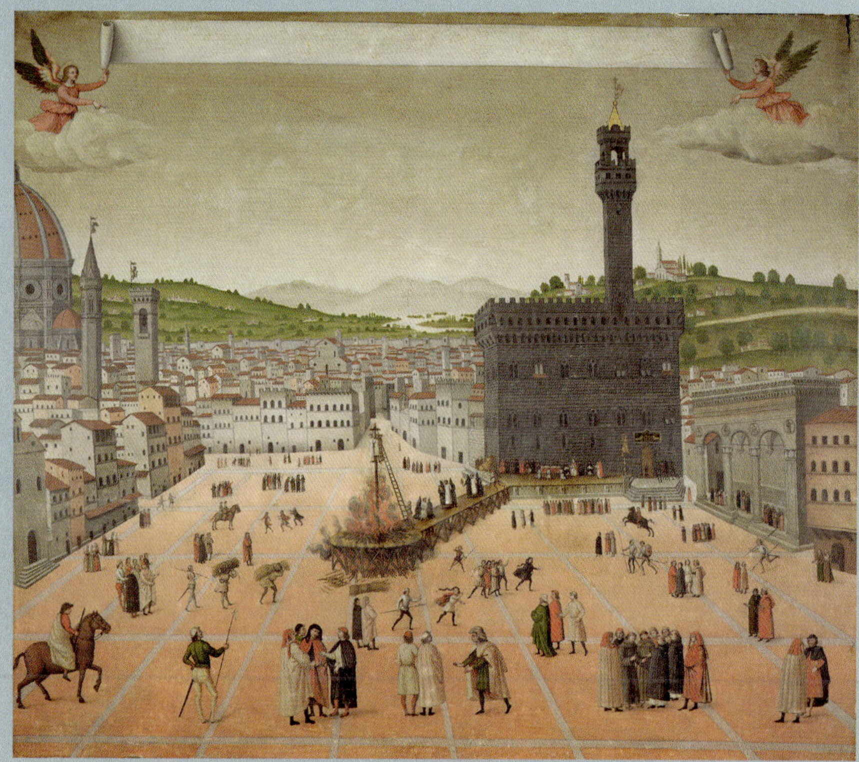

Hanging and Burning of Girolamo Savonarola in the Piazza della Signoria, *artist unknown, c. 1498. On 23 May 1498, the fanatical preacher Savonarola was burned at the stake. His last words were 'The Lord has suffered as much for me.' The artist here has used dramatic linear perspective in this impression of Florence's main square and beyond.*

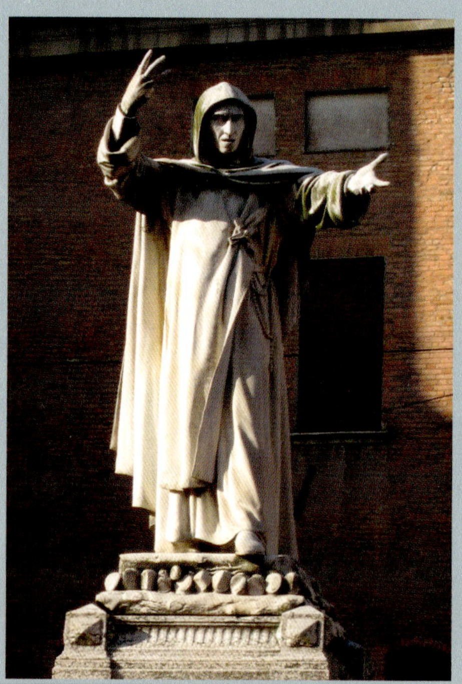

Monument to Savonarola, *Stefano Galletti, c. 1875. This life-sized monument to Savonarola in his birthplace of Ferrara was created in white Carrara marble by the sculptor Stefano Galletti (1832–1905). Galletti presents Savonarola standing on the pyre still preaching fervently, despite his imminent death.*

SAVONAROLA

In 1490, the Dominican friar Girolamo Savonarola (1452–98) became prior of San Marco in Florence, mainly due to Lorenzo de' Medici's influence. However, once he was established in this position, he preached vehemently against what he perceived as widespread depravity and decadence, and he sought to rid the city of vice, as exemplified by the extravagance and excess of his backers, the Medici family. Savonarola's influence grew so rapidly that within a short time he was in effect ruling Florence. From early in 1495, he began his 'bonfires of the vanities': he and his ardent supporters collected objects that he considered to be self-indulgent, including manuscripts, sculpture, paintings, tapestries, books, mirrors, musical instruments, clothes, jewellery, cosmetics and ornaments. All were thrown on to the great bonfires that were lit regularly in the Piazza della Signoria. Countless priceless valuables were consigned to the flames.

Savonarola had the Florentines in his thrall, but in Rome, Pope Alexander VI – Rodrigo de Borja (1431–1503) – was not so impressed, and in 1495, when Savonarola urged the Florentines not to join the Pope's Holy League against the French, the Vatican summoned him to Rome. Pleading ill health and fearful of being attacked on the journey, Savonarola refused to go. At this, the Pope banned him from further preaching, but Savonarola ignored the ban and was excommunicated in 1497. At last tired of his extreme teachings, the Florentines turned against him and arrested him. He was convicted as a heretic, and burned at the stake in May 1498.

the muscles and understand the nude in a more modern way'. Michelangelo and Leonardo both also managed to undertake detailed anatomical dissections, and as a result they set new standards in realism. Gradually more artists studied and dissected corpses, and patrons commissioning art in this period began to expect anatomical accuracy. Until about 1510, artists including Pollaiuolo, Leonardo and Michelangelo knew more about anatomy than was taught in universities.

Also during the 1490s, it is often suggested that Michelangelo bought a large block of marble and with it created a larger than life statue of Hercules which was sent to France but is now lost. His patron for this statue is not known. After heavy snowfalls in January 1494, Lorenzo's heir, Piero di Lorenzo de' Medici, commissioned him to create a snow statue, and Michelangelo again entered the court of the Medici. Soon after the snow statue had melted, the Medici were expelled from Florence and Michelangelo also left the city.

TURBULENCE IN FLORENCE

Lorenzo de' Medici was succeeded by his son Piero in 1492. Known at the time as Piero II, he was later called Piero the Unfortunate because he caused the Medici to be banished from Florence. In 1494, Charles VIII of France invaded northern Italy for a hereditary claim on the Kingdom of Naples. As the French army entered Tuscany, Piero determined to mount a resistance but he did not have the backing of his nobles, and when the huge French army reached Pisa, Piero surrendered. He then agreed to every demand that Charles made, and such a poor handling of the situation made the Florentines furious. They exiled Piero II and restored the republican government.

VENICE AND BOLOGNA

With two companions, in 1494, Michelangelo travelled to Venice, but they stayed for only a few days as money ran out. The fashion in Florence for building on the art of the ancient Greeks and

Romans did not appeal to the Venetians at the time, so no commissions were forthcoming. On their return to Florence, they entered Bologna. However, Michelangelo and his friends failed to follow a local law to identify themselves as visitors by stamping red sealing wax on one thumbnail. They were detained at the tax office and fined 50 small coins called *bolognini* – which they did not have. A local noble and politician, Gian Francesco Aldrovandi

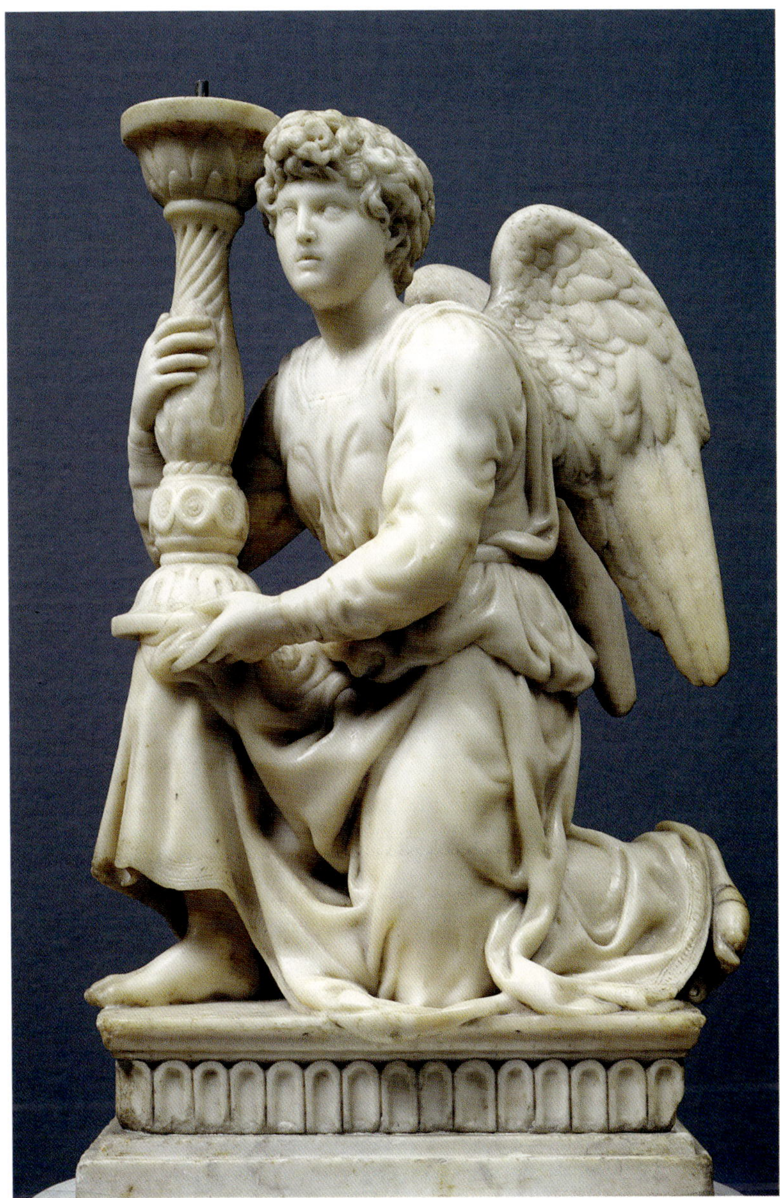

Kneeling Angel Holding a Candelabra, *Michelangelo, 1494–5. Michelangelo created this angel to echo the pose of another angel already in place on the shrine made by a previous sculptor, although this angel looks more realistic and natural than the earlier one. He was paid 12 ducats for this work.*

(birth date unknown–1512) stepped in and used his influence to save Michelangelo from having to pay the fine. (Michelangelo's friends were left to save themselves.) Aldrovandi invited Michelangelo to stay in his nearby palazzo on a grand street in the centre of Bologna, which he did, and every evening Michelangelo read to Aldrovandi from Dante, Petrarch or Boccaccio. Aldrovandi commissioned Michelangelo to create three marble figures for a shrine that had not been finished in the local church of San Domenico. Michelangelo duly produced two marble statues of the saints Petronius and Proculus, and a kneeling angel. They are accomplished works, but do not show the extraordinary standard for which Michelangelo soon became famed. Even so, Michelangelo again aroused resentment among other sculptors. He was treated as a celebrity, lived free of charge in a grand palazzo, and was paid for his work and materials while they had to pay for their own rent and buy their own tools and materials. However, there was not much work to go round, and after about a year Michelangelo returned to Florence.

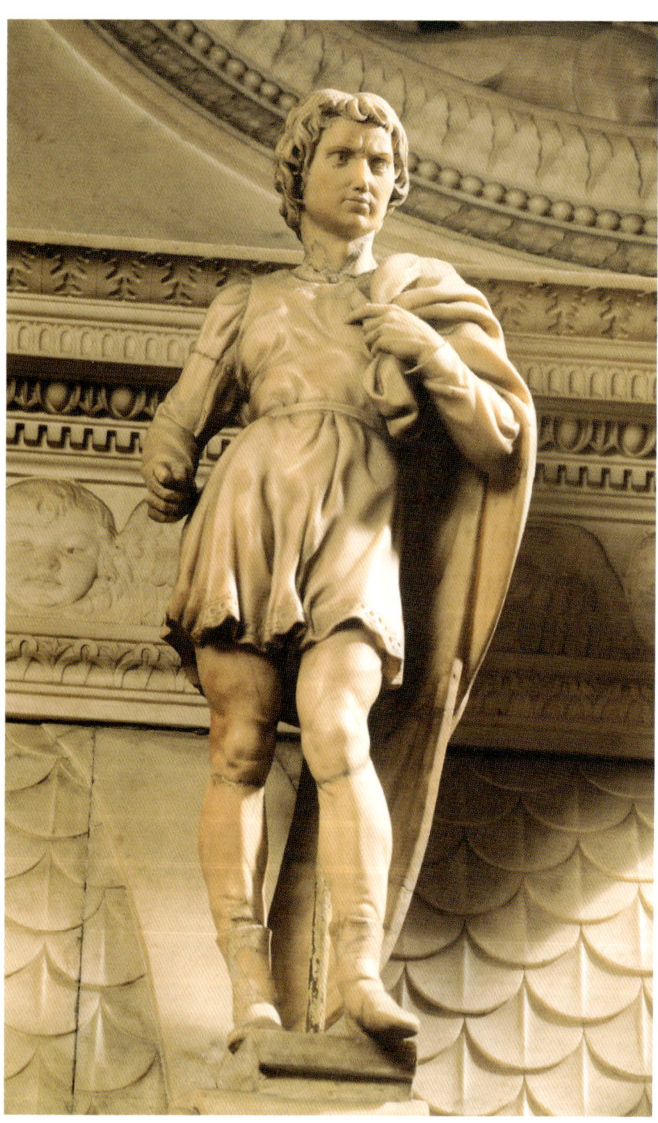

St Proculus, 1494–5. Possibly a self-portrait of Michelangelo, this small statue represents St Proculus, a martyr from Bologna. It is one of two saints carved by Michelangelo for the shrine in the church of San Domenico.

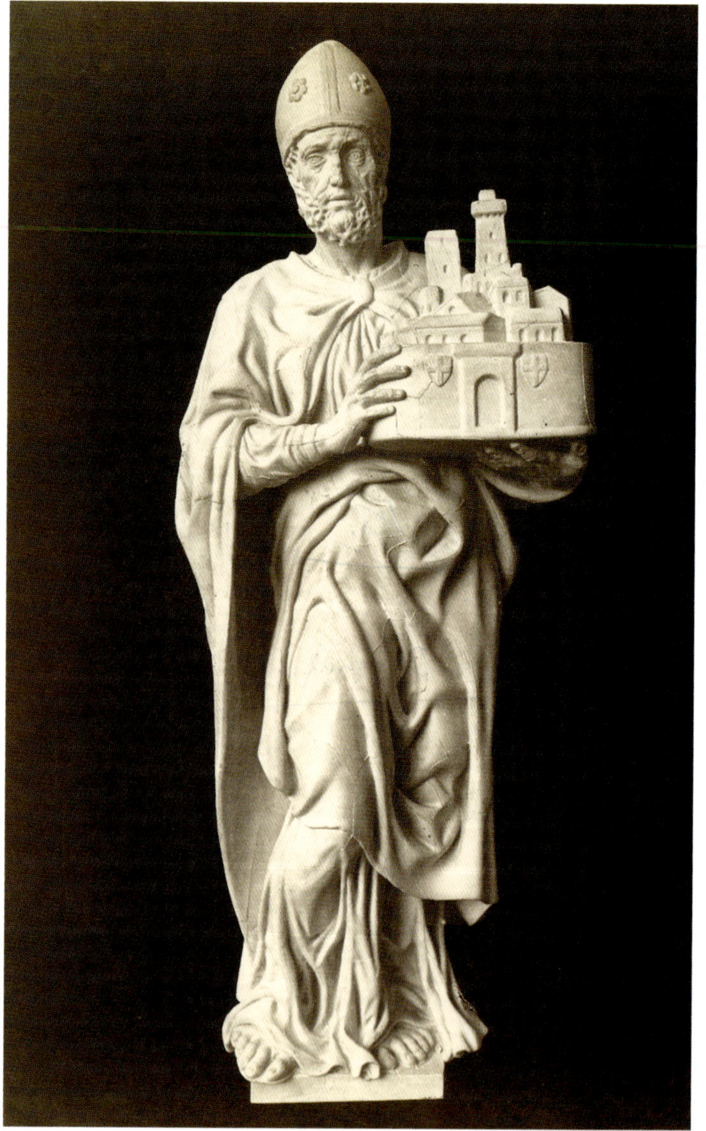

St Petronius, 1494–5. The patron saint of Bologna, St Petronius was one of the three sculptures created by Michelangelo for the Bolognese church of San Domenico. He was paid 18 ducats for the figure.

COUNTERFEIT CUPID

When Michelangelo arrived back in Florence, the city had changed enormously. Savonarola was ruler in all but name, and under his puritanical regime no one from the Florentine government commissioned art. Nonetheless, some younger members of the Medici family who had returned to Florence welcomed Michelangelo's return. Lorenzo di Pierfrancesco de' Medici (1463–1503, nicknamed the *Popolano* – man of the people) was a cousin of Lorenzo and had sided against Piero the Unfortunate, meaning that he was able to return to Florence. He now invited Michelangelo to live in the Medici household once again. Michelangelo accepted, and there he created at least two new sculptures. One was a small statue of a young St John the Baptist and the other was a Sleeping Cupid. Both of these works are now lost, but the Cupid was probably based on an antique sculpture in the Medici collection and was well-known to Michelangelo. It is not clear who decided on the next step – Michelangelo himself or Lorenzo di Pierfrancesco – but the sculpture was artificially aged by being buried to attain a worn patina. Then it was sent to Rome and sold to Cardinal Raffaele Riario (1461–1521) for 200 ducats. When Riario later discovered that he had bought a forgery, he insisted on a refund.

Sleeping Eros, *artist unknown, c. 330–10* BCE. *This ancient Greek statue of a sleeping Eros is along similar lines to the statue sculpted by the 21-year-old Michelangelo while living with Lorenzo di Pierfrancesco and subsequently sold to Cardinal Riario in Rome.*

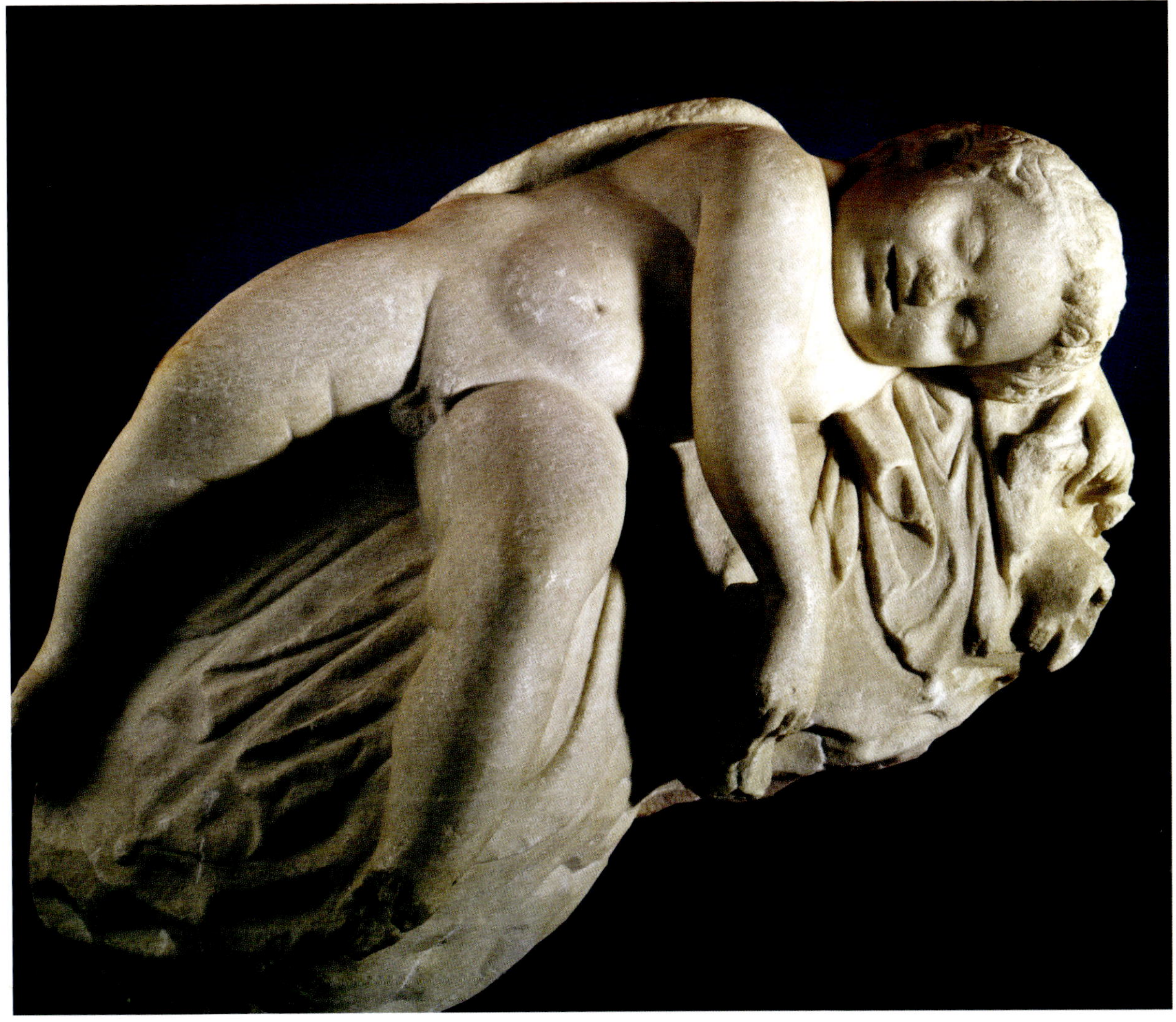

ROME

Rather than feeling resentment towards Michelangelo, Cardinal Riario was intrigued by the young man who had been intimate with Lorenzo de' Medici and who had such skill that he had fooled Riario about the 'antique' sculpture. Riario had one of the greatest collections of genuine antique sculpture at the time, and he sent his banker Jacopo Galli (c. 1460–1505) to Florence to find Michelangelo and bring him back to Rome. At the end of June 1496, Galli returned to Rome with Michelangelo, and for the next two years, Michelangelo lived and worked in Galli's mansion that was located near to the Campo de' Fiori. Cardinal Riario showed Michelangelo his collection of antique sculpture, asked his advice about the art, paid him to assist with the buying of more antiquities, and commissioned him to create a life-sized marble sculpture of Bacchus, the mythical god of wine, to accompany the ancient works. However, when Michelangelo had completed the sculpture in July 1497, Riario rejected it. It is not clear why. Perhaps it appeared too 'modern', or it may have been because the block of marble purchased by Riario for the work was of poor quality, or simply because Riario did not like Michelangelo's interpretation of the pagan god of wine. Whatever the reason, Michelangelo sold the work to Galli instead. In the work, Michelangelo presents Bacchus leaning drunkenly on a rock, wearing an ivy wreath and holding a goblet in one hand, close to his lips. In the other hand, he holds a lion skin. Behind his left leg is a small satyr. Although the work was intended to mimic classical Greek sculpture and was artificially distressed to give it an antique appearance, Michelangelo's Bacchus is more human than idealized. His Bacchus is clearly drunk and his body appears to be lurching, unlike any classical sculpture.

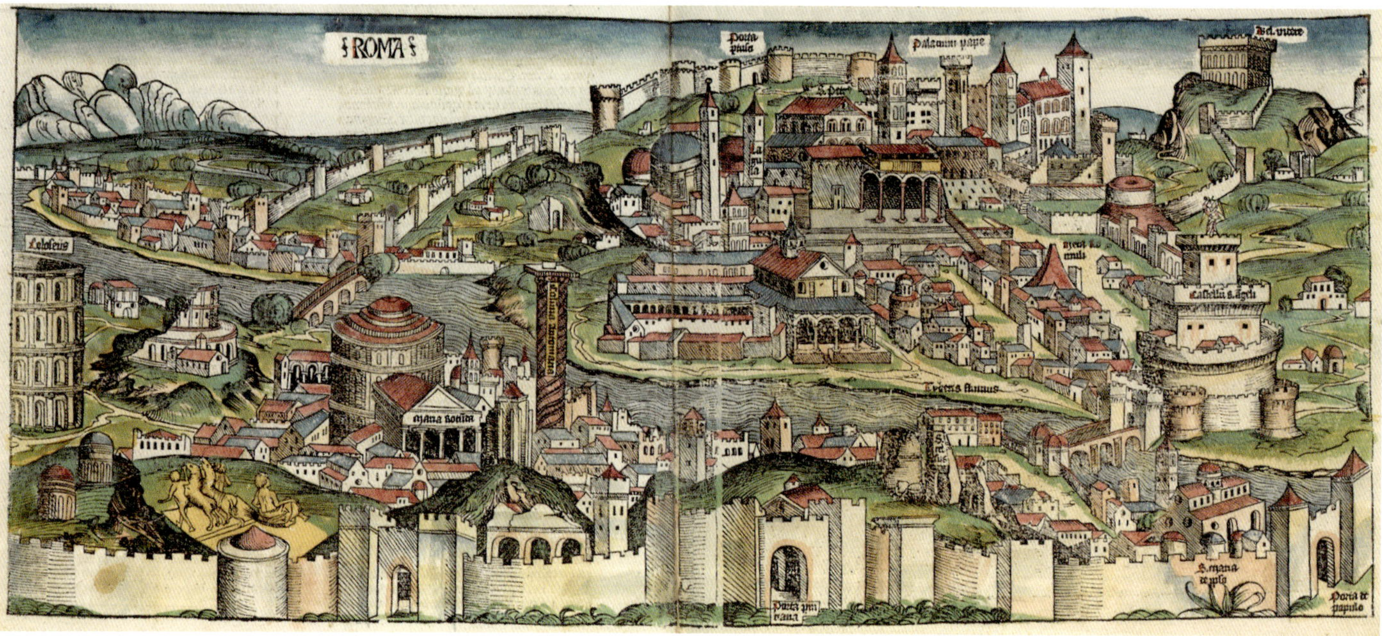

View of the City of Rome, in the Nuremberg Chronicle, *1493. The* Nuremberg Chronicle *is an illustrated book written in Latin by Hartmann Schedel (1440–1514) and illustrated by the Nuremberg artists Michael Wolgemut (1434–1519) and Wilhelm Pleydenwurff (c. 1450–94) during the time that Michelangelo was living in Rome. Along with the histories of several Western cities, the* Nuremberg Chronicle *features some biblical stories.*

Bacchus, 1496–7. Rejected by Riario, this sculpture of Bacchus appears to sway in drunkenness. With his swollen breasts and abdomen, the figure was described by Vasari as having 'both the slenderness of a young man and the fleshiness and roundness of a woman'.

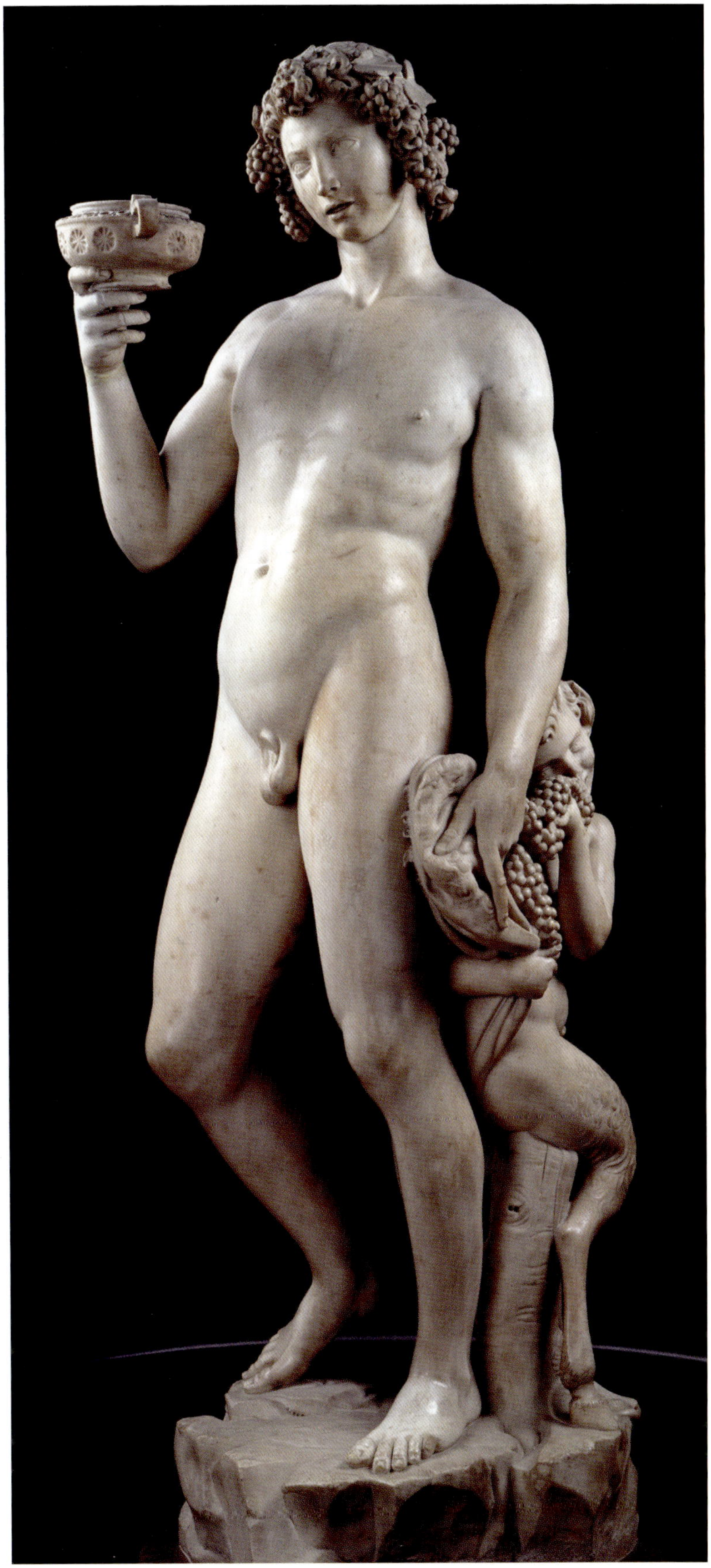

Detail of satyr from adjacent sculpture. This small satyr hiding behind Bacchus eats grapes that are slipping out of the god's left hand. Satyrs were common in pagan myths as half-human, half-goat figures, and often aligned to Bacchus.

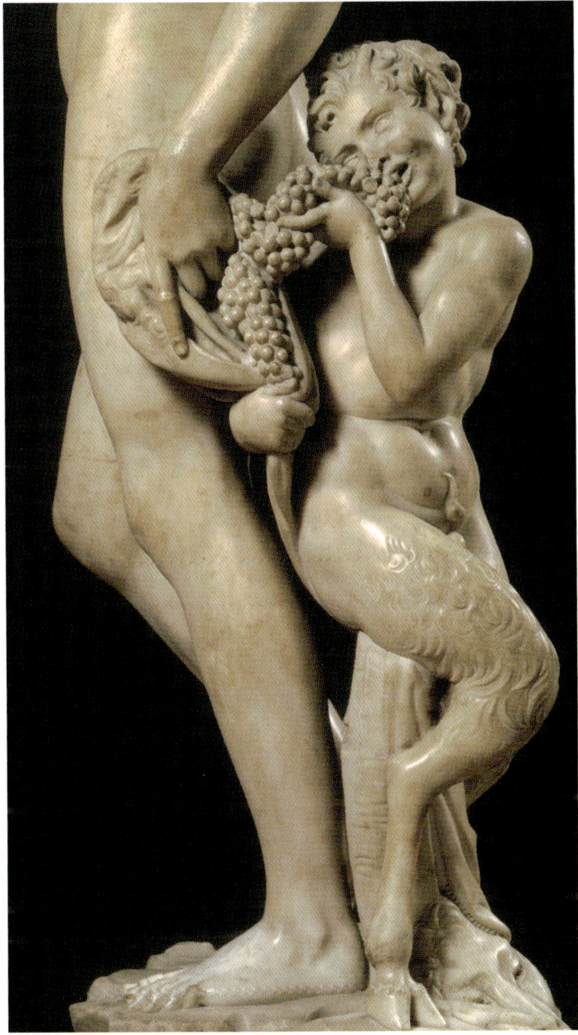

THE MANCHESTER MADONNA

While living in Rome, Michelangelo started work on a panel painting. It is not known who commissioned the work, nor why Michelangelo did not complete it, but some parts are detailed, while other areas have hardly been started. It is likely that he stopped working on it when he received a more attractive commission. With only three of Michelangelo's panel paintings known, this work is extremely rare, and because it is unfinished it shows much of his painting technique. His method here is one that he became known for above other High Renaissance painters and that influenced many later painters: *cangiante*, from the Italian *cangiare* (to change). Characterized by colour changes to describe darkness or lightness, *cangiante* can be seen in the yellow parts of the hair to convey highlighted areas of brown. Using a plain background, Michelangelo placed his figures as if in a sculptural frieze and used strong tonal transitions, all of which reflects his preference for sculpture. The black on the Virgin's cloak would have been used to intensify shadows when he painted lapis lazuli, or bright blue, over it. Probably the earliest of Michelangelo's panel paintings, this has been known as *The Manchester Madonna* since 1857, when it was exhibited in the great Manchester Art Exhibition in the UK and about 1.3 million visitors saw it.

THE COMMISSION

In the autumn of 1497, the French ambassador in Rome for Charles VIII, Cardinal Jean Bilhères de Lagraulas (1434/9–99) commissioned Michelangelo to create a work of sculpture. In a letter, Jean Bilhères wrote that he planned to use this work – a *pietà* (in Christian art, a *pietà*, meaning 'pity', is a depiction of the Virgin Mary cradling the dead body of Jesus) – for his tomb. He wrote: 'We have recently agreed with master Michele Angelo di Ludovico, Florentine sculptor and bearer of this, that he make for us a marble tombstone, namely a clothed Virgin Mary with a dead Christ naked in her arms.' The figure of Christ was to be as 'large as an actual man'. The agreement was made in 1497, although the Cardinal did not sign the contract for Michelangelo to begin the work until the summer of 1498. Nonetheless, the artist been looking for a suitable piece of marble at the quarries of Carrara since the previous November.

PIETÀ

Galli had signed the contract with Jean Bilhères de Lagraulus for the *Pietà* commission on behalf of Michelangelo, agreeing to a fee of 450 ducats for the finished work, the price of the marble to be added on. This was three times the amount that Michelangelo had been paid for *Bacchus*. The Cardinal wanted the statue for his burial chamber, in the chapel of Santa Petronila in St Peter's Basilica, and Michelangelo completed it in less than two years. In a pyramidal composition, the Virgin Mary (more than life-sized) holds her son's lifeless body across her lap. This is the moment after Jesus was crucified and before his body was placed in the tomb – a theme that was more common in northern Europe than in Italy.

The work is deliberately out of proportion although this is not immediately apparent. Mary is too large in comparison with Jesus. This is a technical necessity, so that the

The Madonna and Child with St John and Angels (The Manchester Madonna), c. 1497, possibly as early as 1494. In this unfinished panel painting, Mary sits on a rock with Christ and John the Baptist. The angels around her are not all finished; the greenish underpainting was traditionally used under light flesh tones. Mary's exposed breast implies that she has just fed her baby, who tries to grasp the book she is holding. Hatched and cross-hatched brushstrokes would not have been visible if the work was finished.

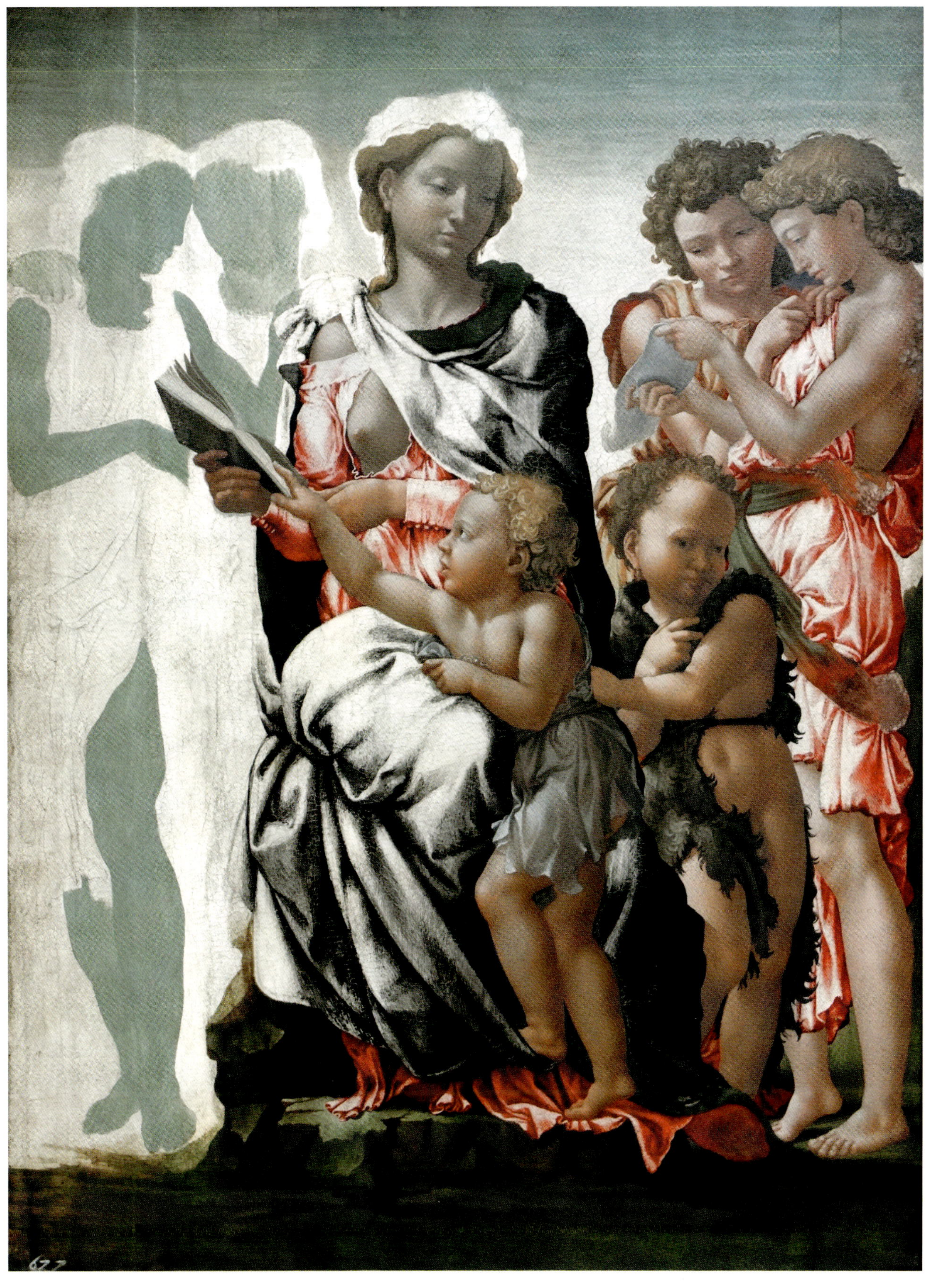

figure of Christ fits across her lap. However, the only criticism was that Mary looks too young to be the mother of a man in his 30s. Michelangelo insisted that her earthly youthfulness was because of her divine, spiritual beauty. This is the only work that he signed. According to Vasari, when it was unveiled, Michelangelo overheard visitors claim that the great work was by 'Our Gobbo from Milan', a reference to the sculptor Cristoforo Solari (*c.* 1460–1527). Irritated, one night he carved on a diagonal sash across Mary's chest, the words: MICHELANGELUS BUONARROTUS FIORENTINUS FACIEBAT or 'Michelangelo Buonarroti, Florentine, made this'. Artists of the period did not usually sign their work, and it was also unusual in that he gave himself the name 'Michael the Angel' – signifying the messenger or archangel sent from God. It demonstrates his pride in his work and belief in his own genius – but afterwards, he regretted his arrogance and never signed another work he produced. By July 1500, the sculpture was installed in the Cardinal's funerary chapel, and Michelangelo became instantly famous.

Pietà, 1498–9. *The* Pietà *combines idealism with naturalism, and Michelangelo's rendition of the theme was unprecedented. His treatment of the cold, hard marble to convey warm, soft flesh and draping fabrics is exceptional, especially for such a young and inexperienced artist. In the eighteenth century, Michelangelo's* Pietà *was moved to a new location in St Peter's Basilica.*

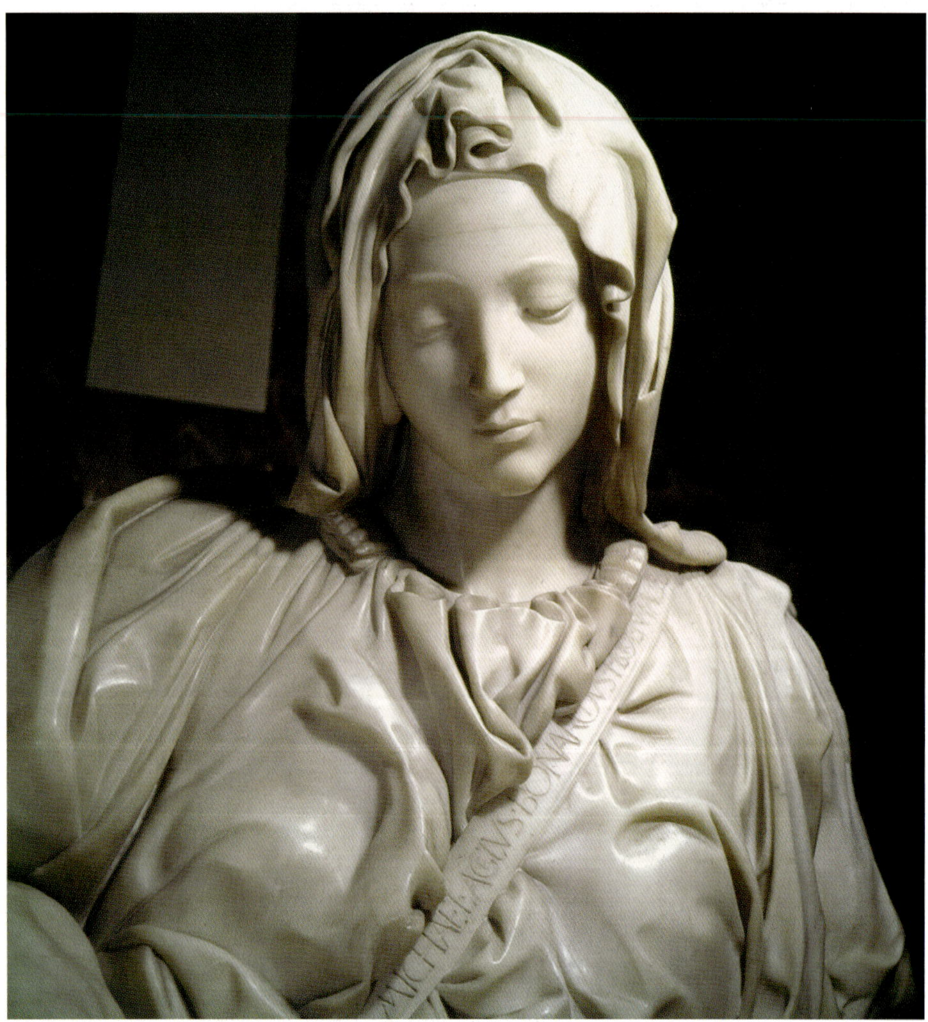

Mary's head, detail of the Pietà, *facing page. Michelangelo created complex, billowing, draped fabrics around the form of the Virgin Mary to conceal her body's over-large dimensions. He refined and polished this work more than any other sculpture he created.*

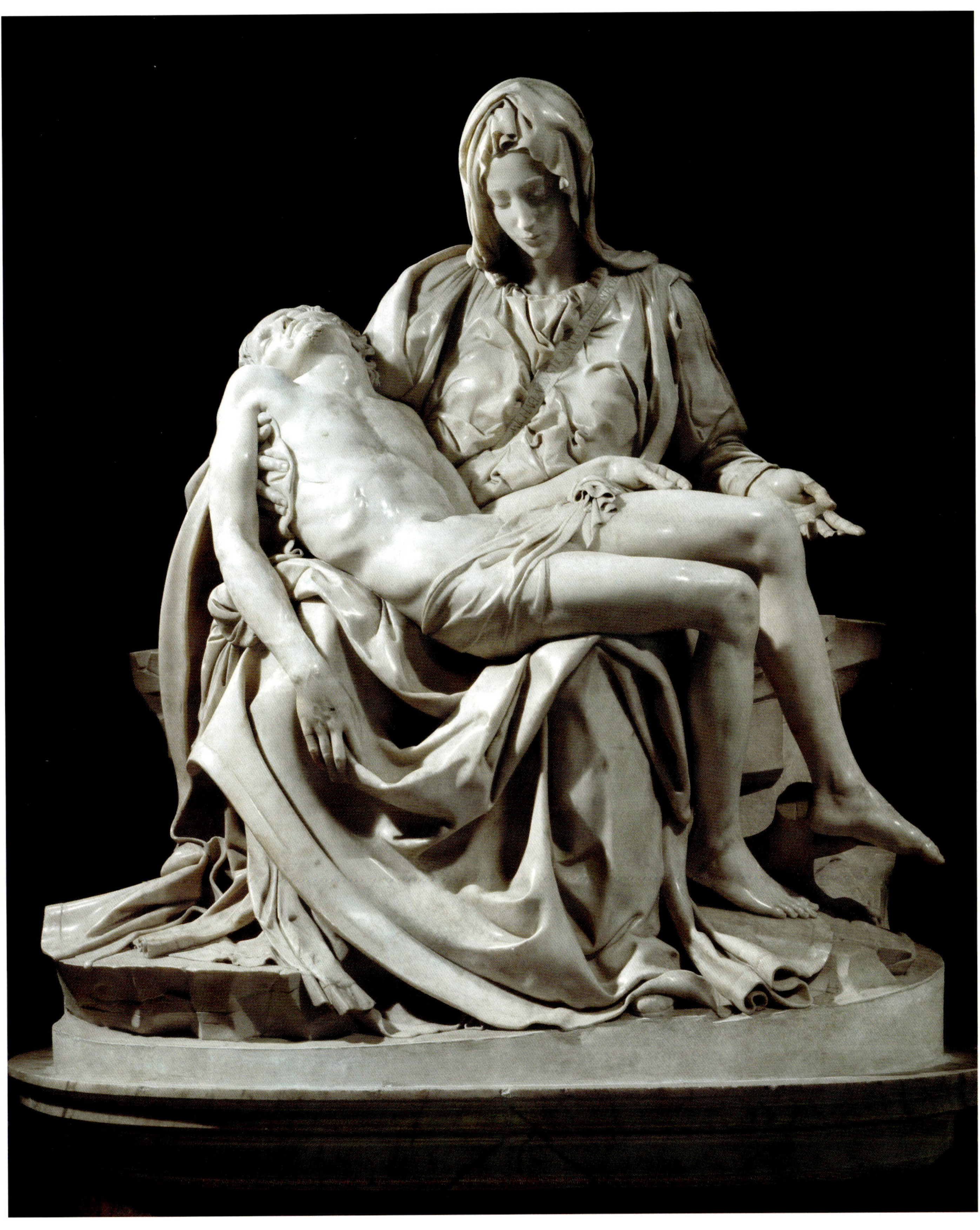

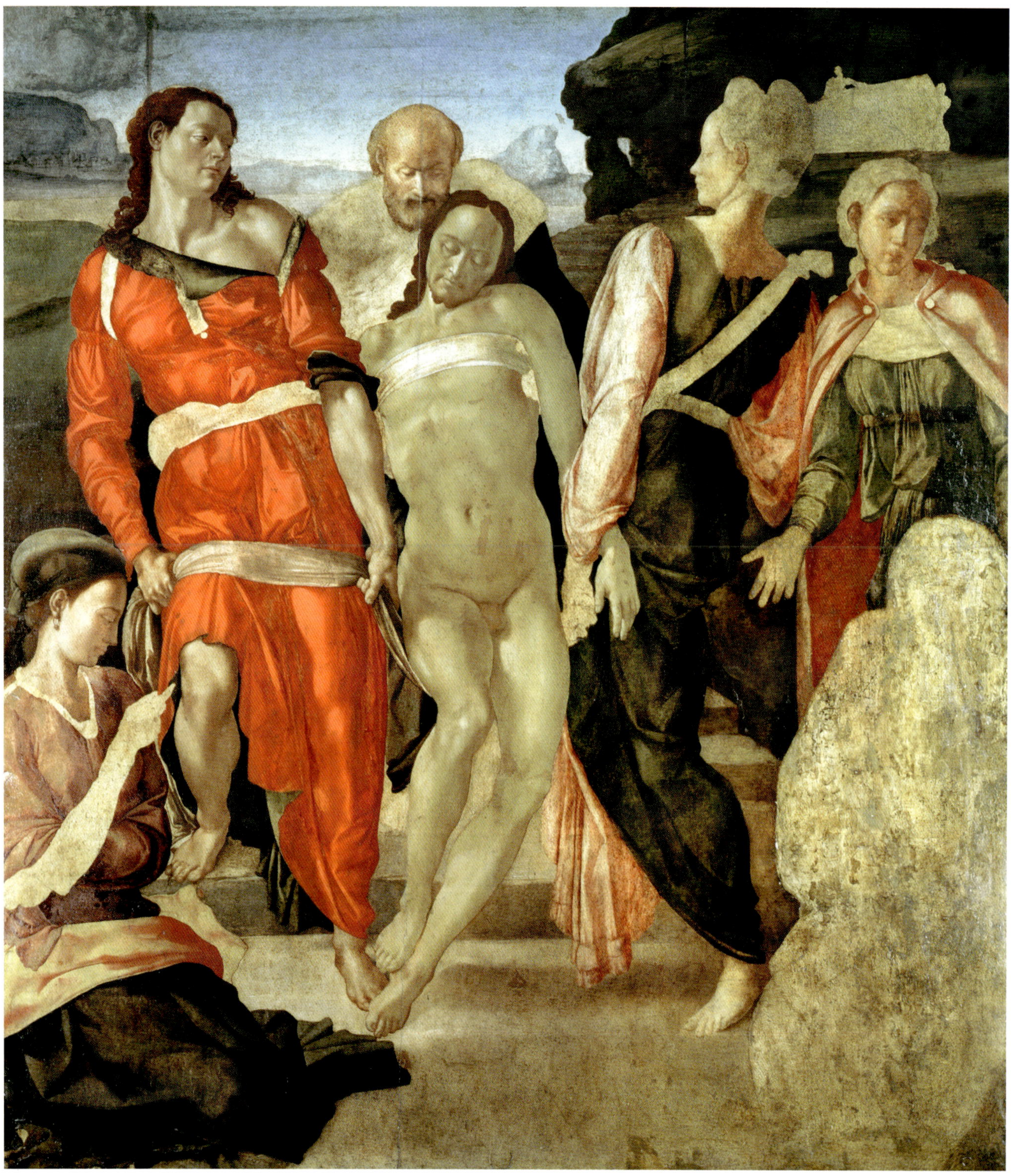

The Entombment, 1500–1. One of only three known surviving panel paintings by Michelangelo, this shows Christ's upright body being carried to his tomb after the Crucifixion. The figure on the left holding Christ's body is probably St John the Evangelist, the man behind is either Joseph of Arimathea or Nicodemus, and partially included are the Three Marys. The painting's unfinished state allows some understanding of Michelangelo's oil painting technique. Following tempera rather than oil painting techniques, he painted each figure completely before the next, and instead of applying transparent glazes over opaque underpainting as was traditional with oils, he blended colours and tones while the paint was still wet.

CARRARA

Used since ancient Roman times, Carrara marble is a particular white or blue-grey marble that is quarried in the city of Carrara in the north of modern-day Tuscany. The Carrara quarries have produced more marble than anywhere else in the world. Among many famous works, the Pantheon (113–125) and Trajan's Column (107–113), both in Rome, are made of Carrara, and along with many other sculptors of the time, Michelangelo favoured it. From the end of November to the end of December 1497, he made numerous trips to Carrara to select the marble he needed for his *Pietà*. He even set up a workshop at Carrara to prepare the stone he chose before it was transported to Rome. When he found it, he declared that the block of Carrara marble he would work on for the Cardinal's tomb was the most 'perfect' marble block he had ever used.

The Carrara quarries in Tuscany have produced more marble than anywhere else in the world. This is one of the Carrara quarries in the province of Massa-Carrara in northern Italy.

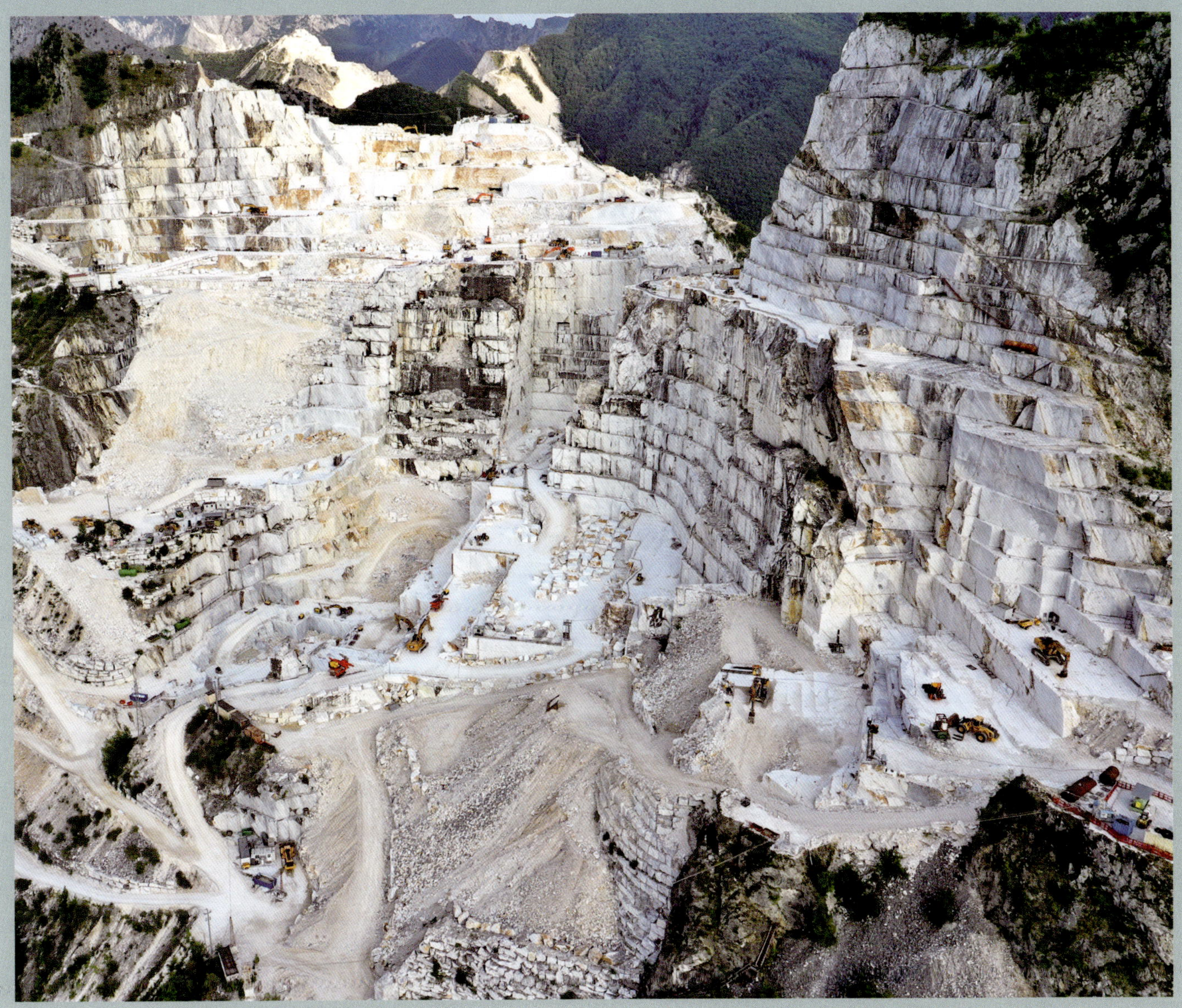

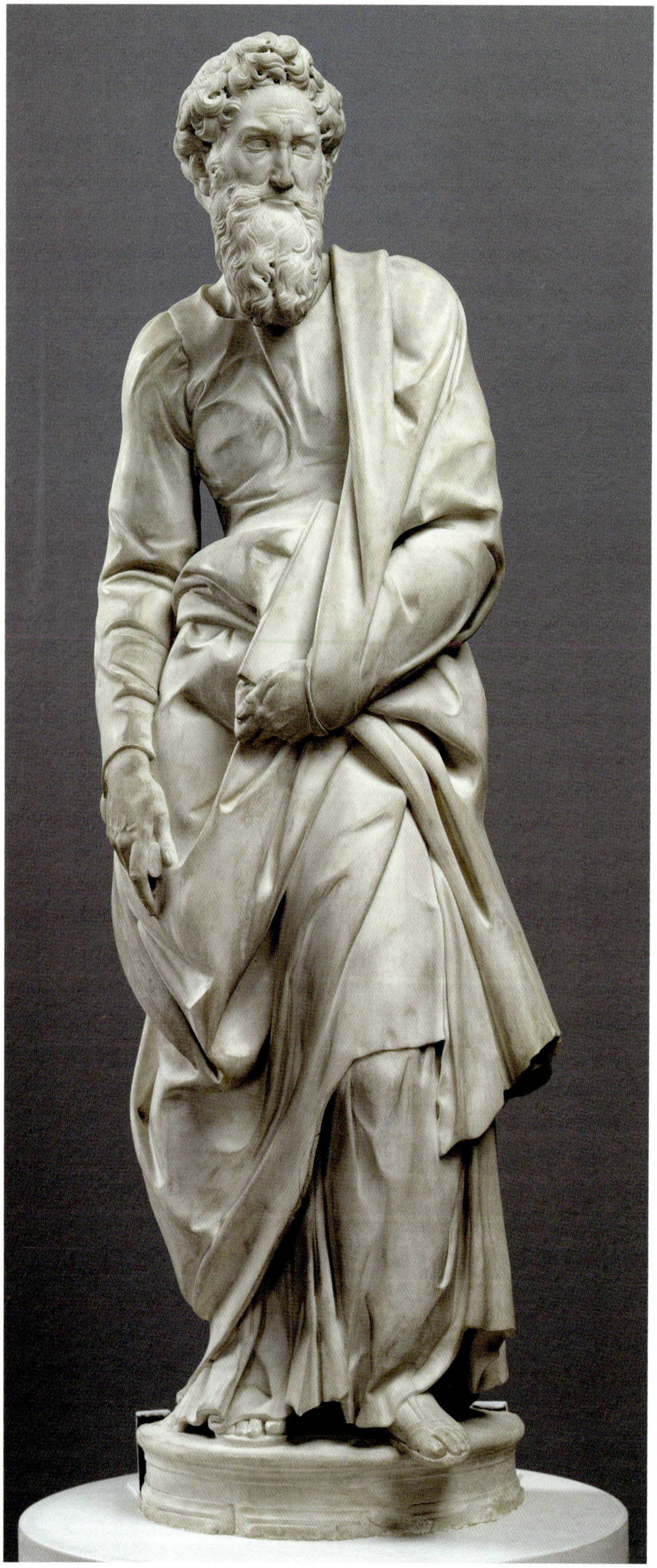

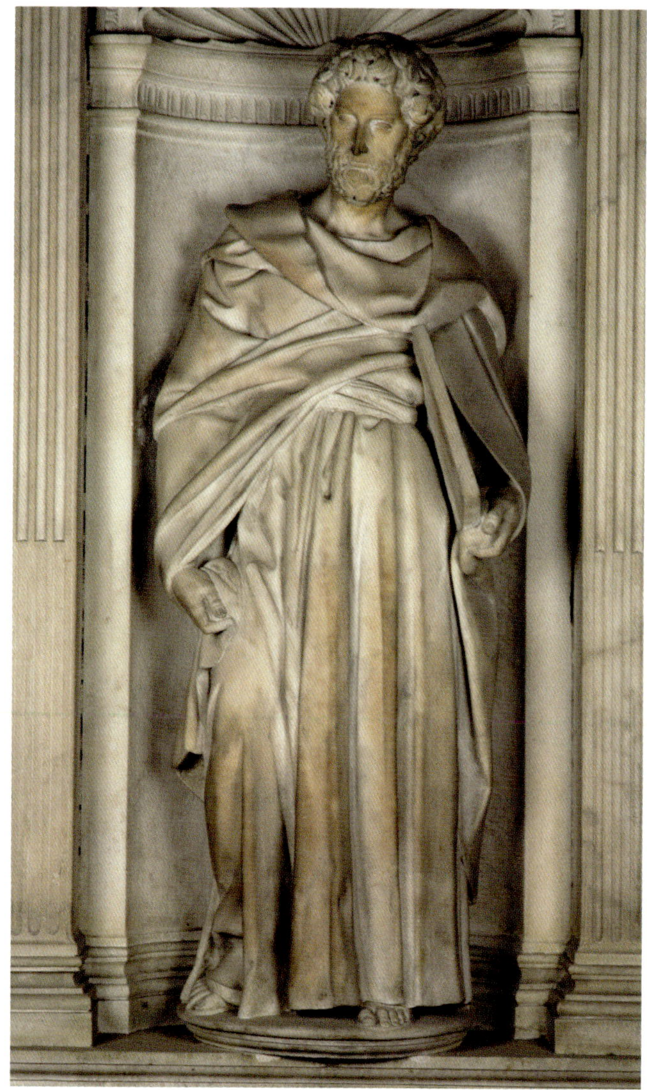

St Peter, 1501–4. The Piccolomini Altarpiece in Siena Cathedral was commissioned in 1481–3 by Francesco Piccolomini (1439–1503), a cardinal who was later briefly Pope Pius III. While waiting to receive the contract for David in Florence, Michelangelo accepted the Cardinal's commission and created four sculptures of the saints Peter, Paul, Gregory and Pius for Cardinal Piccolo. This is his St Peter, who holds his cloak with his right hand and a book with this left.

St Paul, 1501–4. Although Cardinal Piccolomini commissioned Michelangelo to create 15 marble figures for the Sienese altar, he created only four of them before he became too busy. This led to a long dispute between Michelangelo and the Piccolomini family.

THE FLORENTINE CHALLENGE

Soon after completing his *Pietà* in Rome, Michelangelo returned to Florence. Since Savonarola had been executed in 1498, the Republic of Florence was reassessing itself, and an interest in the arts was reviving. In the spring of 1501, after undertaking several other commissions in Rome and amassing considerable savings, the artist arrived back in Florence. Having earned more between 1497 and 1501 than his father had earned in ten years, he was now recognized as a great master.

A century earlier, the *Operai* – the Overseers of the Office of Works of Florence Cathedral, which consisted mostly of members of the influential woollen cloth guild, the *Arte della Lana* – had decided to commission 12 large Old Testament figures to stand on the cathedral buttresses. In 1410, Donatello had made the first of the statues, a figure of Joshua in terracotta. In 1464, the *Operai* commissioned the sculptor Agostino di Duccio (1418–*c.* 1481) to create a sculpture of the biblical hero David. They acquired a block of Carrara marble for this, but Agostino had only started to shape some of the statue when, for unknown reasons, he abandoned the project. Ten years later, Antonio Rossellino (1427–79) was commissioned to finish the work, but his contract was terminated within a short time, again for unknown reasons, and the marble block was left in the yard of the cathedral workshop for a further 26 years. Determined to find an artist who could create a work of art out of the large, expensive piece of marble, which had been started by Agostino, the *Operai* now let it be known that they intended to commission an accomplished sculptor. Andrea Sansovino (*c.* 1467–1529) applied, explaining that he would create the statue using the original block with additional pieces of marble attached. Then Michelangelo applied, explaining that he could make a statue of David using the block and not requiring any additional pieces of marble. In August 1501, Michelangelo was given the contract to undertake this challenging task.

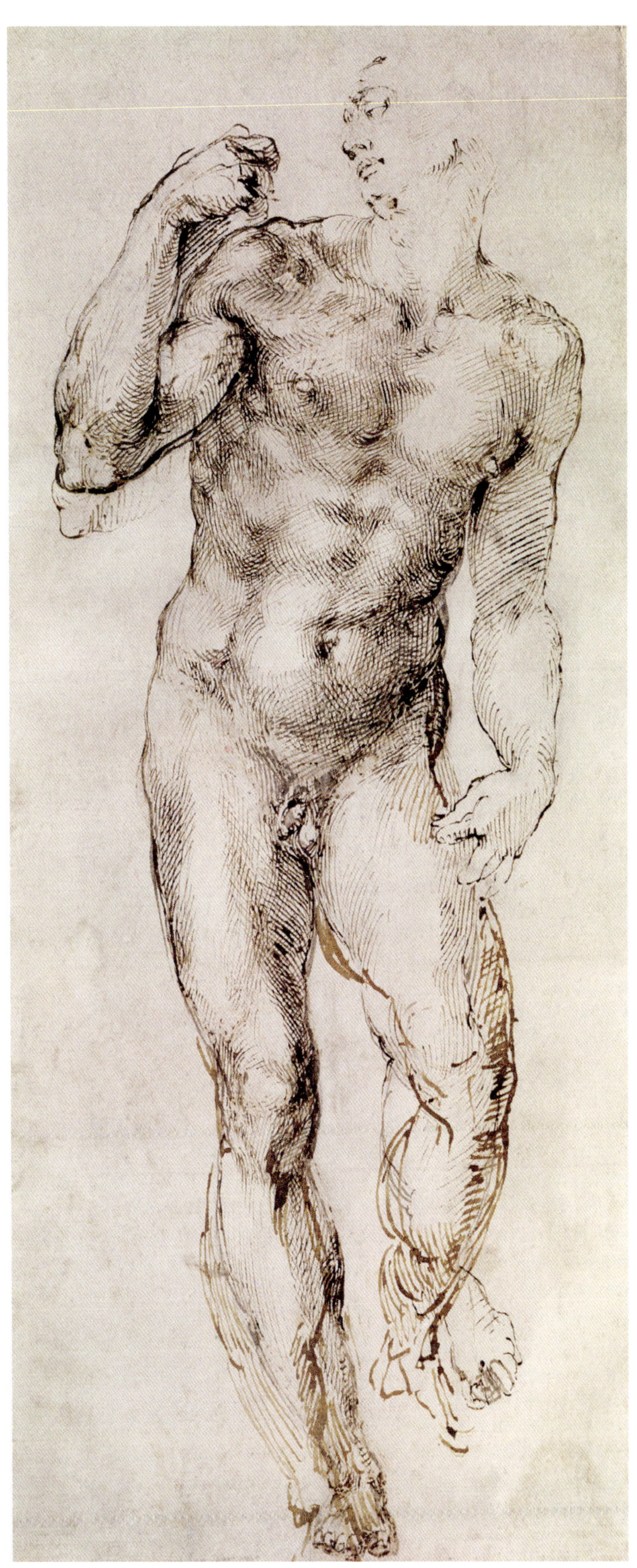

Study for David with his Sling, 1503–4. Michelangelo explored several ideas for his final statue of David. Because so much of the marble block had already been hacked, Michelangelo planned for the figure to be naked but also wanted to show him holding the sling.

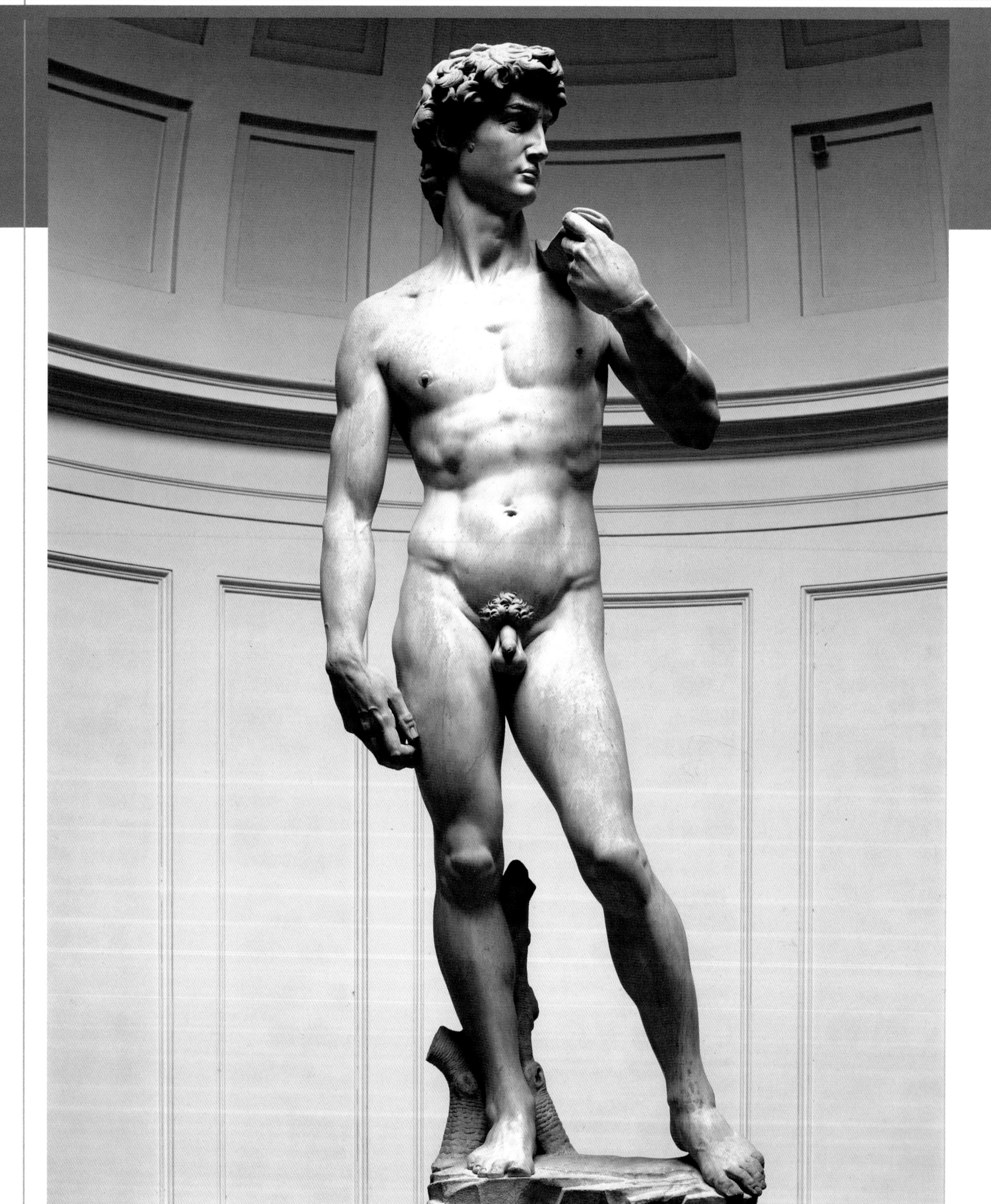

CHAPTER 3
Fluctuating Fortunes

During the medieval period and early Renaissance in Florence, a *Gonfaloniere* was often elected to hold a prestigious post in the government, comparable to a chief magistrate. In 1502, for the first time in the history of Florence, a *Gonfaloniere* was elected for life, to rule the city and to live in the Palazzo Vecchio (then called the Palazzo della Signoria). Piero Soderini (1450–1522) was chosen from a wealthy and prominent family. He proved to be a moderate and thoughtful ruler, and he became Michelangelo's patron and close friend.

DAVID

Michelangelo began carving his statue of David early in the morning of 13 September 1501, a month after he was given the contract, and he worked on it for approximately 21 months. At first, he carved in full view of anyone who wanted to watch him work, but by October 1501, he paid for a wall to be built around the work and in December, he had a roof put over it. By the end of February 1502, he renegotiated his payment for the work and had it increased to 400 gold ducats, a large sum for the period. For St John's Day on 23 June 1503, the *Operai* removed the wall around the sculpture so that anyone who wanted to view the work in progress could do so. By then it had been decided that the statue was too good to be placed high up on the cathedral as the original commission stated, and instead should be where more people could see it in closer proximity. However, no one could agree about where it should go, so the following January, the *Operai* brought together 28 artists and architects to decide where to put it. Among these respected figures were Botticelli, Perugino (1446/1452–1523), Filippino Lippi (1457–1504) and Leonardo da Vinci (1452–1519). After a great deal of deliberation, it was ultimately decided that Michelangelo's *David* would stand in the Piazza della Signoria, the main square of Florence. To move the monumental statue from where Michelangelo had created it to its final location required a feat of engineering – and more than 40 men to turn winches and drag it along. A special cart was made to pull it through the streets, and it was heavily guarded before its unveiling. It took four days to move it a few hundred metres from the yard of the Opera del Duomo to the Piazza del Signoria. When it was unveiled, most viewers marvelled at the magnificent figure and how the cold, hard marble looked soft and warm. Some, however, were shocked at its blatant nakedness. Either way, *David* resembled a Greek god, and signified the might of Florence.

David, *1501–4. Depicting the young shepherd of the Bible who kills the giant Goliath with a sling and small rock, Michelangelo created a strong, narrow body in a* contrapposto *position that conveys strength and beauty, all from a damaged block of marble.*

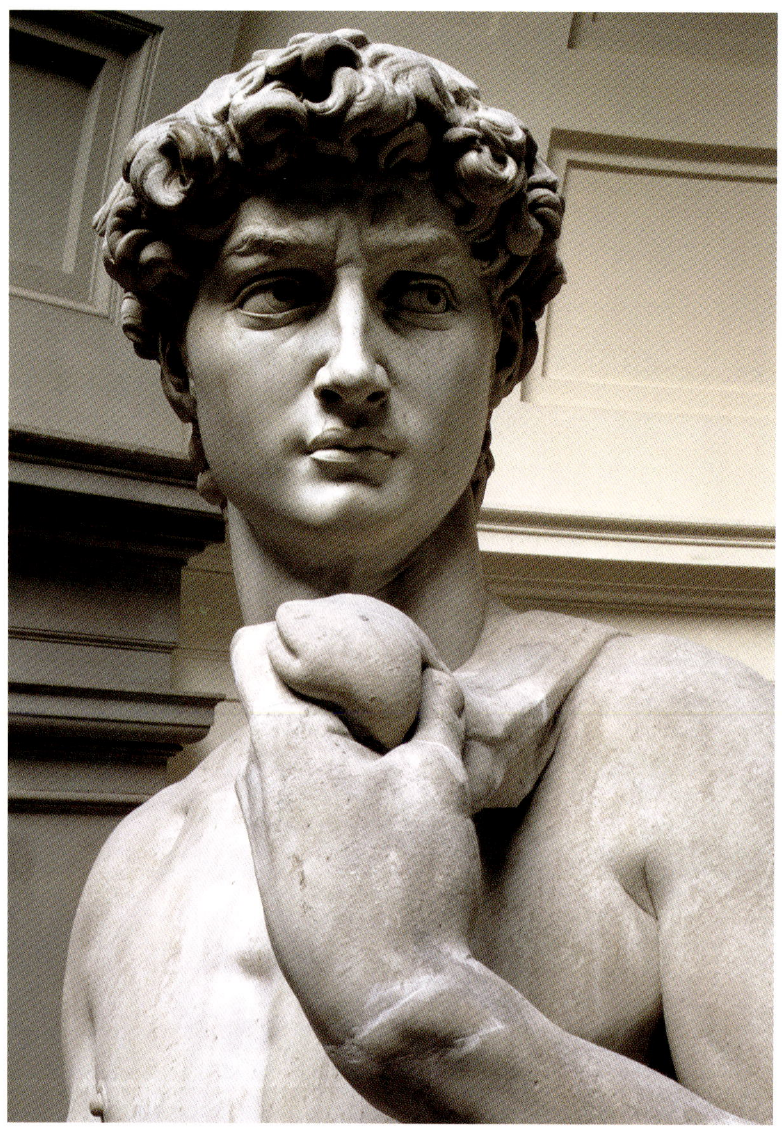

David's head, detail of sculpture on page 38. Vasari relates how, on first seeing the statue, Soderini commented that David's nose was too thick. Taking a chisel and some marble dust, Michelangelo climbed up and pretended to reshape the nose, sprinkling marble dust as he 'worked'. When he climbed down, Soderini observed that Michelangelo had improved the face.

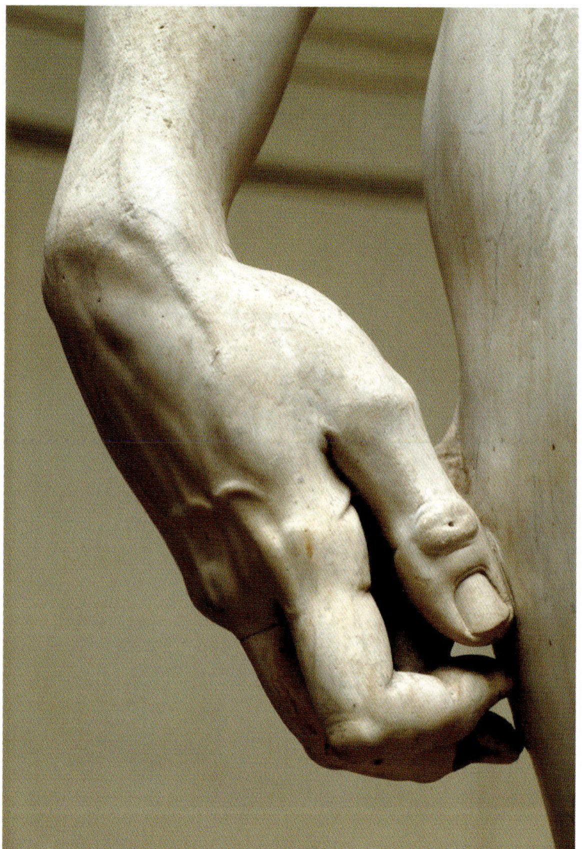

David's hand, detail of sculpture on page 38. David's right hand holds a small rock. Although detailed with prominent veins indicating the tension of the moment, this hand is out of proportion with the rest of the body. This is perhaps to symbolize his nickname, Manu Fortis (Strong Hand), or because when viewed from below it appears balanced with the rest of the figure, or because it conveys the disproportionate limbs of a growing youth.

RIVALS

By now, Michelangelo was a respected, established artist, so while working on *David* he was also working on other commissions. In late 1503, Leonardo da Vinci had been commissioned by the *Gonfaloniere* Piero Soderini to paint *The Battle of Anghiari* on a wall in the Hall of the Great Council in the Palazzo Vecchio (then called the Palazzo della Signoria), where the council of Florence met regularly. It was a prestigious commission in an important place, commemorating a great Florentine victory over Milan in 1440. In the autumn of 1504, Soderini commissioned Michelangelo to paint an equally large mural of *The Battle of Cascina* near to Leonardo's painting. The Battle of Cascina was another triumphant success for Florence, this time over Pisa, in 1364. Although the relationship between Michelangelo and Leonardo is not known, it seems that they probably did not like each other much. No correspondence between them or about each other survives. Leonardo was 16 years older than Michelangelo and was already established in Florence when Michelangelo returned from Rome. Leonardo was described by his early biographers as being kind and generous, while Michelangelo was passionate, quick to anger and harsh on himself. Soderini later claimed he had wanted the competition between them to propel their work. However, this rivalry over the battle paintings did not amount to much. On 6 July 1505, Leonardo began his mural, having made several preparatory works for it. He was depicting the cavalry, soldiers and horses in close combat. Michelangelo made a large cartoon for his work, which was to be a scene of predominantly naked soldiers jumping to action as they are ambushed while bathing in the River Arno. In the spring of 1506, Leonardo would abandon his unfinished painting and move on to other pressing work.

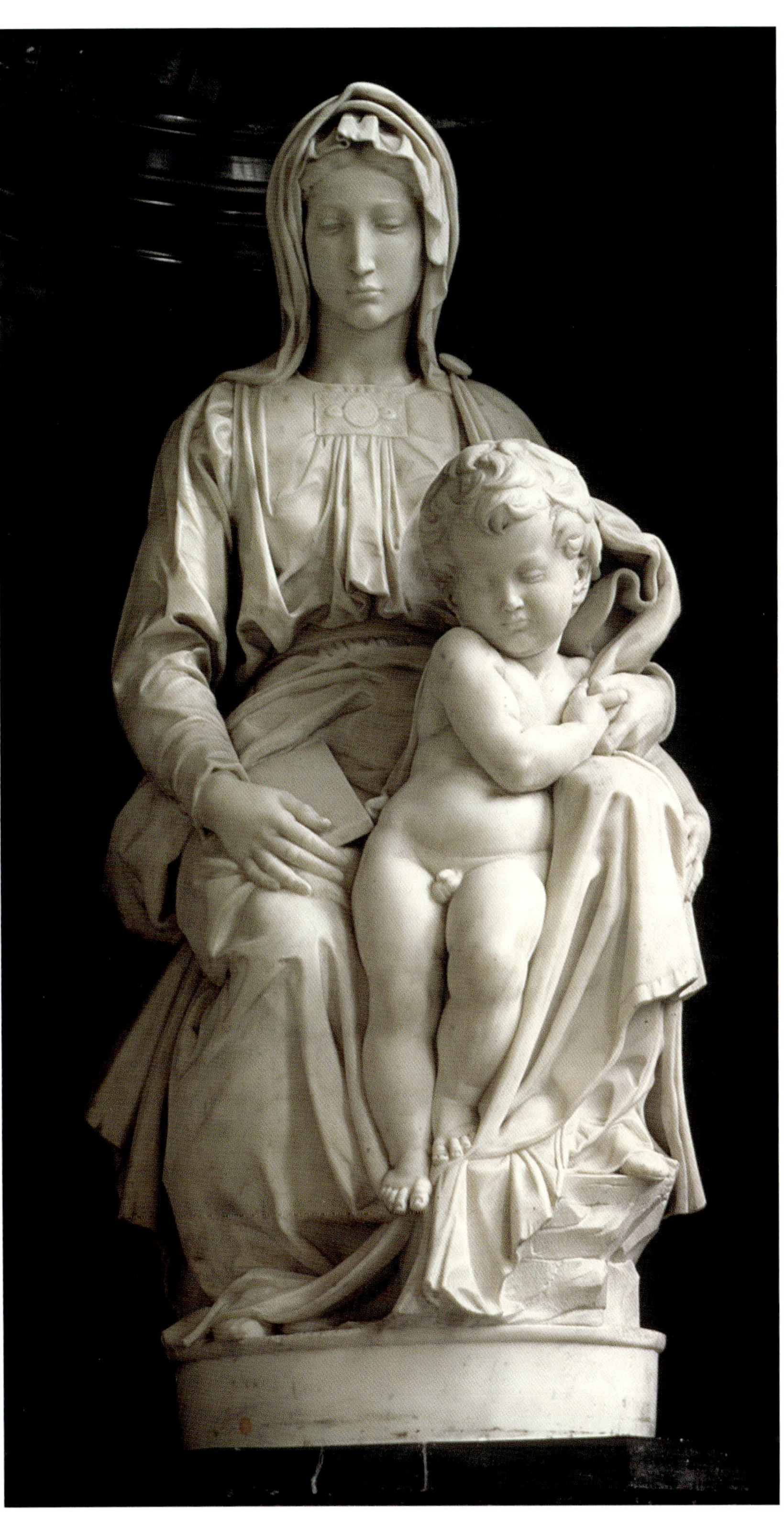

Madonna of Bruges, c. 1504–5. Jacopo Galli obtained this commission for Michelangelo, for two cloth merchants named Jean and Alexandre Mouscheron, for their family chapel in Bruges. The pyramidal composition and the Madonna's face resemble his Roman Pietà, *while unusually, Christ is a standing toddler, leaning on his mother rather than a baby on her lap.*

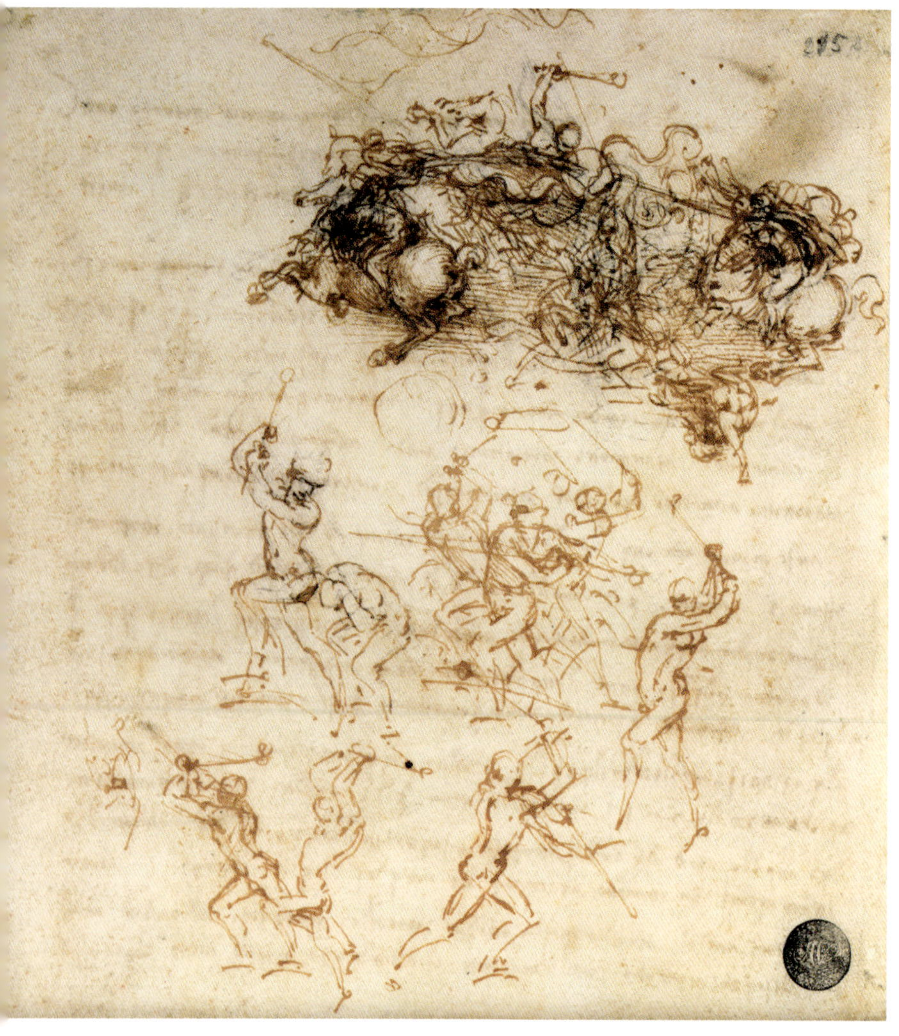

Study for The Battle of Anghiari, *Leonardo da Vinci, 1503–4. When the Republic of Florence decided to create an assembly hall for their most important political committee, they commissioned two large wall paintings to express success and self-confidence, choosing for their subjects two important Florentine victories: the Battle of Anghiari and the Battle of Cascina. This study, depicting horsemen in combat and foot soldiers, was made by Leonardo for his painting and is among the few sketches that remain. He never completed the actual painting, although other artists copied what he did complete.*

Below: The Battle of Cascina *or* The Bathers, after *Michelangelo, Aristotile da Sangallo, 1542. Although Michelangelo's cartoon for* The Battle of Cascina *was much admired and studied by his contemporaries, it did not survive. According to Vasari, the original cartoon was destroyed by one of Michelangelo's rivals, Bartolommeo (Baccio) Bandinelli (1488–1560) through jealousy. Fortunately, his pupil, Bastiano (Aristotile) da Sangallo (1481–1551) made a copy of the central section of the image. Several other artists also copied it, but this is the most well-known copy to have survived. This scene, in which the figures are depicted twisting and moving with great energy, represents an early moment in the battle when the Florentine army was taken by surprise by the Pisans.*

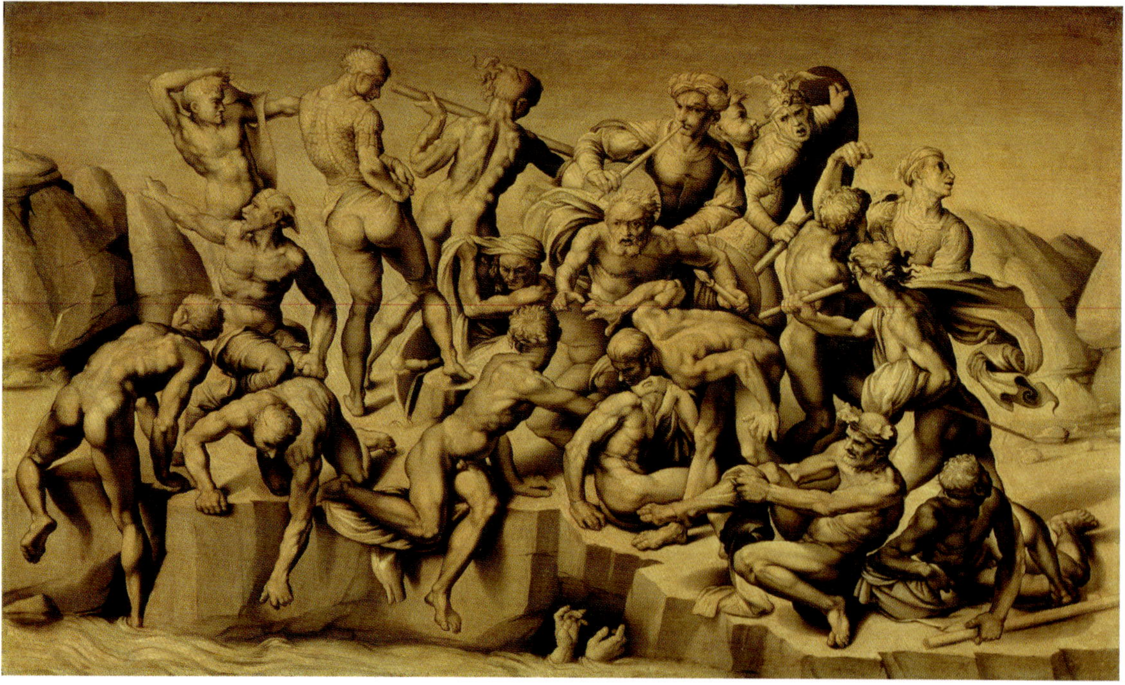

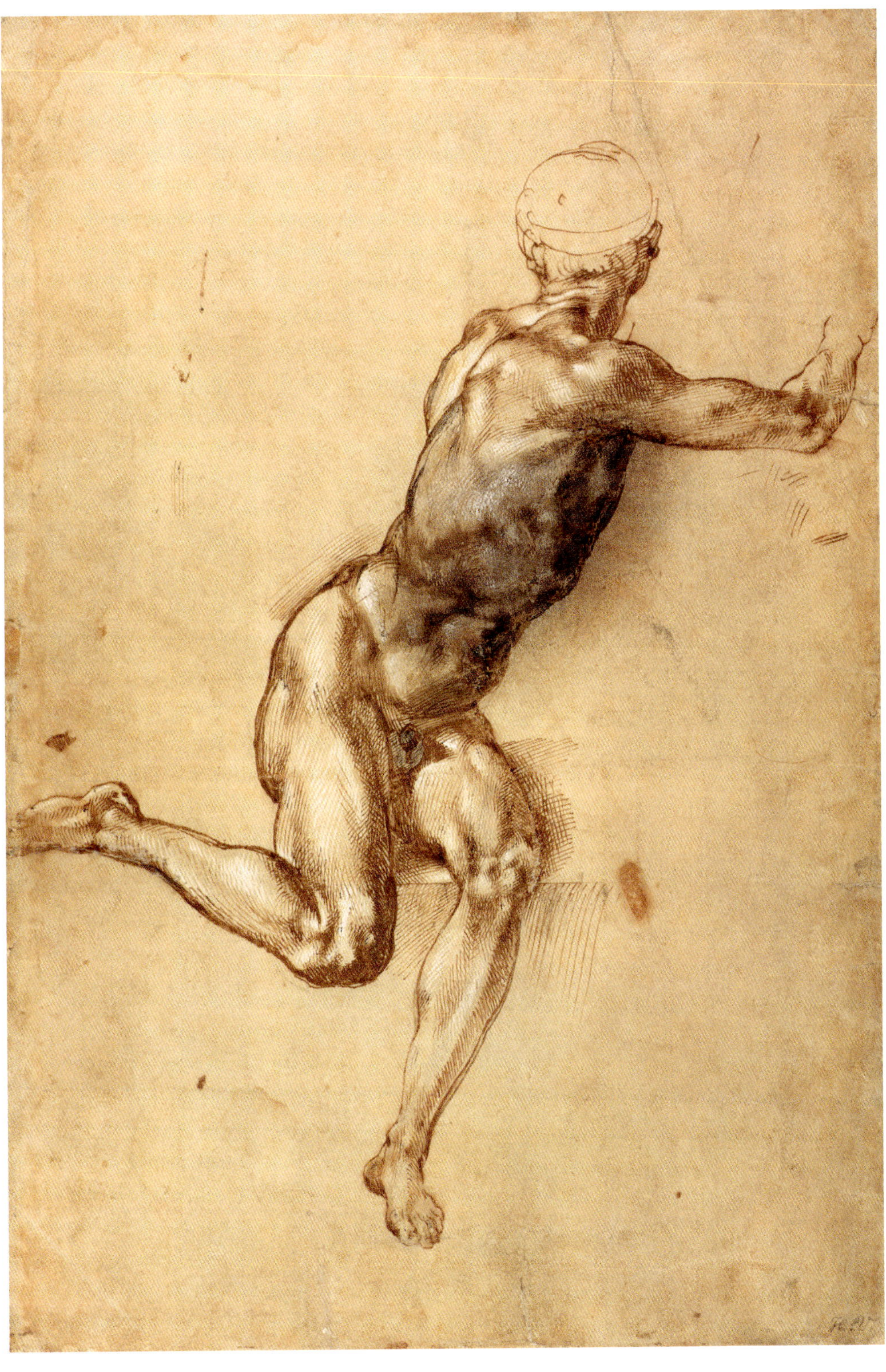

The part of the painting Leonardo had started soon began to deteriorate due to the formula of paint he had used. As for Michelangelo, he had been summoned to Rome by the Pope in 1505, so he never even began the actual mural. Records of what both murals would have looked like remain through copies by other artists, and these had a significant impact on painting throughout Italy. Both works were intense, dynamic and skilful, but Leonardo's focused more on the horses and the battle itself, while Michelangelo's focused on the figures; their anatomy, gestures and emotions.

A seated male nude twisting around, 1504–5. This figure was to be in the centre of Michelangelo's Battle of Cascina. *Although it is an unnatural pose, the figure would have served to draw attention to the figures behind. Michelangelo completed only the cartoon for the work, but all who saw it admired the powerful sense of movement that he created.*

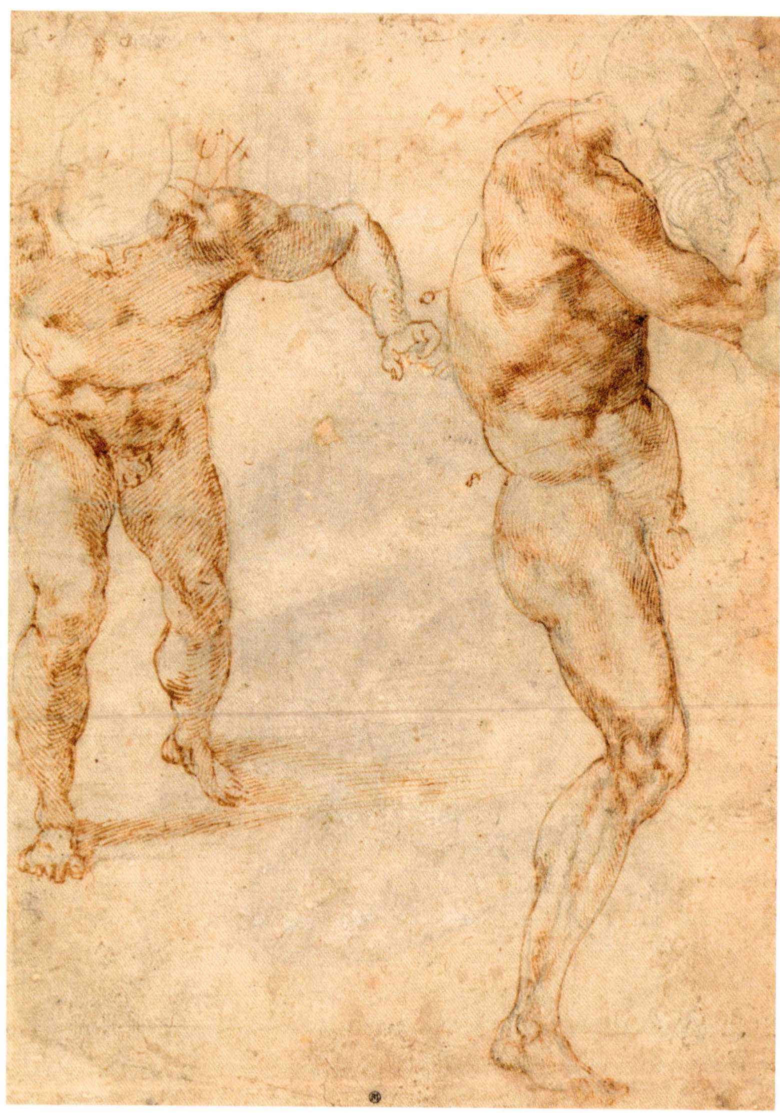

Nude studies of a forward- and a right-facing man, c. 1504. From the age of 17, Michelangelo dissected cadavers in the hospital at the Monastery of Santo Spirito. Pope Sixtus IV had allowed dissection in public of condemned criminals, and the focus on accurate anatomy became an important aspect of art.

DONI TONDO

Probably painted to celebrate the birth of the first child for the wealthy Florentine merchant Agnolo Doni (1474–1539) and his wife, the noblewoman Maddalena Strozzi (1489–1540), this is the only finished panel painting known by Michelangelo and one of only three in total. Sometimes called *The Holy Family*, the painting is in the form of a *tondo*, or circular, which was popular at the time for paintings in grand Italian homes. Michelangelo also designed the wood-gilt frame and painted Jesus, Mary and Joseph in a striking pyramidal composition. Mary is the most prominent figure in the centre, sitting in front of Joseph, on the ground, lifting her hands to take the child from him. She sits on grass, which contrasts with the barren ground behind her. In the background is a landscape including mountains and greenery, while five nude – unnamed – figures appear to be busy amongst themselves. They possibly represent the soul and the intellect. Also towards the back, but slightly closer to the foreground than the nudes, is John the Baptist, the patron saint of Florence. Between him and the Holy Family is a horizontal band. As a sculptor, Michelangelo used his paint in a sculptural manner, making strong distinctions between tones, so especially dark colours have been used for deep shadows and light colours for highlights in the *cangiante* technique. A similar sculptural effect is achieved by the creased fabrics and their draping, while skin and hair have also been rendered flawlessly.

Holy Family with the Infant St John the Baptist (Doni Tondo), 1505–6. This is Michelangelo's only known finished panel painting. The tondo, *or circular shape, was fashionable at the time and the image is created in a sculptural pyramidal composition to fill the space. The plants in the image have been included for their symbolism, such as the cornflower that is a symbol of Christ, and the anemone that symbolizes the Passion of Christ.*

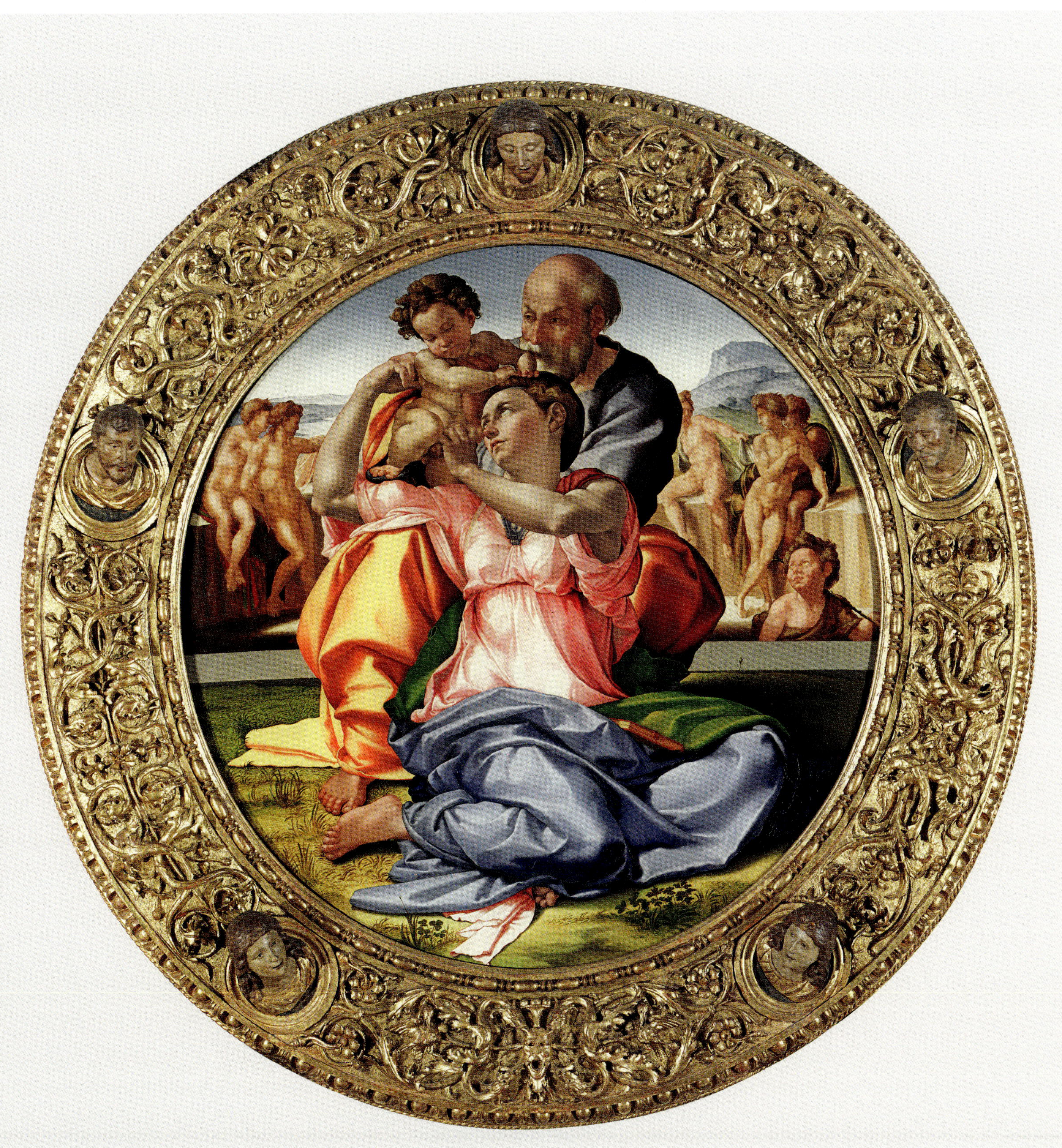

POPE JULIUS II

On 1 November 1503, Cardinal Giuliano della Rovere (1443–1513) was elected Pope Julius II. It is often said that he chose his papal name after Julius Caesar, and his ten-year reign became remembered for its varied achievements, especially war and art. Nicknamed the Warrior Pope or the Fearsome Pope, he was also one of the greatest art patrons of his time. Elected in the shortest conclave in history with a unanimous vote of the cardinals, Julius II spent most of his reign at war with Italian city states. He began by eliminating the most powerful men in Rome, including Cesare Borgia (1475–1507) and the heads of the powerful Colonna and Orsini families. After consolidating his dominance in Rome, he joined with Louis XII of France, Ferdinand II of Aragon and Maximilian I, the Holy Roman Emperor, to suppress the expansion of the Venetian Republic. In 1506, he led his papal troops into battle to free Bologna and Perugia from oppressive tyrants. He was also a Humanist and a Neoplatonist, and through his patronage of art he created a visual fusion of the three doctrines: Humanism, Neoplatonism and Christianity. He amassed a large collection of ancient sculptures and he sought to rebuild Rome, first demolishing the old St Peter's Basilica that had been erected by Constantine the Great (*c.* 272–337) and ordering its rebuilding in a magnificent design. For this, he commissioned the architect Donato Bramante (1444–1514), who laid the foundation stone in April 1506; and to decorate the cathedral and rooms in the Vatican, he commissioned artists including Michelangelo and Raphael (1483–1520). Julius died after a decade as pope, just as he was about to call for a crusade against the Ottoman Empire in order to retake Constantinople.

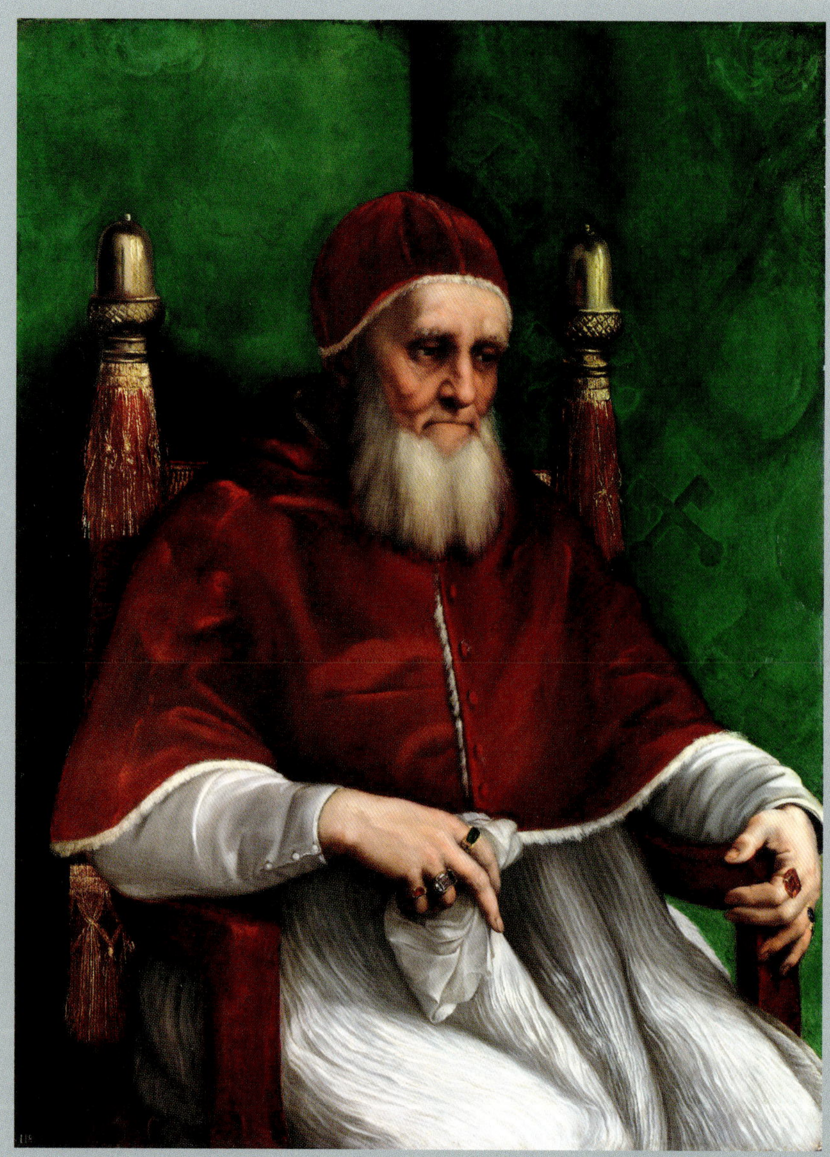

Portrait of Julius II, Raphael, c. 1511. One of three portraits of Julius II painted by Raphael when the Pope was 69 not long before he died. He is sitting, grasping one arm of his chair that features two acorn-shaped knobs on the back; acorns were part of Julius's coat of arms. The image is far more informal and relaxed than any previous papal portraits.

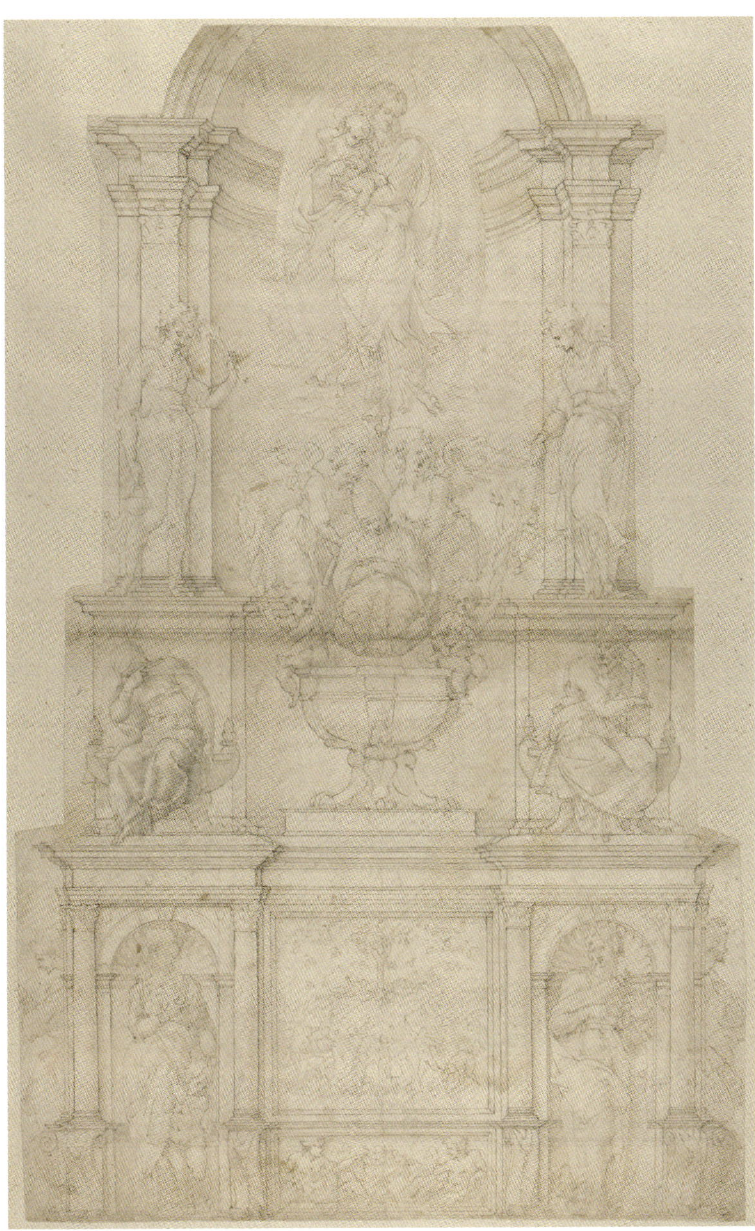

Design for the Tomb of Pope Julius II, c. 1505–6. Michelangelo eagerly accepted the Pope's prestigious commission to create his tomb and produced several drawings, including this, to show how all the statues would be placed in a setting of pillars, arches and niches on three tiers. The Pope was involved with the planning and he approved Michelangelo's design.

SUMMONS TO ROME

In February 1505, Pope Julius II summoned Michelangelo to Rome. After finishing his cartoon for the mural of *The Battle of Cascina*, Michelangelo left Florence, with 100 ducats sent from the Vatican for his travel expenses. By the end of March, he had reached Rome and entered the Papal Court, discovering that he was among several other ambitious artists and architects, including Raphael Sanzio and Donato Bramante. In his ambitions to rebuild Rome, the Pope gathered around him some of the greatest creative minds. Of these, the sculptor and architect Giuliano da Sangallo (1445–1516) recommended Michelangelo for a specific and personal project. The Pope had ambitions for a magnificent tomb to be created for him within St Peter's Basilica, which would surpass any other mausoleum known and commemorate his papacy.

THE POPE'S TOMB

As the new St Peter's Basilica was being constructed, Julius II began planning to have a grand tomb built for himself within it. Michelangelo began his first drawings of it as soon as he was commissioned by the Pope, early in 1505. According to a first (lost) contract, the project was initially going to cost 10,000 ducats and be completed in five years. It was to be a free-standing structure featuring niches containing approximately 40 marble statues. Among these would be 'two angels supporting a bier', one smiling for the joy of Pope Julius's life and one crying with grief at his death. The huge monument would have to be housed in its own area because there would not be enough space for it in St Peter's Basilica. Suggestions included a purpose-built chapel or a chancel that had been started years before but never completed. By April 1505, the Pope and Michelangelo finalized their plans for the extravagant monument and Michelangelo was given a thousand ducats in advance for the work. As well as the large marble sculptures, he planned to create bronze reliefs to illustrate the Pope's accomplishments – rather optimistic because at the time Julius had been pope for less than two years. Michelangelo made several drawings and spent eight months at Carrara choosing and supervising the quarrying and transport of some of the finest marble available. Yet during that time, the Pope's focus changed, and when Michelangelo returned to ask for reimbursement for the purchase and shipping of 100 tons of marble, he was denied an audience every day for a week and then finally told he would not be allowed to see the Pope at all. Julius had become concerned over the cost of the project and fearful that ordering his own grave was unlucky. Besides, he had other plans for the artist.

ENEMY IN ROME

The new project that Julius had in mind for Michelangelo was the repainting of the ceiling of the Sistine Chapel – the Pope's formal place of worship, which had been built by his uncle, Pope Sixtus IV (1414–84). It is commonly believed that Bramante, the architect in charge of rebuilding St Peter's Basilica, was so consumed with envy of Michelangelo that he persuaded Julius to be superstitious about his tomb, and to give Michelangelo the almost impossible task of painting the Sistine ceiling. Michelangelo's contempt of painting – he believed it to be inferior to sculpture – and his lack of skill in fresco was well-known, so it is probable that Bramante, certain his rival would fail, convinced the Pope that Michelangelo should be given the job. However, after Michelangelo had been refused entry into the Pope's presence, he wrote in a fury: 'Most Blessed Father, I was turned out of the Palace today by order of Your Holiness. I must therefore inform You that from now onwards, if You want me, You must seek me elsewhere than in Rome.' Seemingly without fear of the consequences, he withdrew his money from his Roman bank and left for Florence. Even when the Pope dispatched five men to bring him back, he refused. His friends and allies begged him not to anger Julius, but he still refused. He wrote: 'If I stayed in Rome, my own tomb would be made before the pope's. And this was why I left so suddenly.' From Rome, in May 1506, one of Michelangelo's friends, the architect Pietro Rosselli (1474–1521) wrote to him, telling him that he had discussed him at a meeting with the Pope and Bramante. Bramante apparently said: 'I've had a lot to do with Michelangelo and he's told me again and again that he doesn't want anything to do with the chapel ... I don't think he has the heart for it, because he hasn't worked much at figures, and these figures must be high up and foreshortened, which is quite another thing from painting on the ground.' There may have been some truth in Bramante's words because no artist in history had undertaken a project of such epic scale.

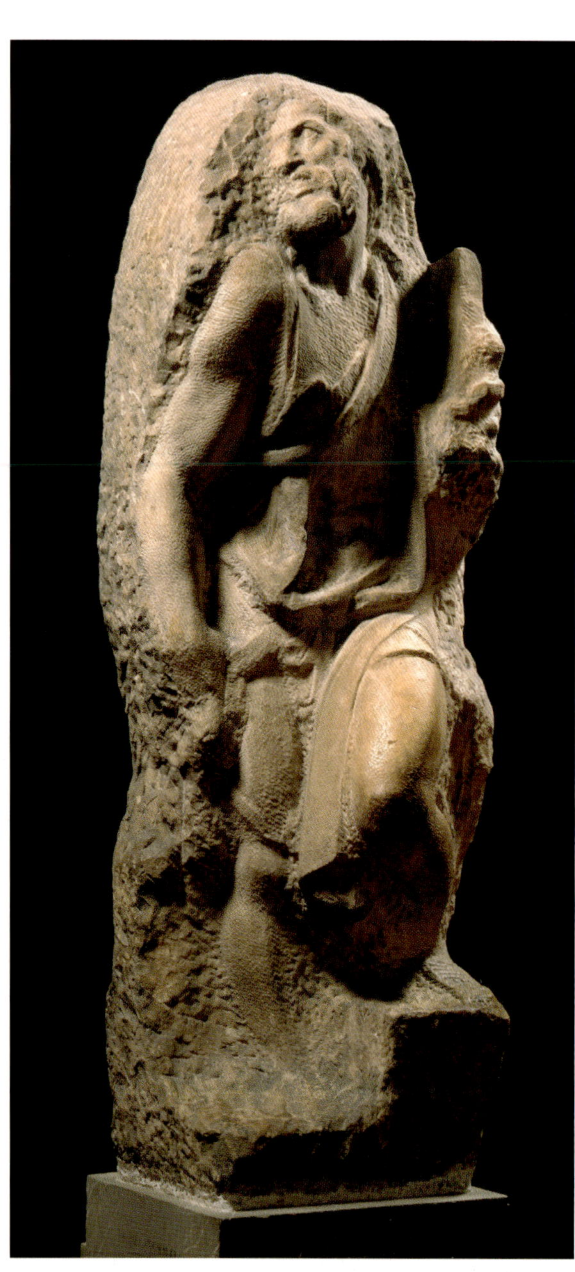

St Matthew, 1505–6. Michelangelo was commissioned to create 12 statues of Christ's Apostles to stand in a niche in the Choir of Florence Cathedral, but he produced only one; this unfinished statue of St Matthew. He was working on it while also planning the mural for the Palazzo Vecchio, but when he moved to Rome in 1505, his contract for the Apostle statues was annulled.

'GIVE ME A SWORD'

Despite Bramante's negativity, Julius ordered Soderini to send Michelangelo back, and eventually the artist responded to the pressure. That November, after eight months in Florence, he travelled to Bologna, where the Pope had just successfully overthrown the controlling ruler, Giovanni II Bentivoglio (1443–1508). On their first meeting after so many months, the relationship between Julius and Michelangelo was strained. Michelangelo had to kneel before him and beg for forgiveness, but they soon became reconciled and Julius immediately commissioned him to make a bronze statue of himself (more than life-sized) to be displayed in the centre of Bologna. Michelangelo set up a workshop and began, creating a clay model of the seated Pope with his right hand raised in blessing. Julius visited regularly to see the work in progress and early on, Michelangelo asked him whether he wanted a book placed in the figure's left hand, to convey his scholarship and intellect. Julius retorted, 'No, give me a sword; I am not a man of letters.' The colossal work took Michelangelo far longer to create than he had anticipated. Yet just three years after it was completed, the Bentivoglio family overthrew the papal troops and retook control of Bologna. The citizens were ordered to pull down the bronze statue of Julius II and sell it for scrap.

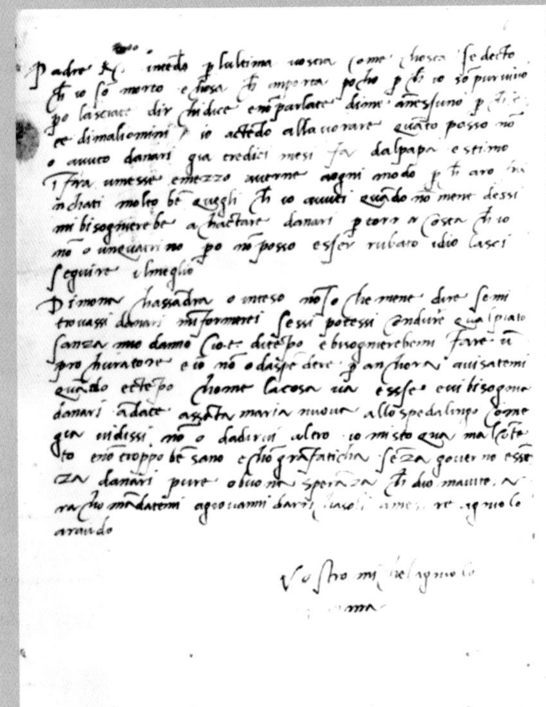

A letter written from Rome by Michelangelo in 1509 to his father in Florence; this contradicts a rumour of his death and complains that he has had no money from the Pope for 13 months. Throughout Michelangelo's time working for Julius there was constant tension over money: he always wanted more and the Pope was reluctant to give it to him.

MICHELANGELO'S LETTERS

Much is known about Michelangelo, mainly because of the two biographies written during his life by Condivi and Vasari, and by his letters, which comprise over 67 years of correspondence. A total of 1,390 letters is known, with almost 500 of them written by Michelangelo himself, and the others written to him. They offer us many facts about his business affairs, family and work issues and the daily events of his life, and also reveal his inner thoughts. Many are letters that he wrote to his father or brothers, such as during the years 1506 to 1508 when he travelled between Florence and Rome and also lived in Bologna. This was one of the most frustrating and miserable periods of his life as he struggled to work for Pope Julius II, who was an unpredictable, capricious autocrat. During that period, he wrote to the papal authorities, asking for more money and to be allowed to create the tomb in Florence: 'Now if His Holiness wants to go on with it, he should place the deposit for me here in Florence and I'll write to tell him where. I have many marbles on order in Carrara which I shall have brought here along with those I have in Rome. Even if it meant a serious loss to me, I shouldn't mind so long as I could do the work here; and I would forward the finished pieces one by one so that His Holiness would enjoy them just as much as if I were working in Rome – or even more, because he would just see the finished pieces without having any other bother.'

THE SISTINE CHAPEL

By 1508, other painters had previously painted the walls of the Sistine Chapel, including Botticelli, Ghirlandaio, Perugino and Luca Signorelli (*c.* 1445/50–1523). The lowest of the three levels is painted to resemble draped hangings. The middle level features frescoes that illustrate the Life of Christ and the Life of Moses, and between the windows on the upper parts of the walls are representations of the first 32 popes. Michelangelo was primarily a sculptor, and remained reluctant to accept the commission, but the Pope had commanded, so in the end he signed a contract on 10 May 1508. Immediately, Michelangelo began planning. The initial agreement was for the pendentives (curved triangular sections of vaulting formed by the intersection of a dome with its supporting arches) to feature portraits of the 12 Apostles, and the rest of the ceiling to be decorated. For this, he would be paid 3,000 ducats.

Study for the Libyan Sibyl, c. 1510–11. Michelangelo made these sketches for the Libyan Sibyl before painting the actual figure on the ceiling about three times life-size. Although the painting from this study represents a female, this study is of a young male figure. In the painting, the twisting figure holds up a large opened book.

Scheme for the Sistine Chapel ceiling, c. 1508. This is one of two surviving initial studies made by Michelangelo as he planned his designs for the Sistine Chapel ceiling. The diagrammatic drawing on the left was made soon after he signed the contract for the work, while the hands and arm on the right were drawn later.

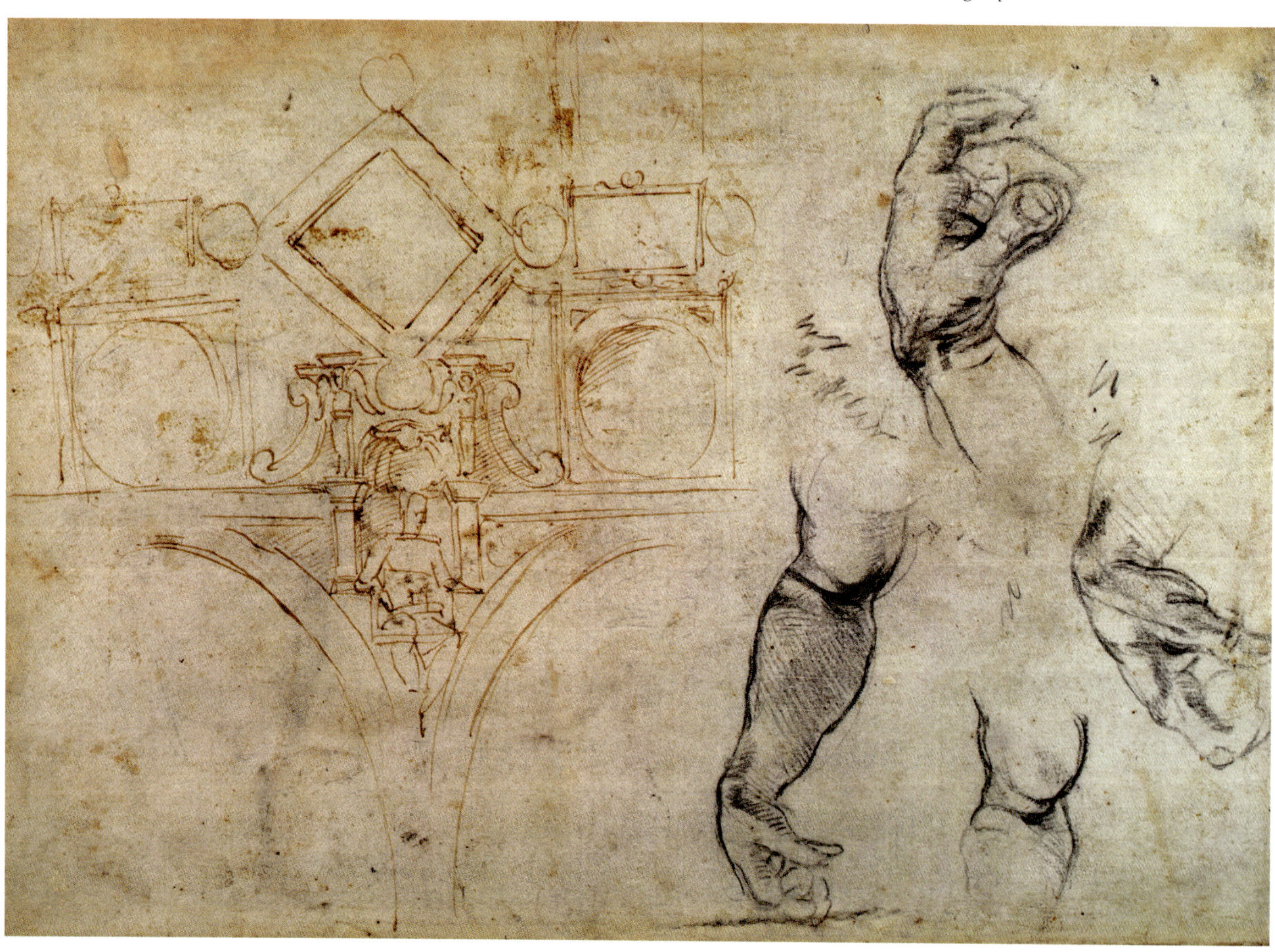

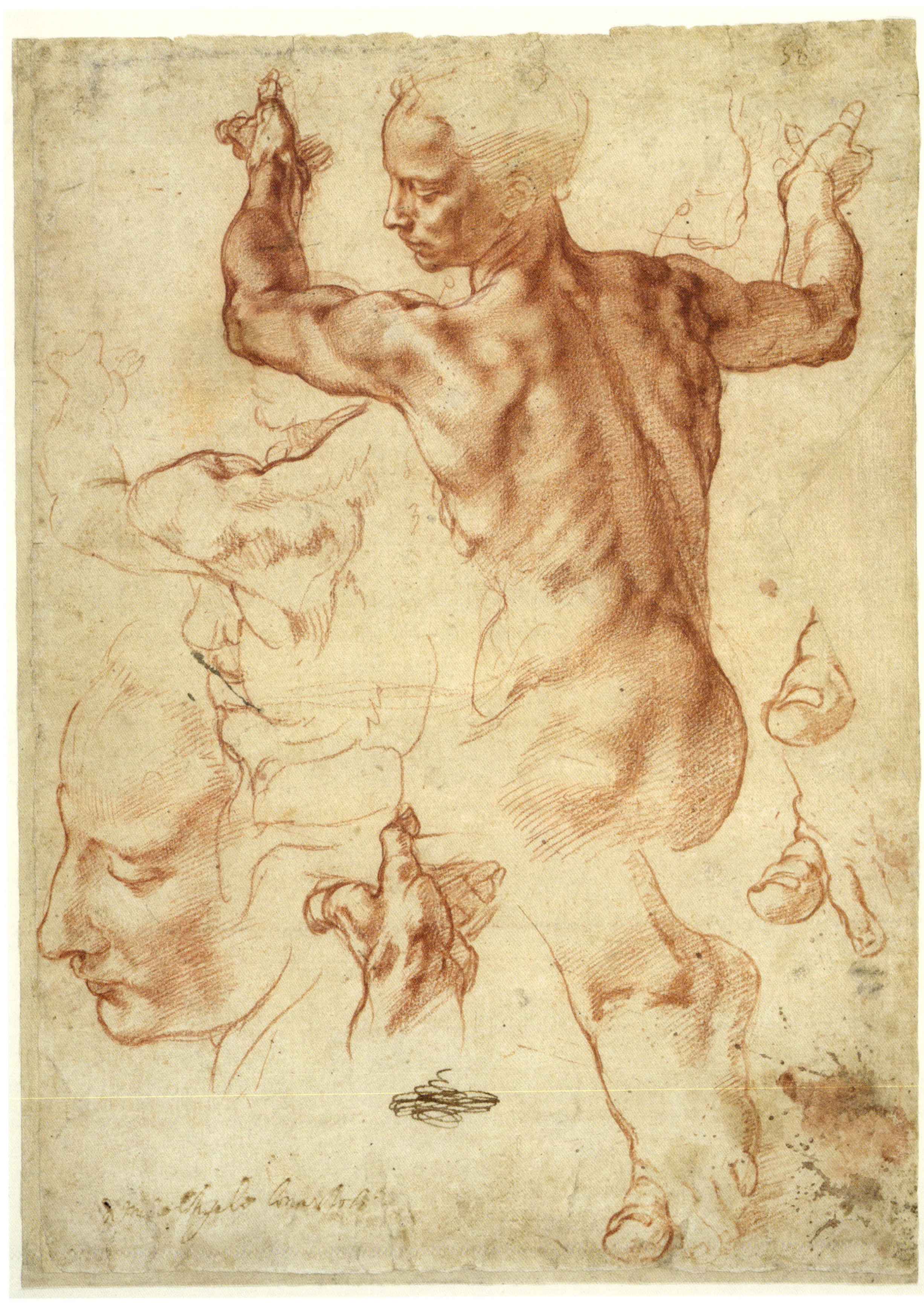

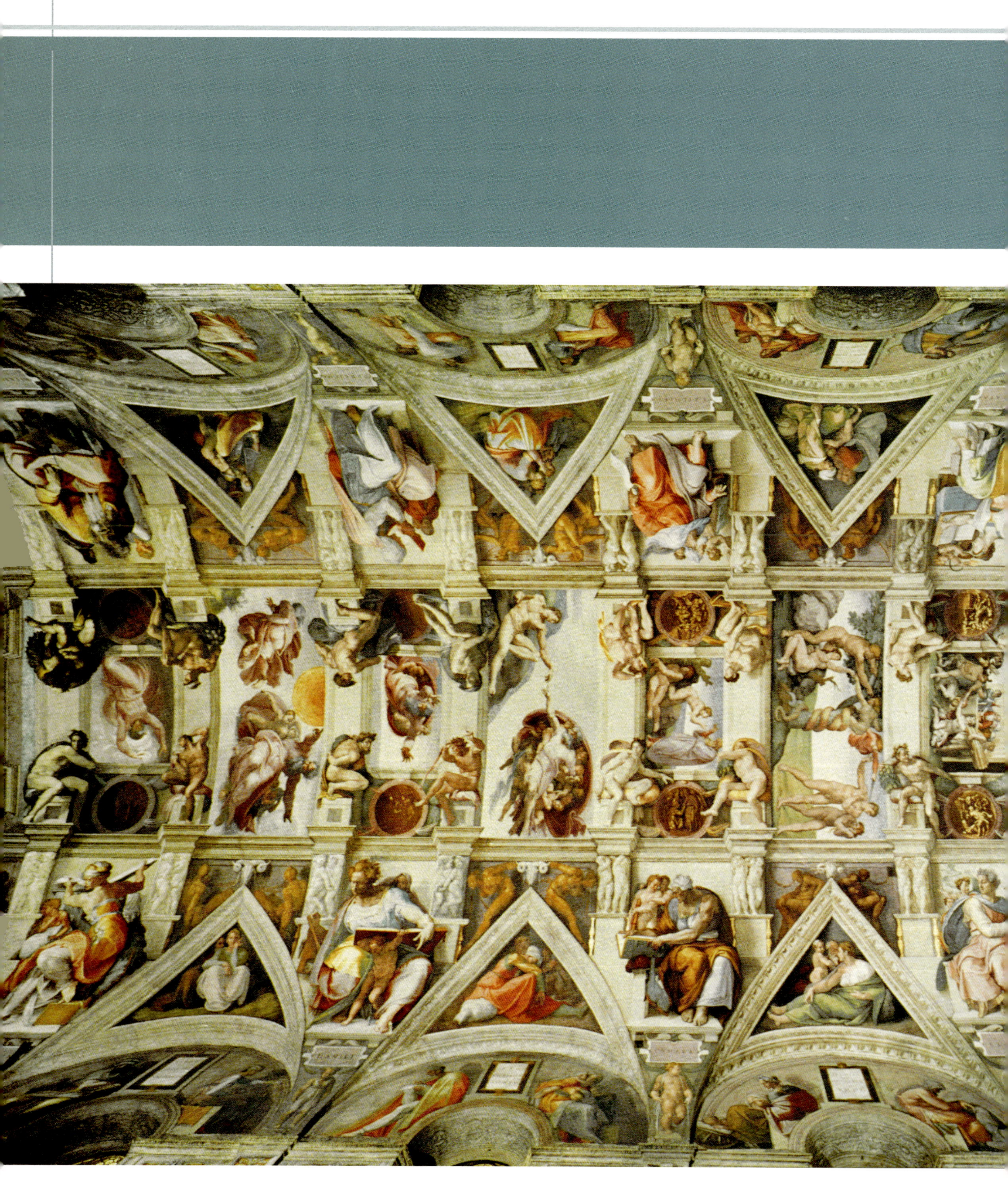

CHAPTER 4

Il Divino

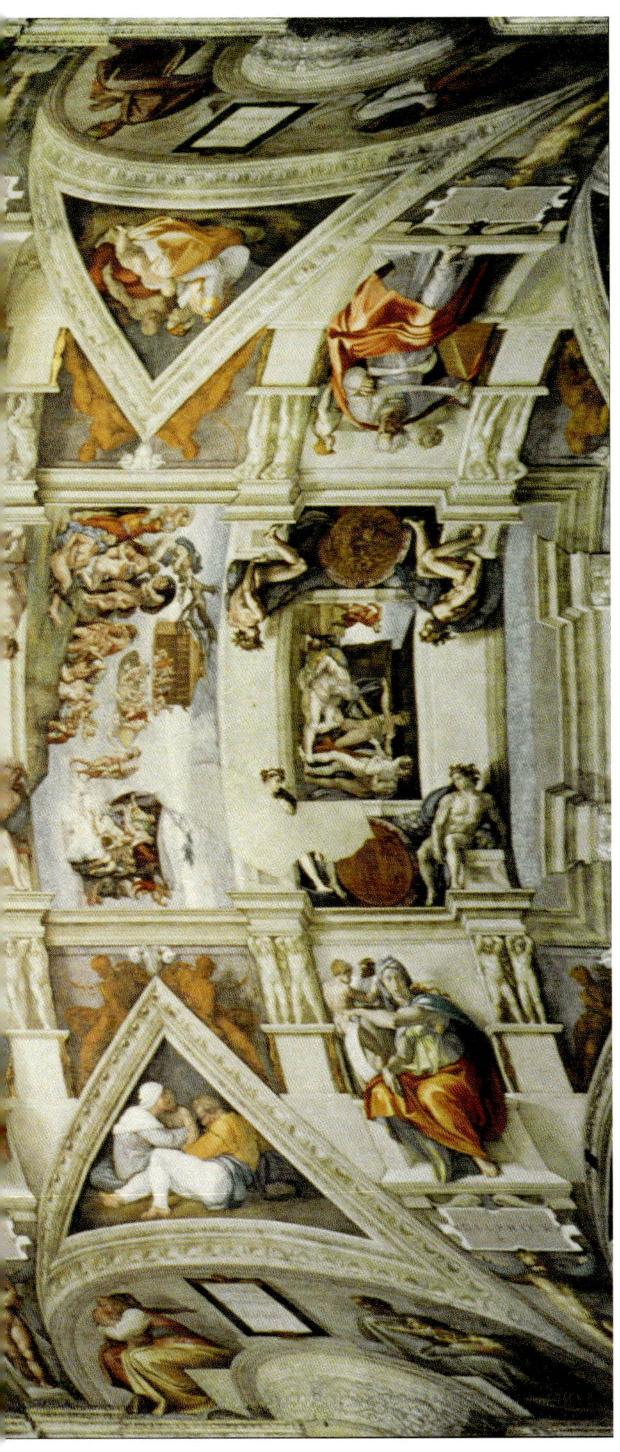

The height of the vaulted ceiling of the Sistine Chapel is 20.7 metres (68 feet) and its dimensions are a vast 40 × 14 metres (131¼ × 46 feet). When he began working on it, Michelangelo enlisted the assistance of his rival Bramante, who was working on St Peter's Basilica. Bramante put up the scaffolding for Michelangelo to reach the ceiling, but when this caused damage, Michelangelo had it all taken down. In its place, he created an innovative wooden platform that was held up by brackets and inserted into holes in the wall. As he completed each stage of the painting, he moved the scaffolding across the chapel. Another problem faced him, however. Although he had trained with Ghirlandaio, he was not confident with his own skills in fresco, so initially he asked the advice of several other painters, including Ghirlandaio. Even then, once he had started work, the plaster became infected with mould, so he had to scrape it all off and start again. Probably his biggest problem of all was the excruciating pain he endured as he spent hours standing with his head bent back and his arm up to paint.

The Sistine Chapel ceiling, 1508–12.
Michelangelo divided the stories and figures
on the Sistine Chapel ceiling with architectural
elements, painted as trompe l'oeil; *to appear*
from below as if it really is divided by manmade
stone structures, including lunettes, spandrels
and pilasters.

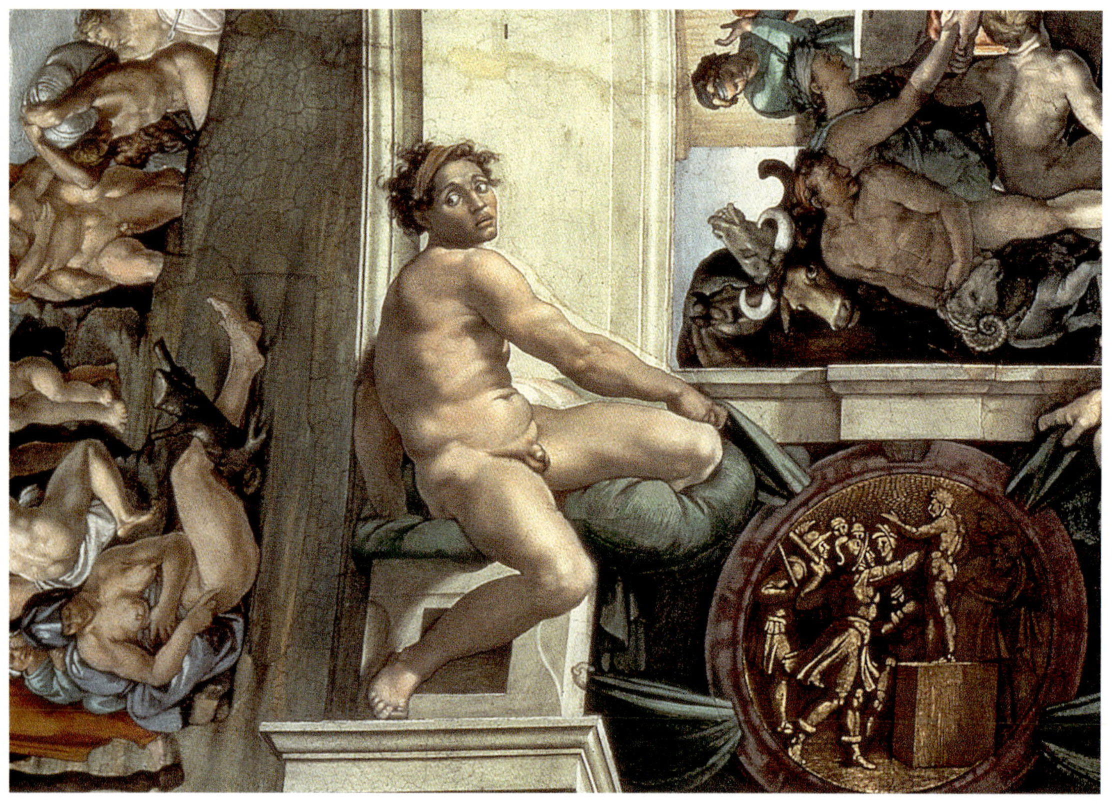

Detail of an ignudi, *1509. At the junctions of the cornices on the ceiling are 24 ignudi, painted to resemble living statues. Ignudi (from the Italian adjective* nudo, *meaning 'naked') are young men who appear to combine male and female traits. They are not related to the biblical scenes surrounding them but seem to have been included in the scheme simply for their beauty.*

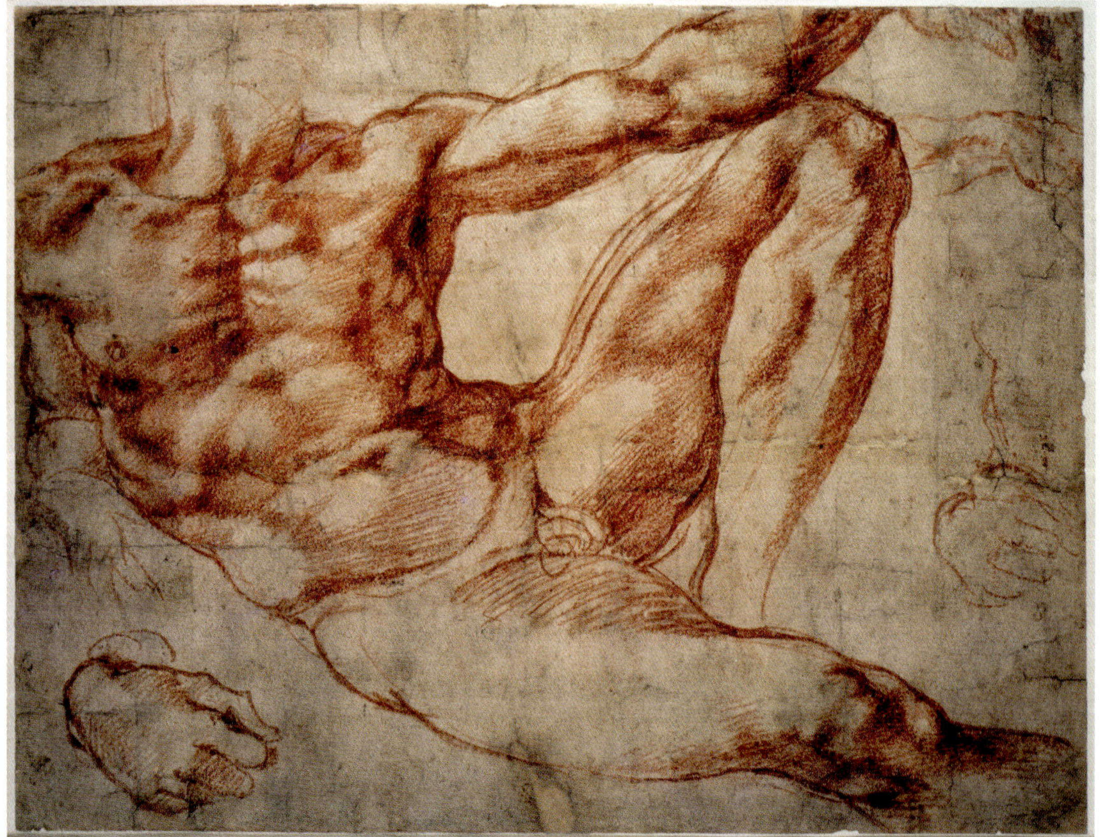

Study for Adam, 1511. This reclining male nude is Michelangelo's study for Adam for the Sistine Chapel ceiling and one of the few drawings of that period to have survived. In the fresco, Adam reaches out to God who grants him life. Known for its dynamism and power, The Creation of Adam *(see page 6) has become the most famous section of the ceiling.*

FRESCO

An ancient method for painting on walls and ceilings, fresco is created through a chemical reaction between lime plaster and water-based pigments that permanently fuse to the surface. There are two different methods: *fresco secco* and *buon fresco*, and Michelangelo used both. With either method, artists have to work quickly. *Buon fresco*, also called 'true' fresco, is made of three coats of a mixture of plaster, sand and sometimes marble dust which is painted on to wet plaster. As the first two coats dry, the artist transfers the outlines of his design – or cartoon – on to the surface. A final, smooth coat – *intonaco* – of plaster is then applied to as much of the wall or ceiling as can be painted in one day, and the artist paints on this third layer of plaster while it is still damp. As the plaster dries, the pigment becomes an integral part of the surface. *Fresco secco*, or 'dry' fresco, is made by soaking the plastered surface of a wall or ceiling with lime water and then painting on the damp surface before the plaster sets. The pigments do not penetrate the plaster as permanently with this method as they do in *buon fresco*. With *buon fresco*, the plaster is laid in new sections each day, called a *giornata*. While it was customary for fresco painters to use a full-sized detailed drawing, a cartoon, to transfer a design on to a plaster surface, Michelangelo broke with convention and drew directly on to the ceiling. In the 1980s, the Vatican began an extensive restoration of the Sistine Chapel ceiling, with Italian and international experts carefully cleaning away centuries of dirt and grime. It revealed unexpectedly brilliant colours.

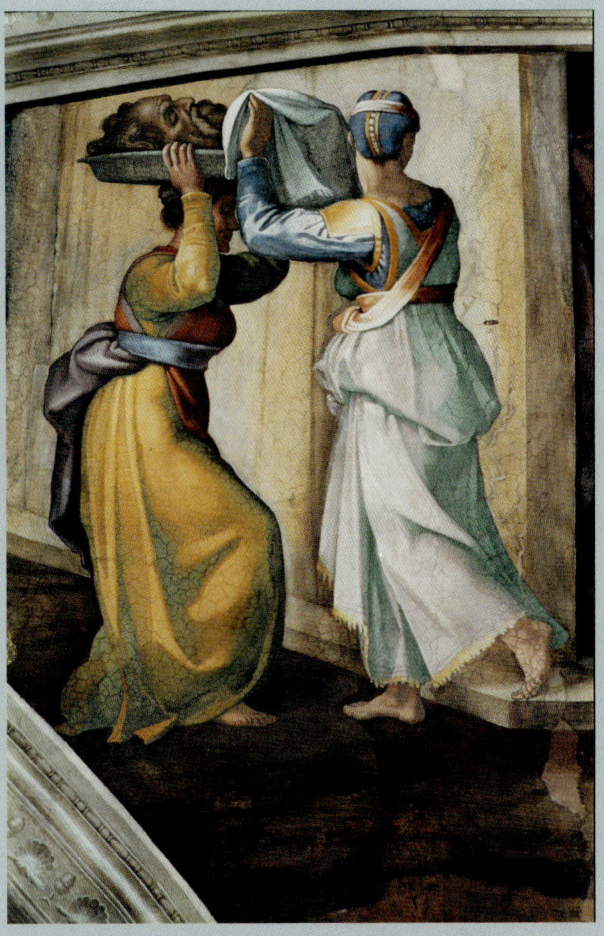

Judith and Holofernes, *1509 (post-restoration). Soon after Michelangelo applied the* intonaco, *mould grew because the surface was too wet. He had to remove it all and start again. He then tried a new formula created by one of his assistants, Jacopo Torni, or l'Indaco (1476–1526), which resisted mould.*

THE CEILING

Although the Pope's plans for the ceiling were for just the 12 Apostles within the triangular pendentives, Michelangelo had other ideas. He persuaded Julius to allow him more freedom and proposed a complex scheme of depictions of Bible stories that would portray the Creation, the Fall of Man, the Promise of Salvation through the prophets and the genealogy of Christ. The Pope agreed, and Michelangelo painted the entire ceiling with over 300 figures. At the centre are nine episodes from the Book of Genesis divided into three groups: God's creation of the earth; God's creation of humans; and their fall from God's grace. On the pendentives are men and women who prophesied the coming of Jesus, prophets of Israel, sibyls (ancient Greek oracles who received divine inspiration from the gods) and *ignudi*. Using the *buon fresco* technique, Michelangelo worked in great discomfort, as Vasari explained: 'The work was carried out in extremely uncomfortable conditions, from his having to work with his head tilted upwards.' Michelangelo also described his pain with a witty sonnet and sketch, including these lines:

...My stomach's squashed under my chin, my beard's
pointing at heaven, my brain's crushed in a casket,
my breast twists like a harpy's. My brush,
above me all the time, dribbles paint
so my face makes a fine floor for droppings!
My haunches are grinding into my guts,
my poor ass strains to work as a counterweight...

Michelangelo began the ceiling at the end of the chapel furthest from the altar, depicting the latest of the stories and progressed towards the altar with scenes of the Creation. Yet he had underestimated the ceiling's scale, and as he moved across it, his figures increased in size and his application became looser. He painted the final scene, *The Creation of Adam*, in one day.

The Creation of the Sun, Moon and Plants, 1511. *This is the second in the sequence of Michelangelo's nine scenes from the Book of Genesis. Depicting the third and fourth days of God's Creation, on the left, God is shown from behind, extending his arm towards a plant, and on the right, He points towards the Sun and Moon. The foreshortening and positions of the figures create a powerful sense of movement.*

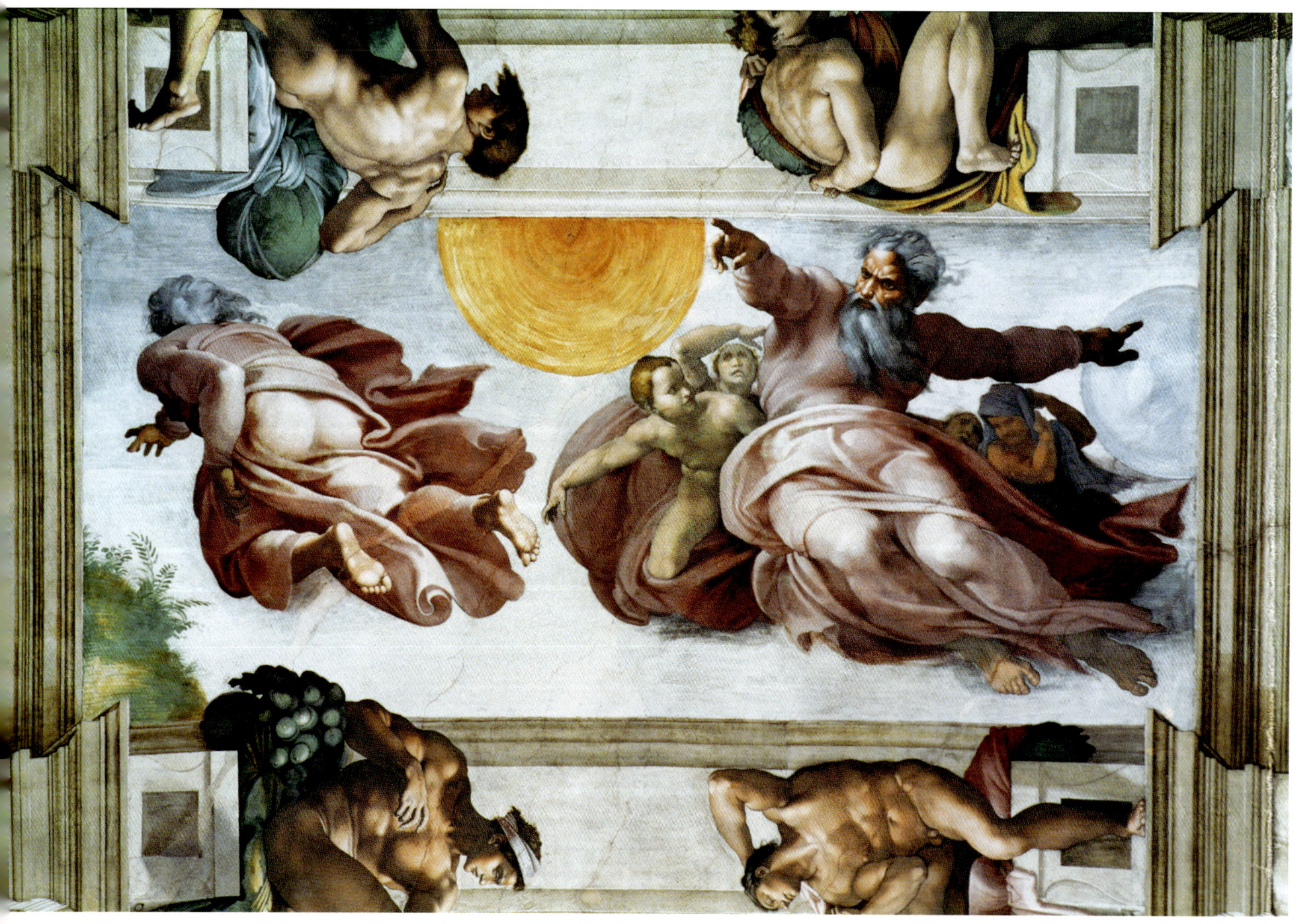

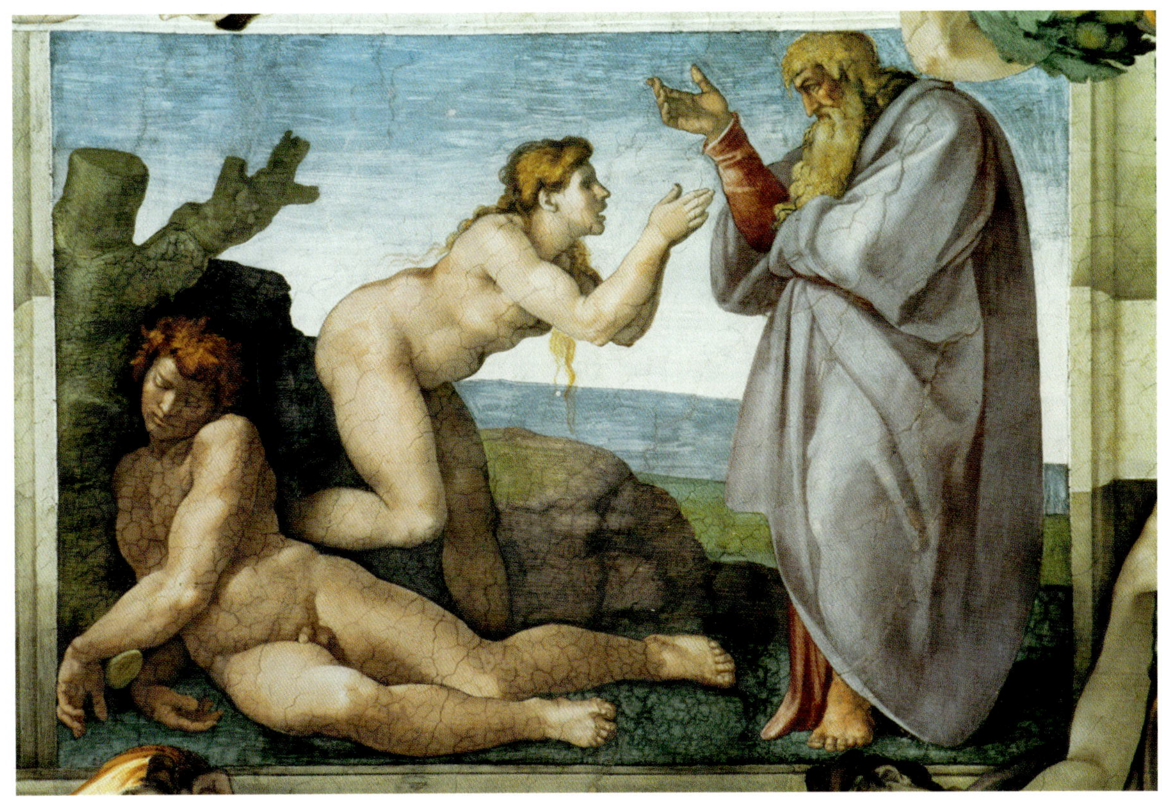

The Creation of Eve, *1508–10. From the Book of Genesis, this image shows how, according to the Bible, the first woman was created. It is probably based on a relief in Bologna created by Jacopo della Quercia (c. 1374–1438) on the door of the Basilica of San Petronio.*

The Fall of Man *and* The Expulsion from Paradise, *1508–12. From the left, Adam grabs the branches of a tree as Eve sits beneath, reaching out to take the apple from the serpent. Behind the serpent in the sky, an angel casts the couple out of Paradise. This part of the Sistine ceiling shows a sequence of two stories, or one story and its consequences.*

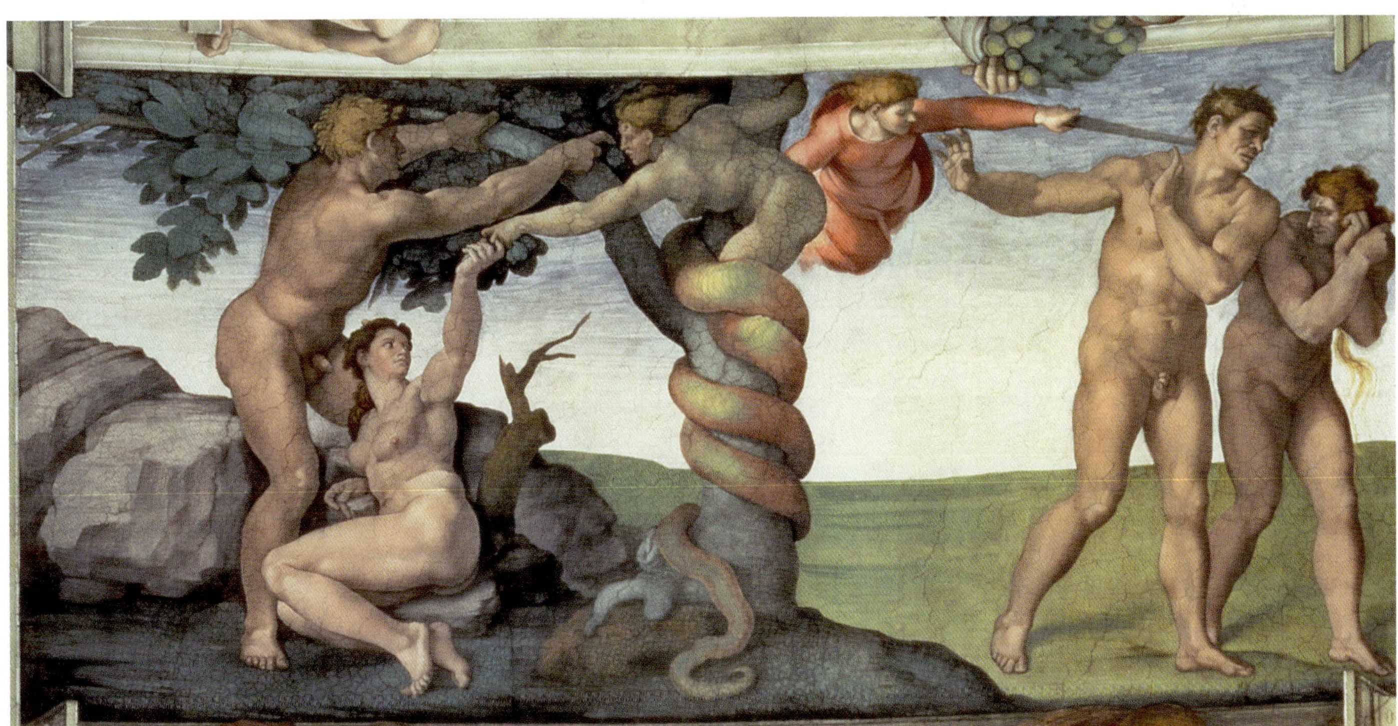

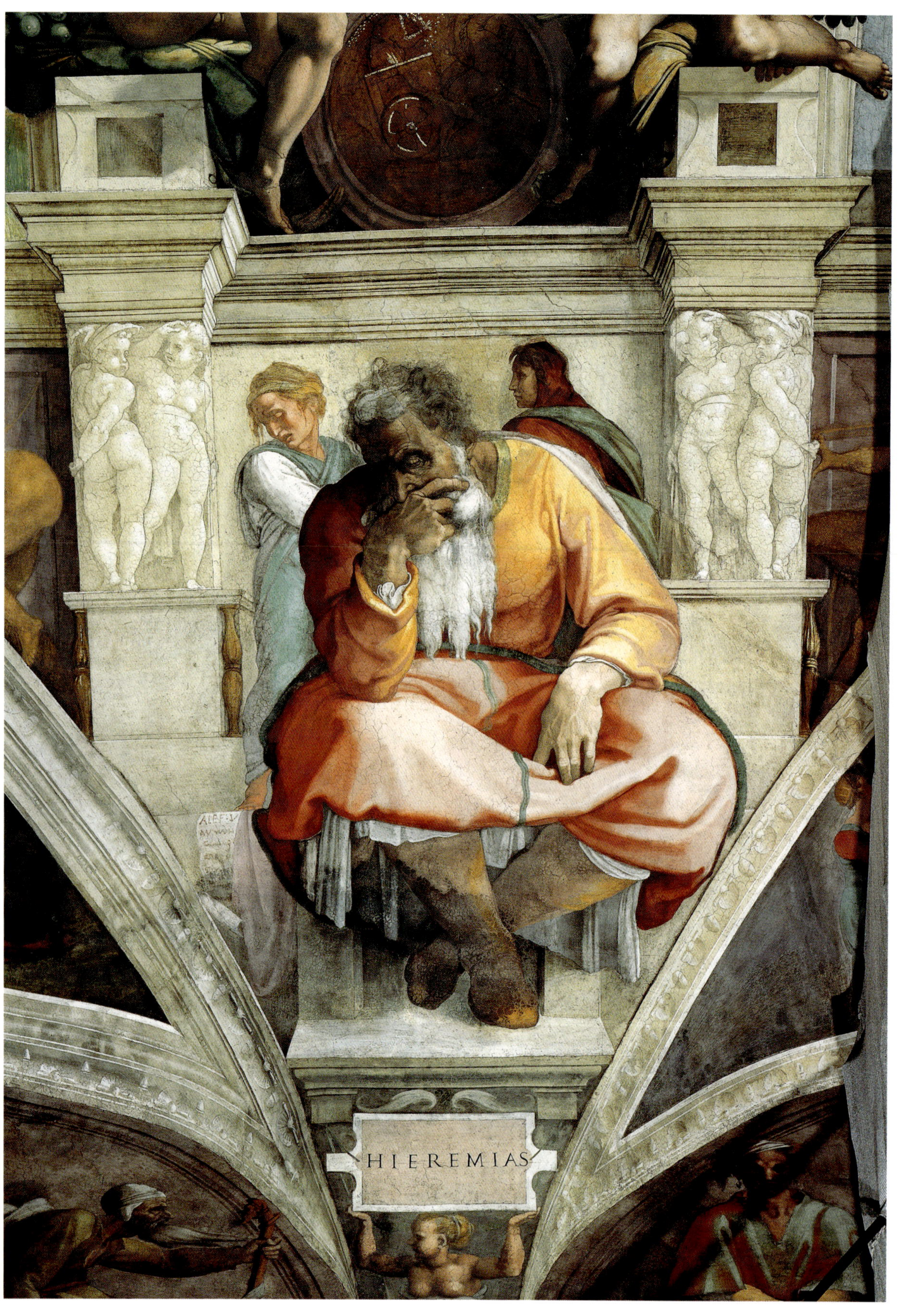
HIEREMIAS

The Cumaean Sibyl, *1510.*
Sibyls were female seers or
prophets from antiquity
who were thought to have
predicted the coming of
Christ. This is the Cumaean
sibyl, the priestess in charge
of the Apollonian oracle
at Cumae, near Naples.
Michelangelo depicts her as
powerful and commanding.

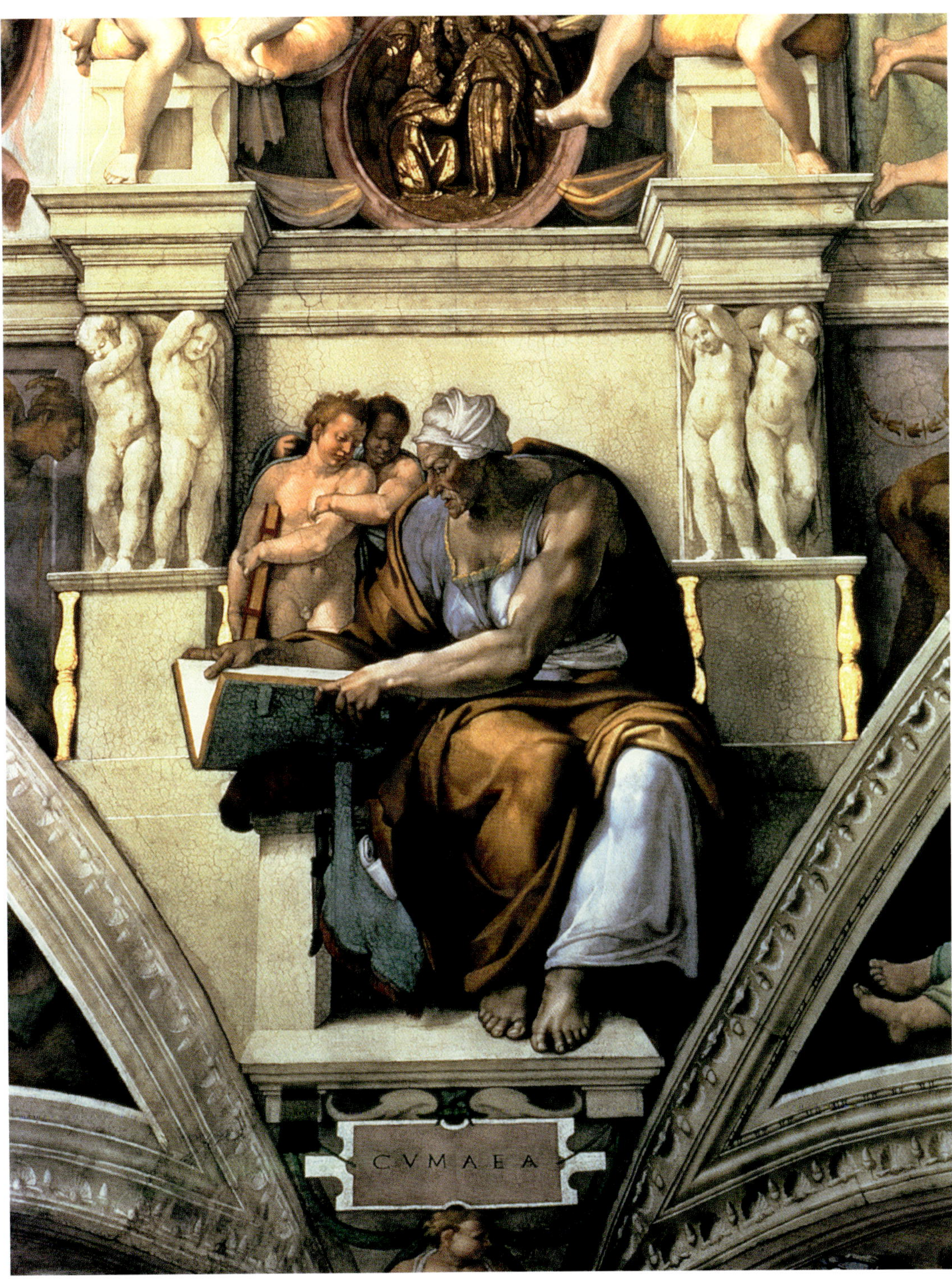

Opposite: The Prophet Jeremiah, c. 1508–12. *One of the seven prophets of*
the Old Testament, Jeremiah is written about in the Book of Jeremiah and The
Lamentations. Here, Michelangelo depicts him lamenting over the Destruction
of Jerusalem. The anatomical accuracy, strong tonal contrasts and use of
foreshortening were unprecedented.

TRIUMPH

For the four years that Michelangelo worked on the ceiling, his relationship with the Pope remained turbulent. Several times he determined to abandon the project, but the Pope forbade him. Several times, because he took so long – and painted in secret behind closed doors – Julius threatened to have him thrown off his scaffold if he did not hurry up. Then, four years after he began, on 31 October 1512, he completed the project. On 1 November 1512, the Feast Day of All Saints, the Pope inaugurated the chapel. All who saw the ceiling were amazed at the breadth of expression, the power of the figures and the clarity of the stories depicted. Nothing before had been painted on such a scale and with so much naturalism, expressiveness and dynamism. Julius did ask why the figures were not gilded, but Michelangelo explained that holy figures despised riches – and the Pope was delighted. Bramante's hopes that Michelangelo would fail had been dashed: rather than disgrace himself, the artist had triumphed. Across the vast ceiling, the 343 figures appear to move, twist, bend and writhe, narratives are clearly conveyed, and decorations include the Pope's della Rovere acorns throughout. The

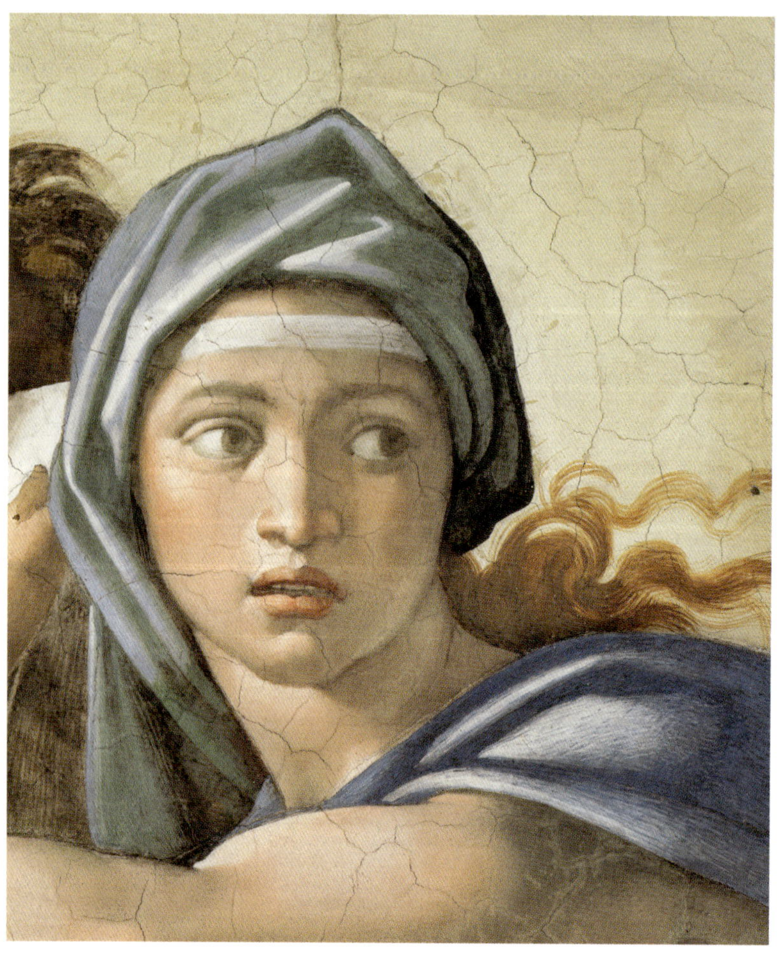

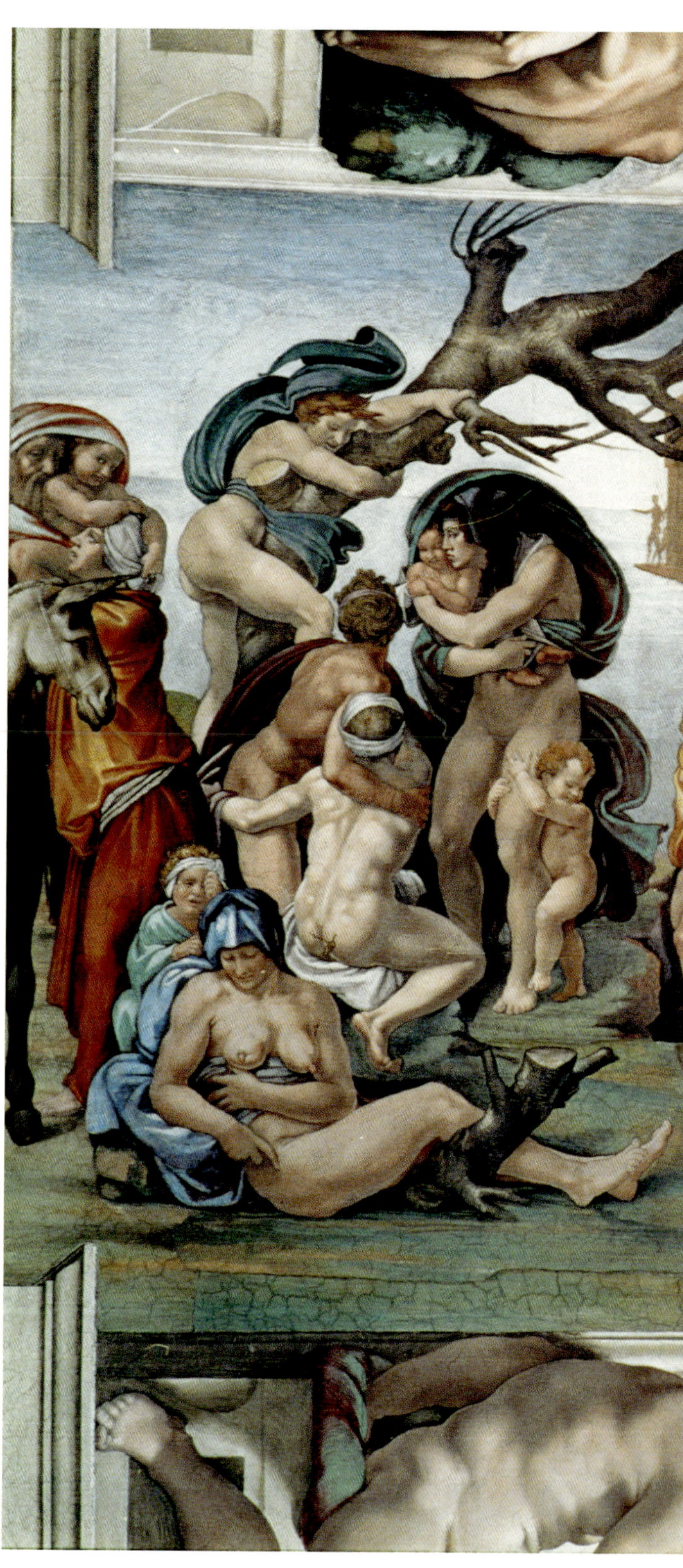

The Delphic Sibyl, 1509. According to Greek and Roman legend, there were many sibyls throughout the ancient world. The beautiful Delphic Sibyl was the voice of Apollo (the Greek god of music, poetry, prophecy and medicine), and here she turns her head away from her scroll to gaze into the future.

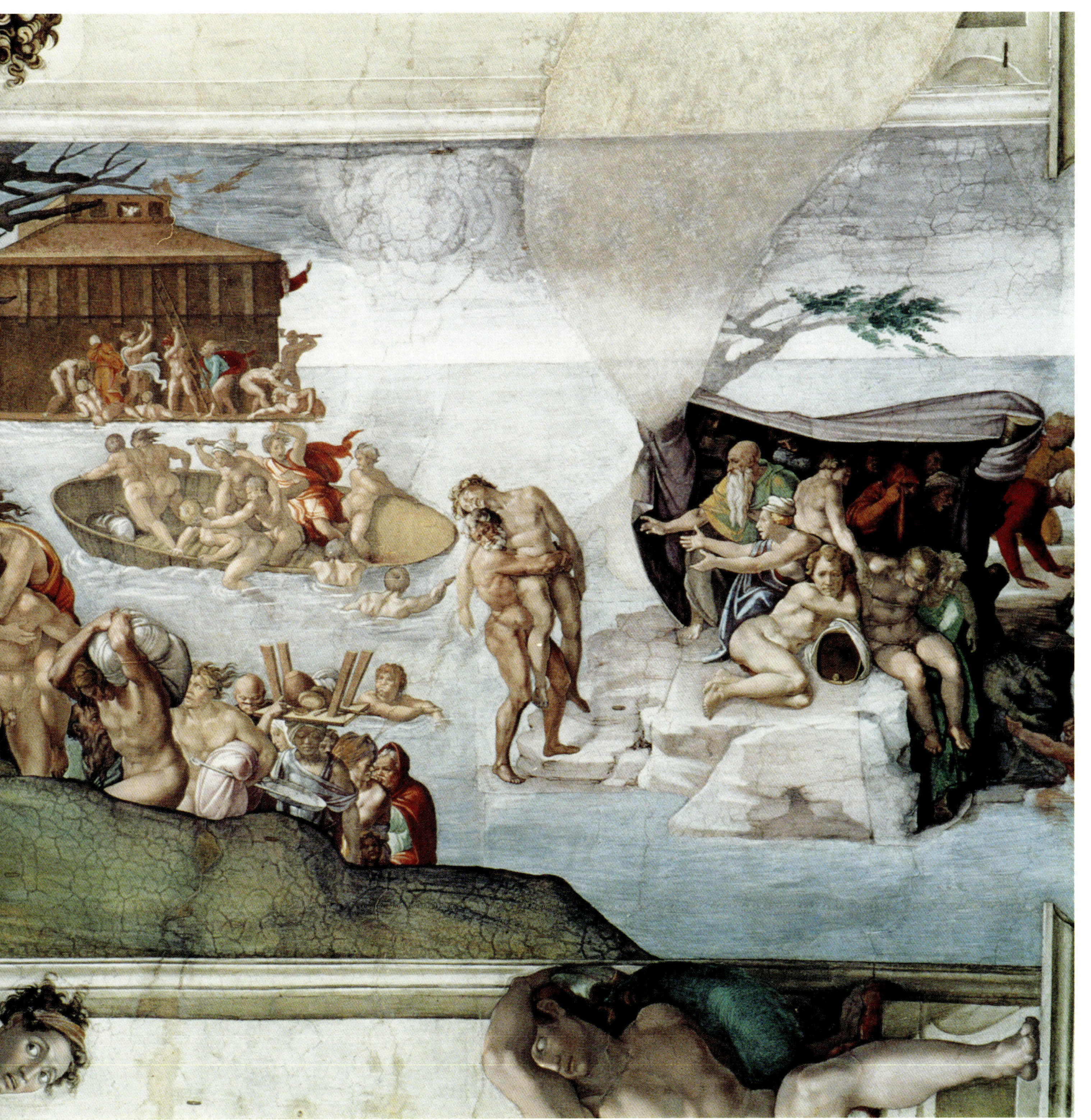

The Flood, *1508–12. The smallest of the nine stories from the Book of Genesis,* The Flood *features a mass of bodies, including a long line of people struggling up a hill as they try to escape the rising flood waters. One figure clings to a tree while another carries a lifeless body from the water.*

colours and realism were astonishing. At last, Michelangelo believed, Julius would not put anything in the way of the tomb project and he would be able to create it as he had planned seven years before. However, just two months later, in January 1513, the Pope took to his bed, and before the end of February, he was dead.

THE TRAGEDY OF THE TOMB

Michelangelo was eager to return to sculpture, and just before his death Julius had ordered the work on his tomb to be restarted. He had stipulated that it be built on a less imposing scale and left approximately 10,000 ducats for its completion. Papal bankers put the vast sum of 2,000 ducats into Michelangelo's bank account. In his biography of Michelangelo, Ascanio Condivi described the entire project as 'the tragedy of the tomb'. With its many problems, this tragedy continued for 40 years. After Julius died, Michelangelo went to stay briefly with his father in Florence, then returned to

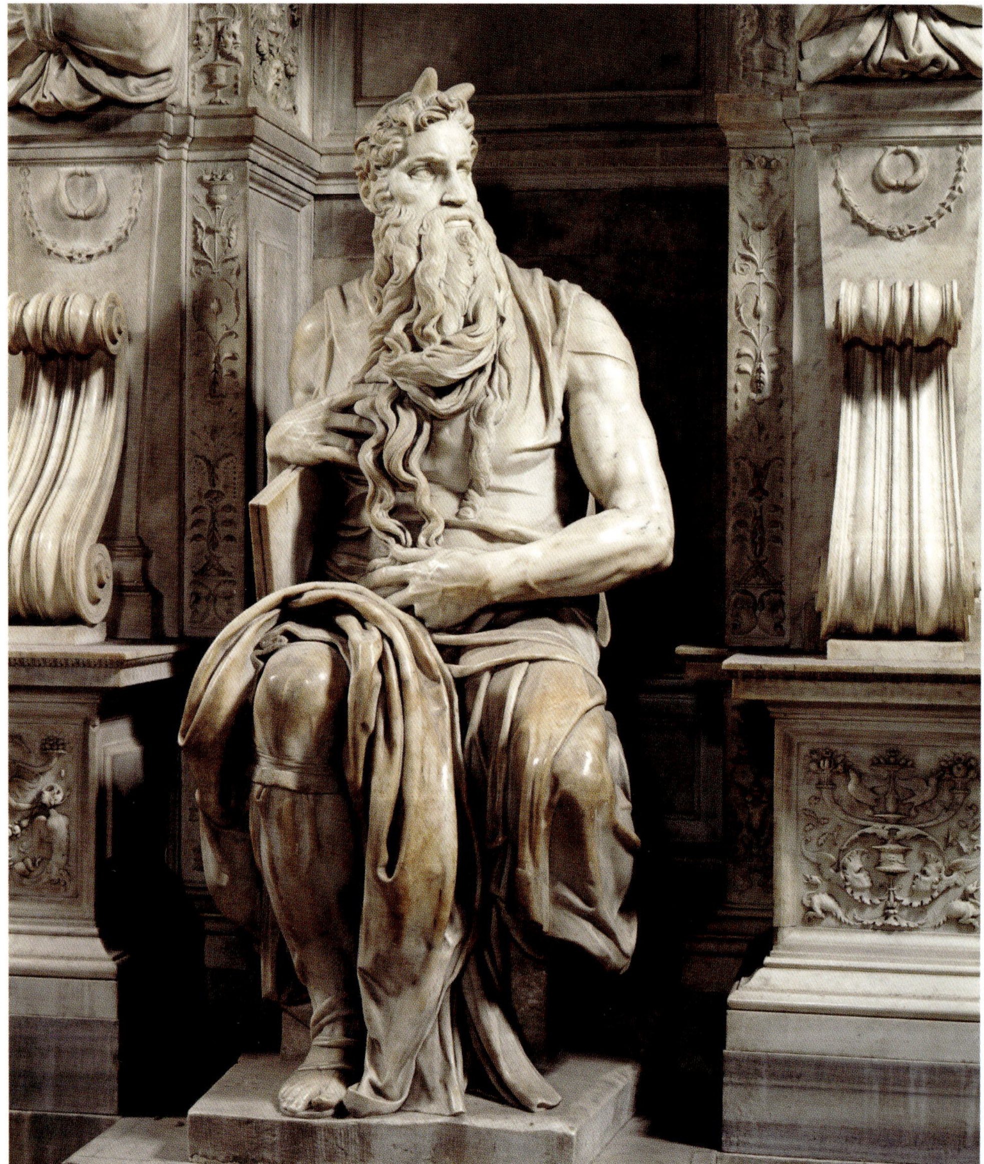

Left: Moses, 1513–15. *Seated on a chair between two decorated columns,* Moses *was originally meant for the upper part of the original tomb where the prophet would have been seen from below, which is why his proportions are distorted. Michelangelo put horns on his head because these derived from an incorrect early translation of the Bible.*

Opposite: Tomb of Pope Julius II, *1505–45. After the death of Pope Julius II in 1513 and many further setbacks, delays and changes, Michelangelo's tomb for the former pope was finally erected in San Pietro in Vincoli in Rome in 1545. It is on a far more modest scale than had been originally planned, and it follows classically harmonious proportions.*

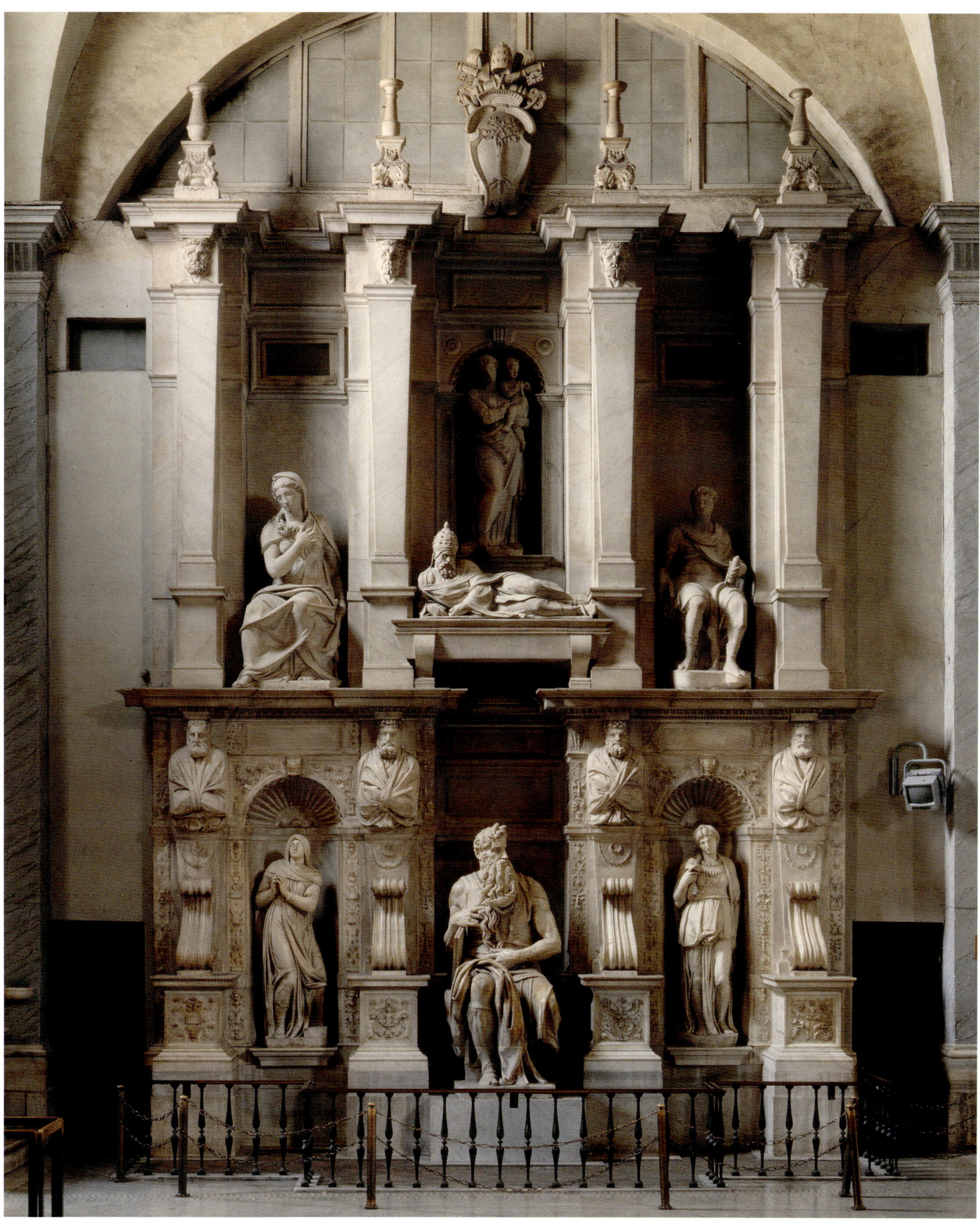

Rome and agreed with the late pope's nephew, Francesco della Rovere, Duke of Urbino (1490–1538), to create a tomb that featured more Christian elements than had been in the original design. With almost 40 sculptures, it would still be large and impressive and Michelangelo was instructed to complete it in seven years, and to be paid 16,500 ducats in total. Della Rovere specified that Michelangelo should not undertake any other projects while working on it and Michelangelo began work straight away, immediately creating *Captive (The Rebellious Slave)* and the *Dying Slave*. The della Rovere family gave him a house in Rome to live in while he worked on the project, and in around 1513 he commenced his colossal statue of Moses. However, problems began when the relationship soured between the della Rovere family and the new pope,

Leo X (1475–1521), born Giovanni di Lorenzo de' Medici and the son of Lorenzo de' Medici. The project was halted, the contract changed and the completion date extended. For the next three decades, Michelangelo found himself caught between successive popes and the della Rovere family, and the project was interrupted and altered. After Leo X died in 1521, he was succeeded by Adrian VI (1459–1523), born Adriaan Florensz Boeyens, who had no interest in the arts. Adrian was followed in 1523 by Clement VII, Giulio di Giuliano de' Medici (1478–1534), who also caused the project to be stopped and started. Michelangelo finally completed the tomb on a much-reduced scale in 1545 and it was placed in San Pietro in Vincoli.

THE SLAVES

An icon of Hellenistic art, the figurative Greek sculpture known as the *Laocoön Group*, or *Laocoön and His Sons*, is a monumental marble copy of a bronze sculpture, which

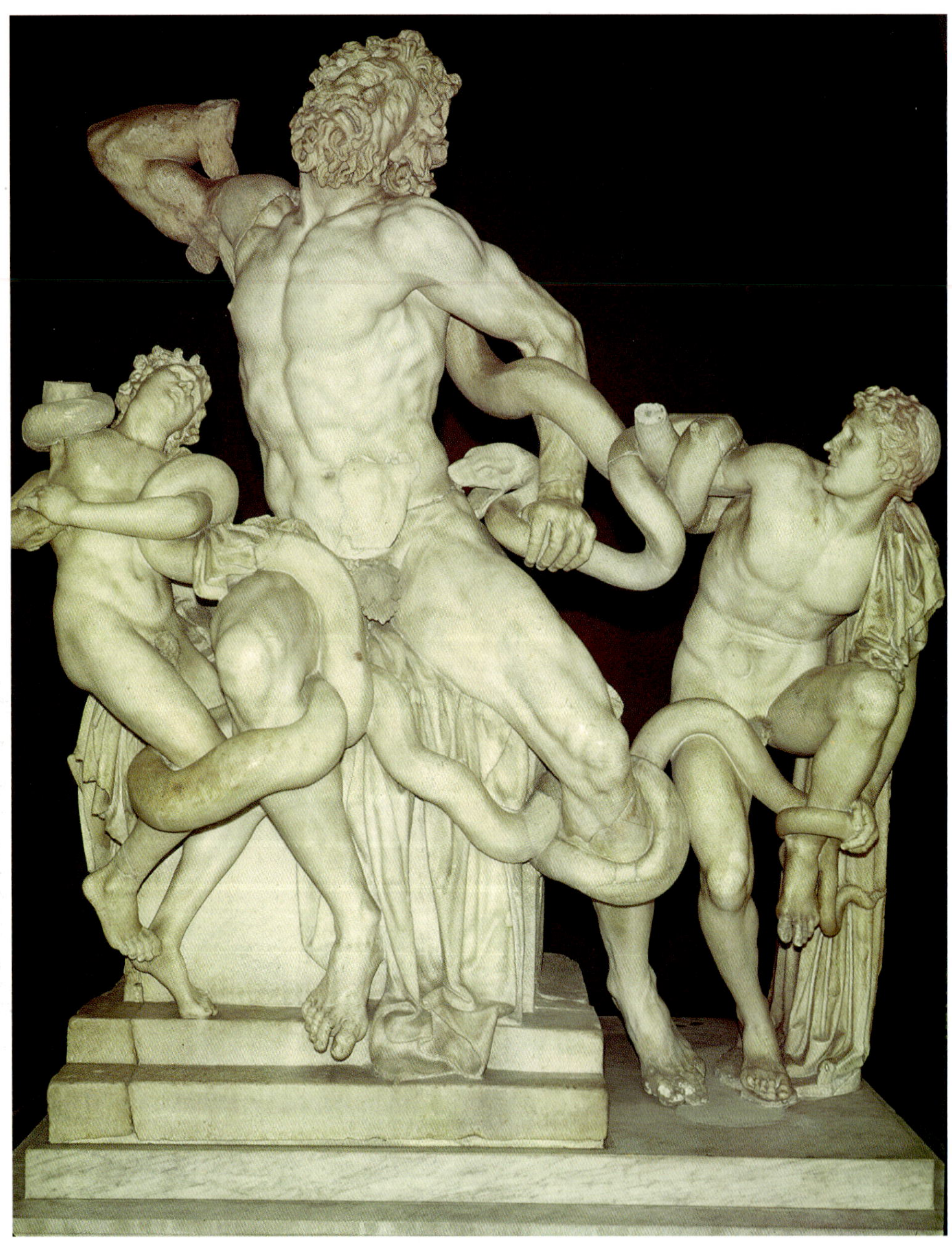

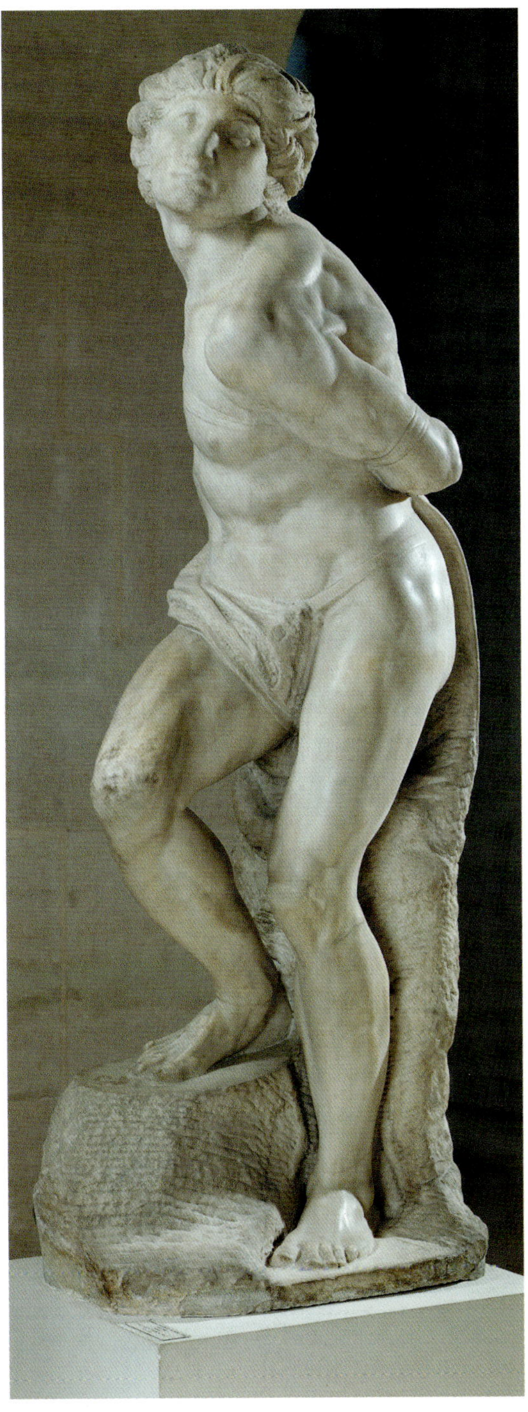

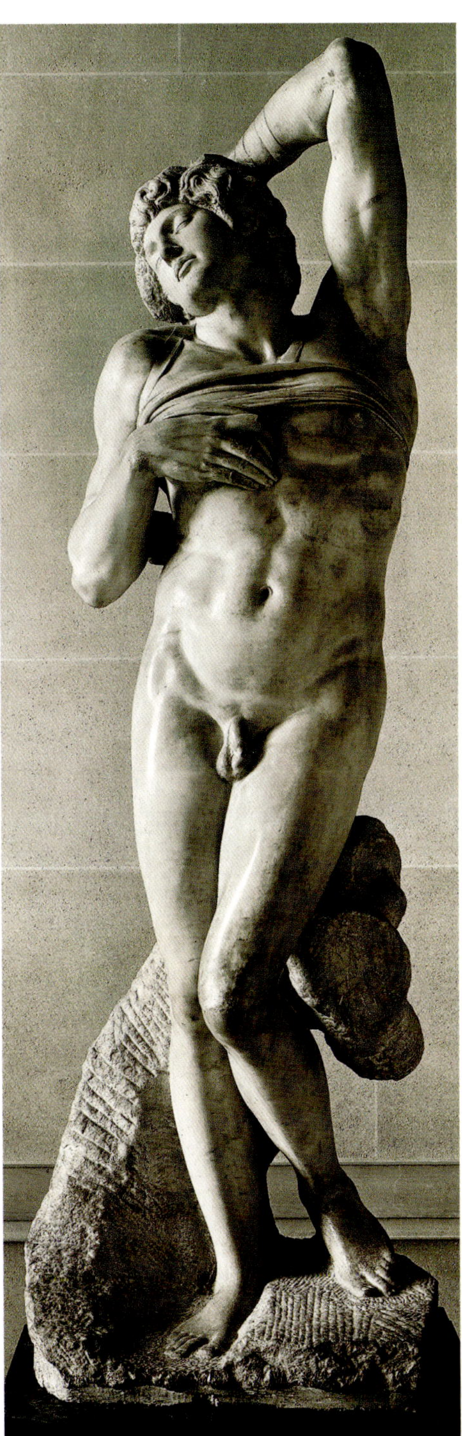

Opposite: Laocoön and his Sons, *Hellenistic original, first century.* One of the most famous Greco-Roman works of sculpture, these near life-sized figures portray the Trojan priest Laocoön and his two sons. One of Poseidon's priests, Laocoön was killed with his sons after attempting to expose the secret of the Trojan Horse.

Captive (The Rebellious Slave), *1513. One of two chained slaves that Michelangelo made for Pope Julius's tomb in 1513. This man seems to be involved in an aggressive struggle, which contrasts with the* Dying Slave *(see right). It is not clear why the two statues were intended to form part of the tomb, although they were designed as part of the initial project in 1505. It seems that Michelangelo did not finish them; he often abandoned a work if he felt he was not achieving perfection.*

Dying Slave, *1513. Between c. 1520–34, Michelangelo created four further 'slaves' that remained unfinished. Named posthumously as* The Awakening Slave, The Young Slave, The Bearded Slave *and* The Atlas, *these incomplete figures have been interpreted in many ways. Commonly, all of the slave figures, including the* Dying Slave *above, are seen as trying to free themselves from the marble.*

was described by the Roman writer Pliny the Elder (23–79). It depicts characters from the epic poem the *Aeneid*, written by the Roman poet Virgil (70–19 BCE). The Trojan priest Laocoön, and his two sons Antiphas and Thymbraeus, are being attacked by sea serpents, and when the work was discovered in January 1506, buried in the grounds of a Roman vineyard, Michelangelo was one of the first experts to attend the excavation site. Also unearthed were some less well-preserved statues and several attempts were made to repair them, but this was done so badly that Michelangelo insisted the renovations should stop. Pope Julius II ordered the work to be brought to the Vatican and installed in the Belvedere Court Garden. Michelangelo spent a great deal of time studying these ancient sculptures and was profoundly influenced by them. His unfinished statues such as *Captive (the Rebellious Slave)* and the *Dying Slave* twist in counterpoint to each other, much like Laocoön's sons. Michelangelo was devoutly Catholic and he believed that these writhing figures, which seem to be trapped in the stone, metaphorically convey the struggle of the soul to free itself from the physical world.

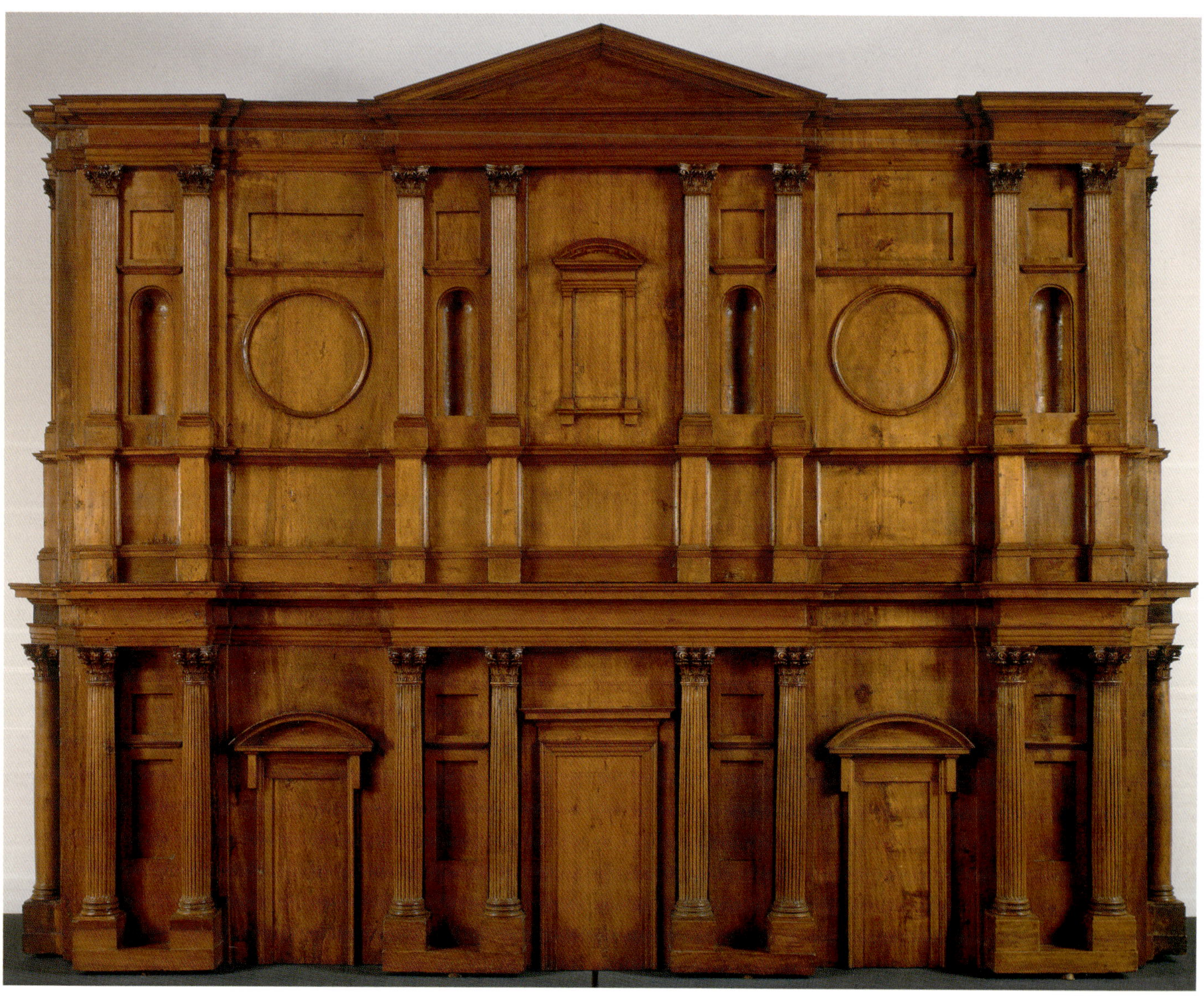

SAN LORENZO

The Duke of Urbino specified that Michelangelo was not to work on anything but his uncle's tomb. However, in 1516 Pope Leo X asked him to decorate the façade of San Lorenzo, the Medici parish church in Florence. The Pope had been Michelangelo's childhood friend; they had lived together in the Medici household. Michelangelo was reluctant to accept the commission, despite the Pope's assurances that he would be able to continue working on Julius II's tomb. Ultimately, however, he could not refuse his close friend, and went to Carrara to select the marble for San Lorenzo, stopping work on the tomb. Next, Leo X insisted that the marble should come from Pietrasanta rather than Carrara, as Pietrasanta was under Florentine jurisdiction, so the marble would be cheaper. This caused Michelangelo great frustration: he had signed a contract with Carrara, did not want to start searching for marble all over again, and new roads had to be created through the mountains from Pietrasanta to Florence to transport it, which delayed the project considerably. The architectural design that Michelangelo produced for the façade of San Lorenzo was quite unique, adapting the classical proportions of the original frontage to follow the ideal proportions of the human body. For him, the bones of every building were its structural elements; aspects of a building that hold other parts together or are weight-bearing, for instance, are the equivalent of muscles and the ideal proportions of the human body could be translated into different aspects of architecture, such as windows, doors, heights and widths. In this way, Michelangelo linked the human figure inextricably to his architectural designs.

THE MEDICI CHAPEL

In 1520, when Pope Clement VII was still Cardinal Giulio de' Medici, he asked Michelangelo to create a new sacristy as part of San Lorenzo. This was to be a mausoleum specifically for Lorenzo the Magnificent (who had taken Michelangelo into the Medici household so many years previously) and his brother Giuliano de' Medici, who had been murdered on Easter Day in 1478 during mass in Florence Cathedral. At that time, artists were also employed as architects, and so, even though he had limited experience of architecture, Michelangelo designed and completed the structural works for the new Medici Chapel in 1524, then worked on the sculptures and sarcophagi for the interior. However, through unforeseen circumstances, the only statues that he completed were those of Lorenzo, Duke of Urbino (1492–1519), Giuliano di Lorenzo, Duke of Nemours (1479–1516), four statues representing Day and Night and Dawn and Dusk, and a Madonna and Child. The *Dawn* and *Dusk* and *Day* and *Night* sculptures are allegories of time. Because of events in Rome, however, Michelangelo never did create tombs for the older Medici members and the chapel was left unfinished, to be completed later in his absence. While creating the Medici Chapel, Michelangelo also designed the adjoining Laurentian Library (see page 86) to contain books bequeathed by Pope Leo X. Before that, most libraries were housed in convents. Michelangelo's design was unique, often described as the first example of Mannerism as an architectural style because it intentionally emphasizes stylization and abandons harmony and classicism.

Opposite: Wooden model after Michelangelo's design for the façade of San Lorenzo, after a drawing by Michelangelo, c. 1518. After a competition between several architects, the design of the façade of San Lorenzo was given by Pope Leo X to Michelangelo, who devised a clever method for applying classical orders on the irregular church façade. Although the project was never completed, this large wooden model shows what the façade would have looked like.

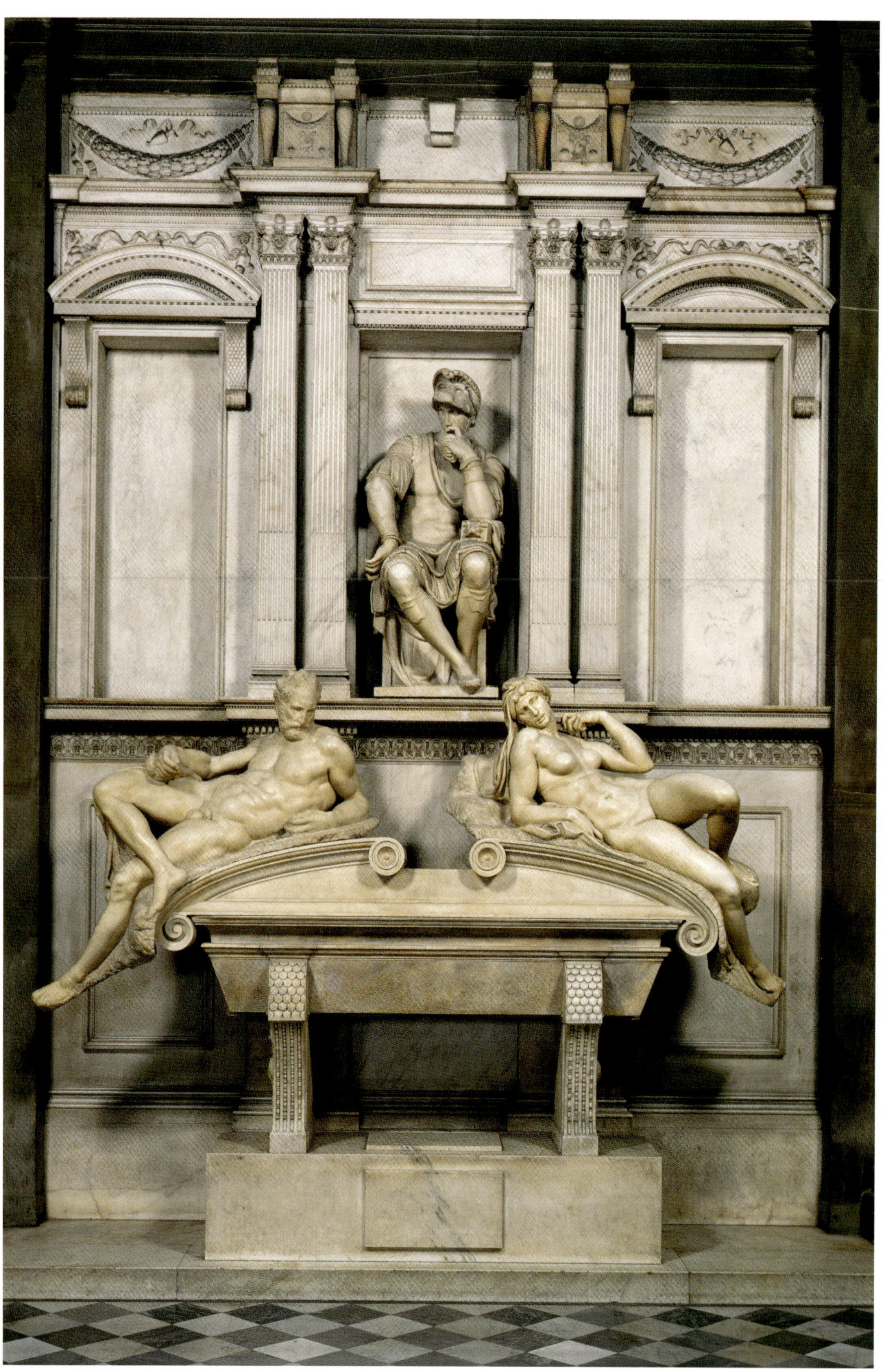

Dawn *and* Dusk, *1524–31. These elongated, elegant curving figures helped to initiate the new art movement of Mannerism. As usual with Michelangelo, all his figures are anatomically accurate – for males. Even his female figures follow the powerfully muscular masculine form. Along with* Night, Dawn *is the only female nude that he ever sculpted.*

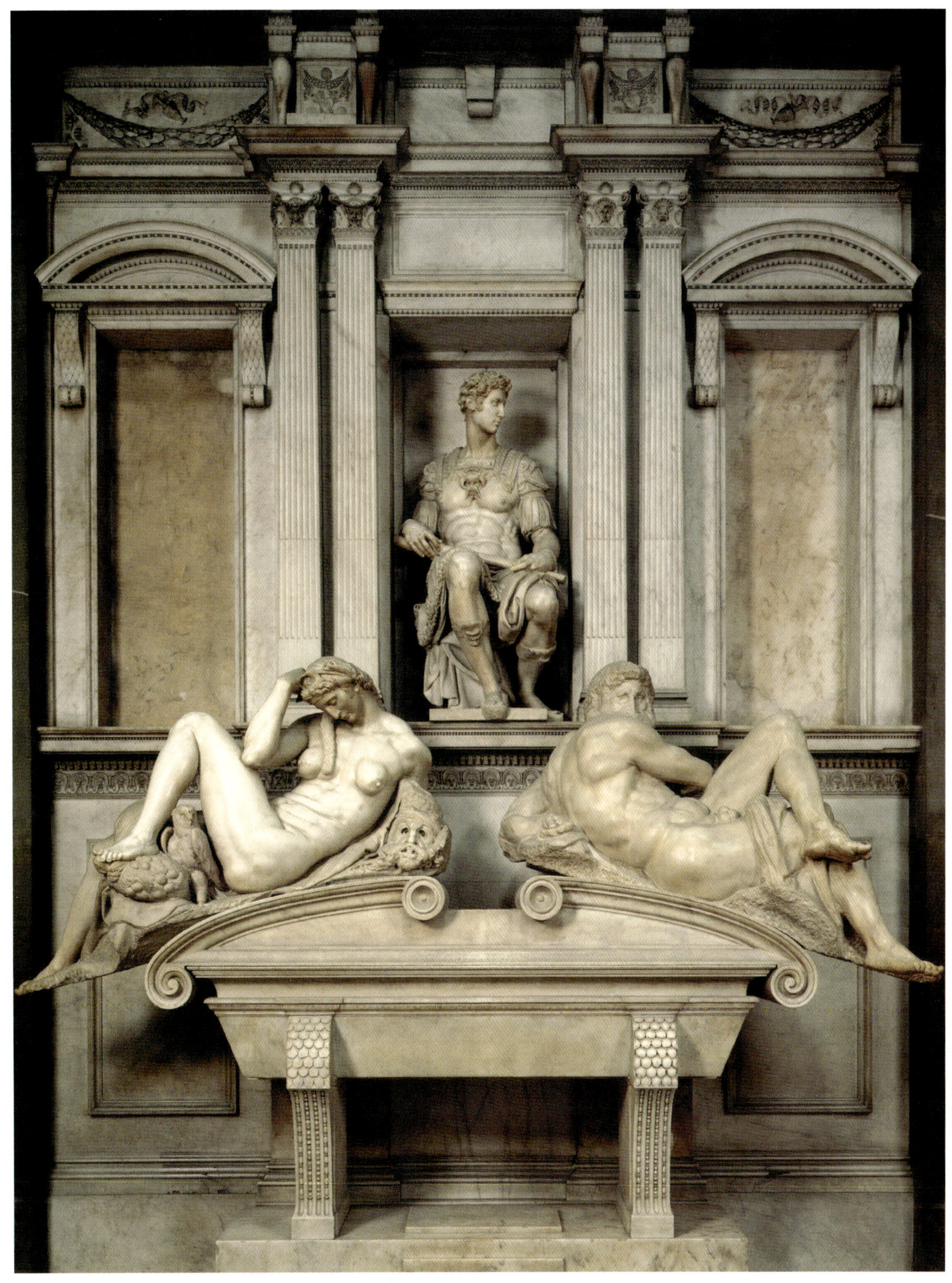

Day *and* Night, *1526–31. Reclining on the sarcophagus of Giuliano di Lorenzo de' Medici are these two allegorical figures representing Day and Night. Day on the left-hand side, is sleeping, while the unfinished statue of* Night *twists and stares outwardly. Once again, the female figure can be seen to be based on a male physique.*

THE SACK OF ROME AND THE SIEGE OF FLORENCE

The Sack of Rome began on 6 May 1527, led by the Italian, German and Spanish mercenaries of Charles V, the Holy Roman Emperor and King of Spain (1500–58). It lasted until the end of 1529 and led to the Siege of Florence. Pope Clement VII had decided that the increasing power of the Holy Roman Emperor was a threat to the Catholic Church. He formed an alliance with Charles V's enemy, King Francis I of France (1494–1547), and the two established the League of Cognac, a treaty that opposed Charles. This led to Charles attacking – and defeating – the French in Italy. However, when he did not pay his soldiers for weeks, they sacked Rome, pillaging and looting houses, churches and the Vatican, assaulting and slaughtering the citizens. Pope Clement fled to the relative safety of the nearby Castel Sant'Angelo, while the Emperor's troops massacred the Swiss Guard and remained in Rome for months, terrorizing, torturing and murdering. It was not until June 1529 that a truce was struck when Clement surrendered, and he and Charles signed the Treaty of Barcelona. He also paid Charles a huge ransom and gave him substantial territory. While

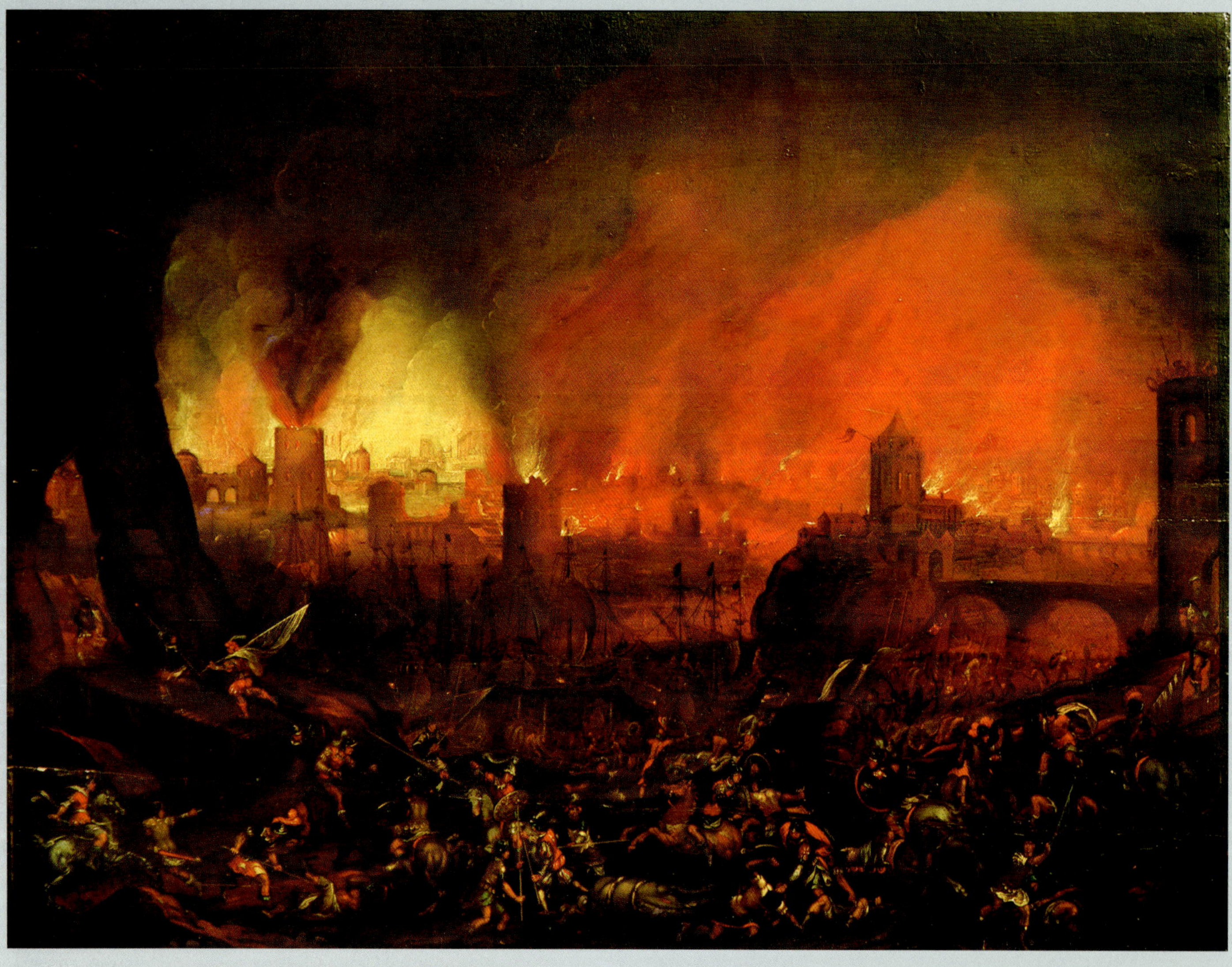

Rome was being sacked, the citizens of Florence expelled the Medici and restored the Republic. Michelangelo owed his career to the Medici, but in 1529 he joined with other Florentines who had grown weary of Medici rule and wanted a more democratic government. The Florentine Republic supported the French during the Sack of Rome, but after Charles defeated them, Florence was on its own. Clement VII was a Medici pope and determined to reinstate his family. So after the Treaty of Barcelona, Charles sent his troops to seize Florence and return the Medici to power. For ten months, Charles's troops held the city under siege, and by August 1530 the Medici were back in control.

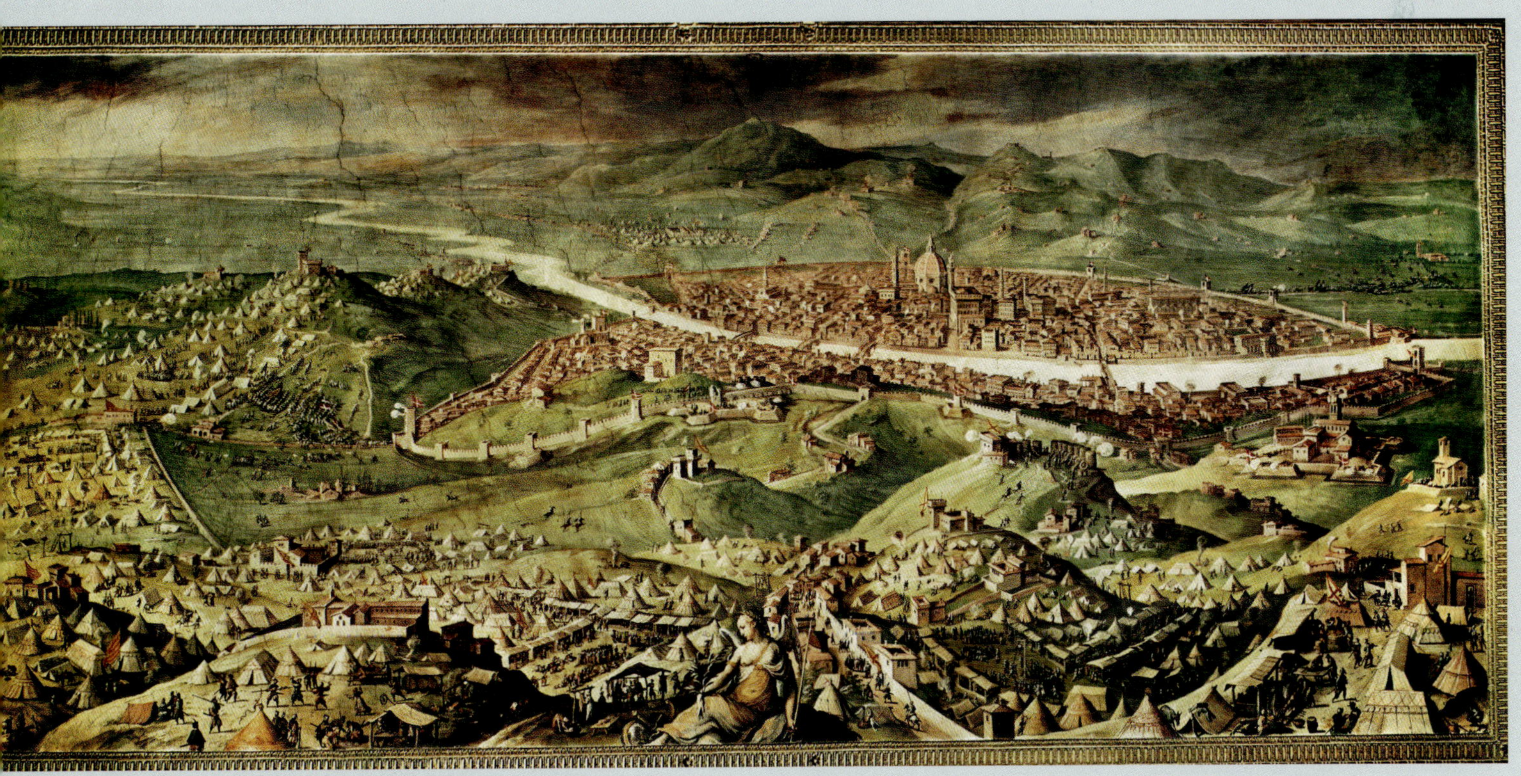

The Siege of Florence, *Giorgio Vasari, c. 1558–60. Painted 30 years after the event, this is Giorgio Vasari's impression of the Siege of Florence, showing the Imperial troops of the Holy Roman Emperor besieging the city in order to force the return of the Medici.*

Opposite: The Sack of Rome, 6 May 1527, *an Italian master, sixteenth/seventeenth century. Painted by an unknown Italian artist, this conveys the violence of the Sack of Rome by Spanish and German troops under Charles V, which lasted for many months, as innocent Romans were assaulted and slaughtered.*

DEATH WARRANT

When the Medici were expelled from Florence, Michelangelo's work on their chapel ceased. Now 54, he was recognized as one of the foremost artists of the time. Known as *Il Divino* (The Divine One), he had dramatically changed the perception of artists, until then viewed as labourers. He was also admired for his *terribilità*, understood as the ability to instil a sense of awe through his art. His importance grew, and in January 1529 he was elected as one of the *Nove della Milizia* (the Council of Nine for the Militia), which was a prominent position in the Florentine government. That April, he was appointed to a new post: Governor and Procurator General of the city's fortifications, for which he received one golden florin a day. However, just as he was appointed, he was sent away from Florence to strengthen the citadels of Pisa and Livorno and then on to Venice and Ferrara – while Florence was under siege. After ten months, in July 1530, Florence was captured, Alessandro de' Medici (1510–37) was installed as ruler of Florence and Baccio Rival (1477–1537), the papal commissioner, ordered a death warrant for Michelangelo for his support for the Republic rather than the Medici. The Pope alleged that Michelangelo had been working for the King of France. To save his own life, Michelangelo fled into hiding in an underground chamber of the Medici Chapel and remained there until the death sentence had been lifted. During this time, it is believed that Michelangelo completed a commission promised some years earlier to Alfonso d'Este, Duke of

Ferrara (1476–1534), a tempera painting of Leda and the Swan, that now exists only in copies.

After several months, Clement decided he needed Michelangelo's services to boost the prestige of the Medici dynasty and he was pardoned. On 21 November 1531, a papal brief was issued, forbidding him from working for anyone but the Pope, and three years later, Clement summoned Michelangelo to Rome.

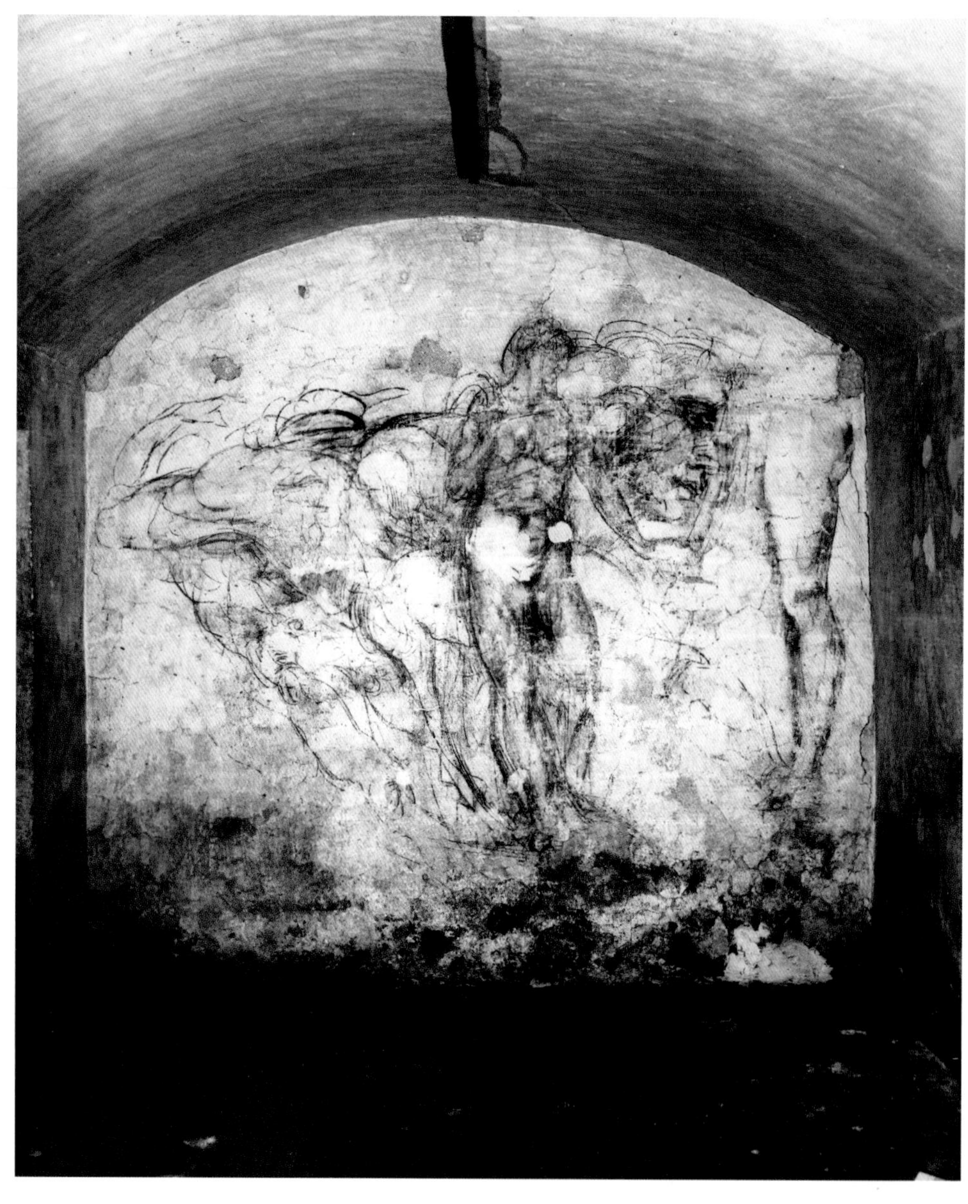

Wall drawings of nude figures, c. 1530. For several months, Michelangelo hid in the basement chamber of the Medici Chapel under the protection of the prior of San Lorenzo. To assuage the boredom he must have felt, he drew large figures on the walls in charcoal that remain there today.

MICHELANGELO'S POETRY

As well as working as a revered artist, architect and engineer, Michelangelo wrote poetry. He was inspired by Plato, Petrarch and Dante Alighieri, and between 1503 and 1560 produced over 300 sonnets, poems and madrigals, often rewriting parts of them many times. Many of his poems explore ideas about love and death, and also beauty, spirituality and Neoplatonic theory. One, written soon after the death of his father in 1530, explores the intensity of grief on losing a loved one: 'The highest love between father and son / Increases in heaven, where every virtue grows.' Although he was exceptionally proud, bordering on arrogant, about his painting and sculpture, Michelangelo was modest about his poetry, describing it as 'something foolish'. In 1534, he met the widowed Marchioness of Pescara and poet Vittoria Colonna (1492–1547), after which he wrote many poems about her. This is an excerpt of one of the poems he wrote for her: 'No mortal thing enthralled these longing eyes, When perfect peace in thy fair face I found; But far within, where all is holy ground, My soul felt Love, her comrade of the skies: For she was born with God in Paradise.'

Manuscript of a poem, c. 1539–47. As with all Michelangelo's poetry, this sonnet was influenced by Plato, Petrarch and Dante – as well as his lengthy conversations with his close friend, the poet Vittoria Colonna.

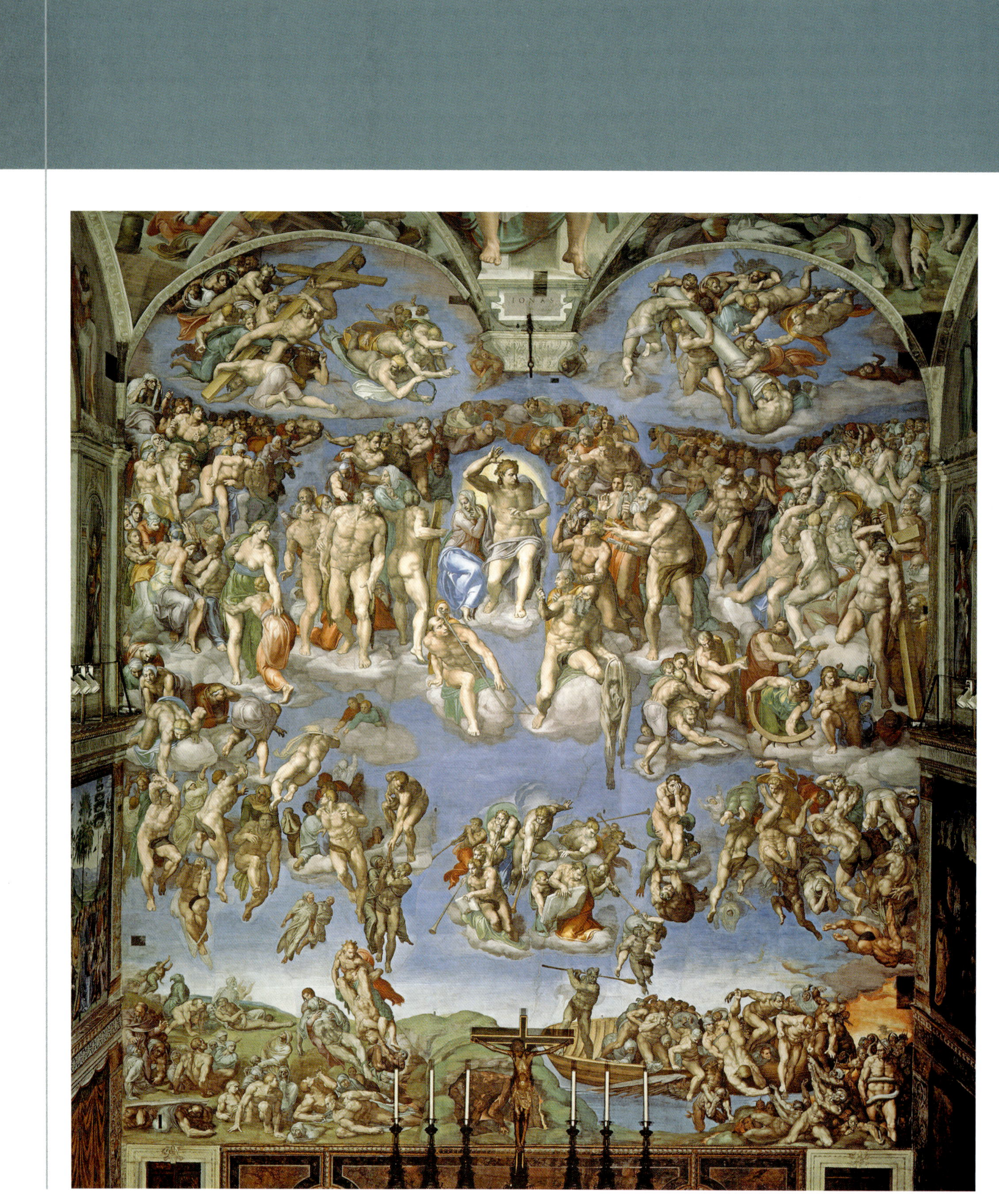

CHAPTER 5
The Genius

Clement VII wanted Michelangelo to create another large fresco for the Sistine Chapel, but Michelangelo had mixed emotions about the idea. When he returned to Rome at the Pope's request, he hoped to secure some more sculpture projects, but another fresco – back in the Sistine Chapel – disheartened him. Now 60 years old, he had not created such a large and important fresco since painting the ceiling over 20 years earlier, and he argued against taking it on, but the Pope was determined.

THE LAST JUDGEMENT

Clement gave Michelangelo complete freedom to depict the story of the Last Judgement from the Book of Revelation, the final book of the Christian Bible. Having only recently won back the Pope's confidence, Michelangelo could not refuse. However, in September 1534, a year after calling Michelangelo to Rome, Clement VII died. He was succeeded by Alessandro Farnese (1468–1549) as Pope Paul III. Michelangelo took the opportunity to forget the Sistine commission and continue working on the sculptures for the Julius tomb, but mindful of his predecessor's commission, the new pope sent several cardinals to see how he was progressing with the cartoons for the fresco. They reported back that Michelangelo was occupied with Julius's tomb, so the Pope arranged with the Duke of Urbino to free Michelangelo from his contractual obligations and insisted that he concentrate on the fresco. From the end of 1534 to October 1541, Michelangelo painted the fresco of *The Last Judgement* on the Sistine Chapel's altar wall, depicting the Second Coming of Christ and his Judgement of souls. Abandoning classical conventions, he portrayed Jesus as a massive, muscular figure, youthful, beardless and naked. He is surrounded by saints, among whom St Bartholomew holds a drooping flayed skin that bears a self-portrait of Michelangelo, while the dead rise from their graves, to be sent to either Heaven or Hell. Following Dante's ideas, Michelangelo's interpretation of *The Last Judgement* is distorted, stylized and dramatic, and at its unveiling, several viewers were alarmed, believing that the nude depictions of Christ and the Virgin Mary were sacrilegious. Some even campaigned to have the fresco removed or censored, but the Pope would not hear of it. At the Council of Trent, shortly before Michelangelo's death in 1564, it was decided to obscure the genitals, and one of Michelangelo's apprentices, Daniele da Volterra (1509–66) was commissioned to make these amends with painted draperies.

The Last Judgement, *1534–41.*
Covering the entire altar wall of the Sistine Chapel, this depicts the Second Coming of Christ and the final judgement by God of all humanity. The souls of humans can be seen, rising or descending to Heaven or Hell. Once more, Michelangelo painted over 300 figures, predominantly nudes.

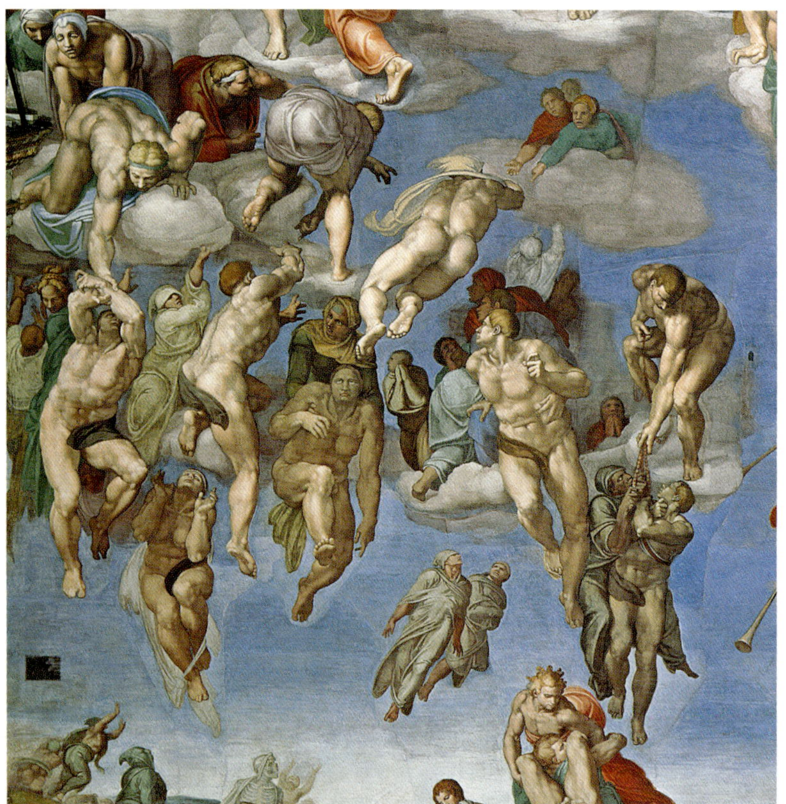

Detail of The Last Judgement, *1534–41. In this part of the fresco, saved souls are separated from damned souls: saints pull the saved up to Heaven, and demons pull the damned down to Hell. The work took Michelangelo over six years to complete. He was nearly 67 when he finished it.*

SUCCESS AND SADNESS

As soon as Michelangelo finished *The Last Judgement*, Pope Paul commissioned him to create two further large frescoes for his private chapel, the Cappella Paolina in the Vatican. Michelangelo was reluctant to undertake yet more fresco work, but he had to obey the Pope's command, and in 1542 he began work. One illustrates the conversion of St Paul on the road to Damascus, and the other portrays the crucifixion of the first Catholic pope, St Peter. At the same time, Michelangelo was also organizing the architectural frame for Julius II's tomb. In January 1544, one of his assistants, the 16-year-old Cecchino dei Bracci (1528–44), died suddenly. His devastated uncle, banker Luigi del Riccio (d. 1546) and a friend of Michelangelo, begged the artist to design the boy's tomb and write some verses as an epitaph. It seems that Michelangelo was particularly close to the boy, describing him as follows: 'Bereft of handsome eyes and jaunty air … in whom my soul now lives.' The frescoes of saints Paul and Peter were to be placed on the wall at either side of the altar of the Cappella Paolina, and Michelangelo's Mannerist style is apparent. No longer were they classical, ideally proportioned figures as on the Sistine Chapel ceiling. Instead they are elongated, slightly distorted and rather stylized.

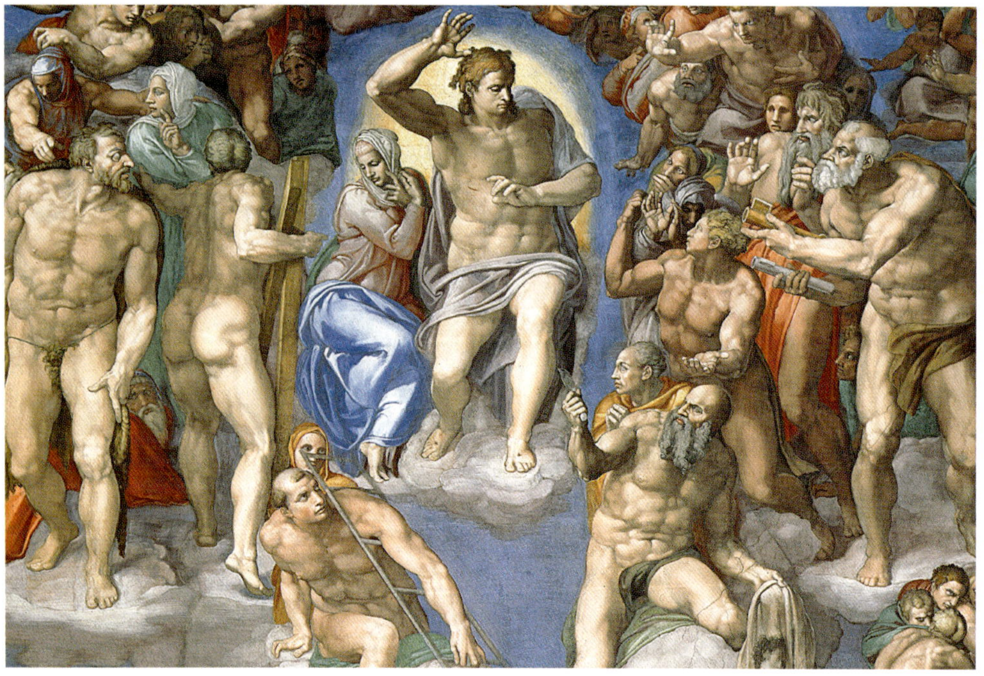

Detail of The Last Judgement, *1534–41. At the centre of the image, Christ announces the final judgement. At his right side, his mother the Virgin Mary intercedes to help the suffering, while around them are muscular saints and angels, mainly painted with pinkish flesh colours and brilliant blue. The style of this expressive painting helped to inspire the Mannerist art movement.*

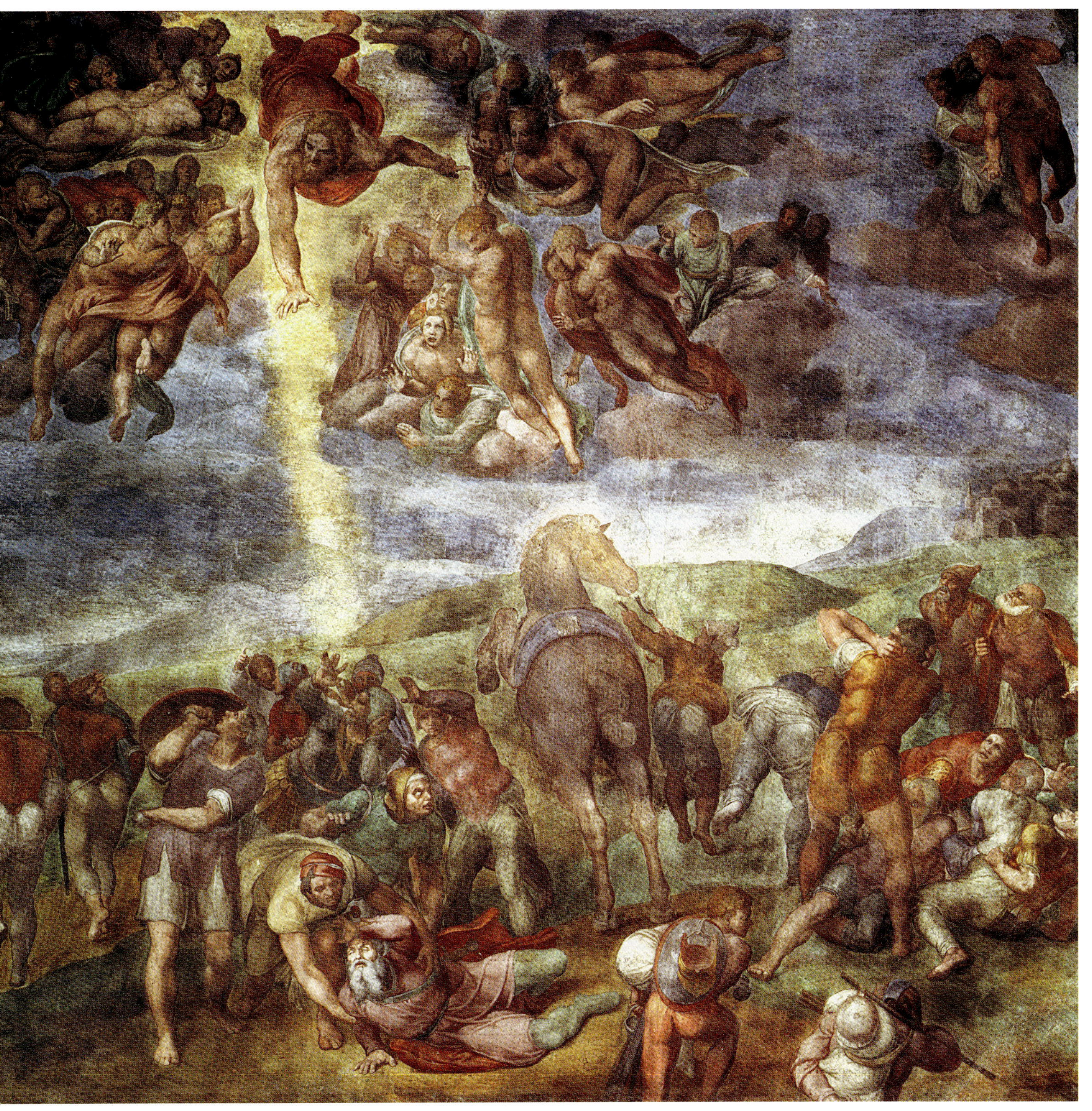

The Conversion of St Paul, c. 1542–5. In the top left corner of the fresco, Jesus enters the scene, bathed in light that radiates down to a group of figures on the ground, including the Roman soldier Saul of Tarsus, who is on the road to Damascus, intending to arrest Christians. As he experiences this divine intervention, Saul is converted to Christianity – and later becomes St Paul.

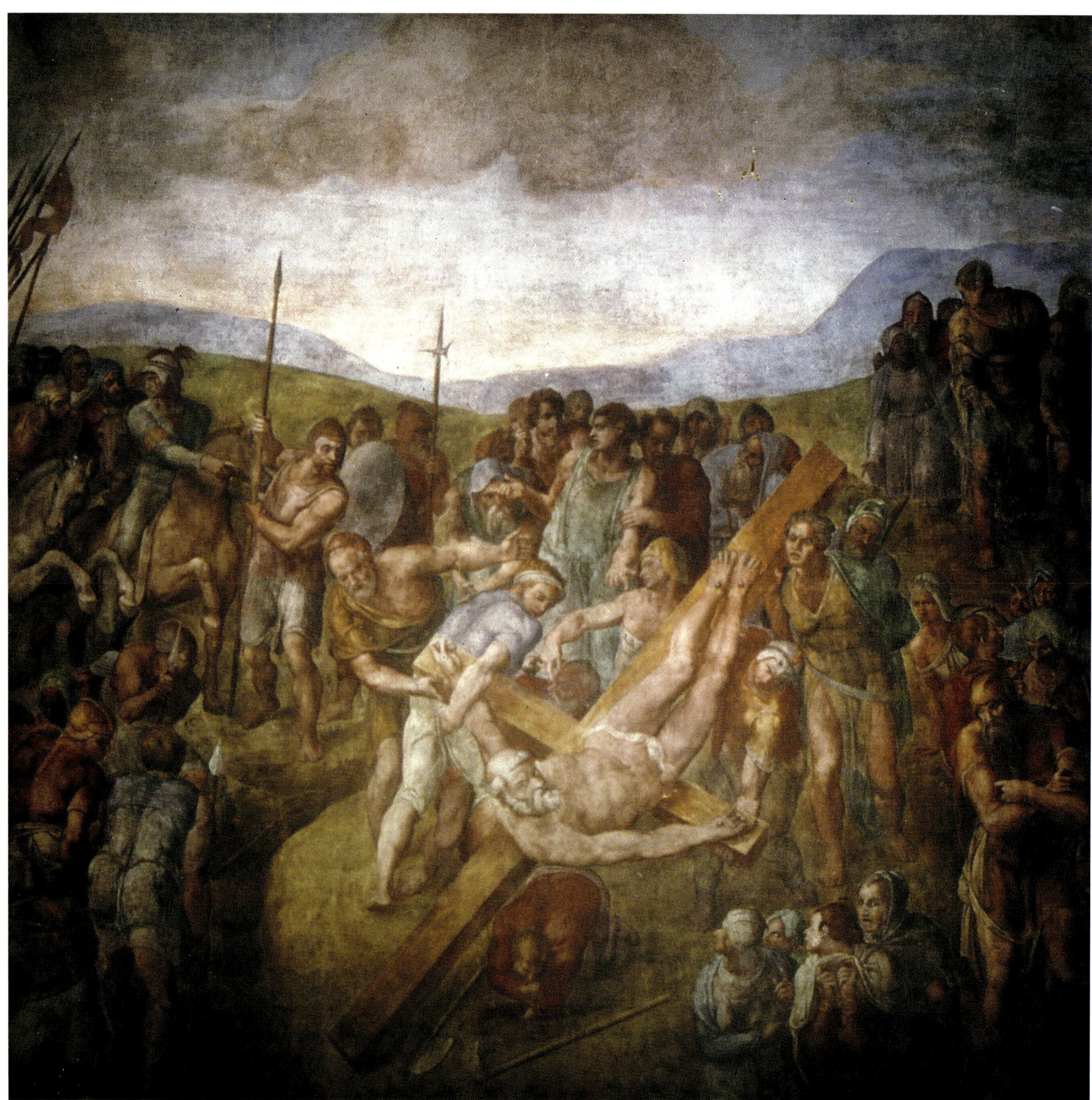

The Crucifixion of St Peter, *1546–50. Although the story is not relayed in the Bible, it is traditionally believed by Christians that St Peter was captured and crucified head-down in Rome during the reign of Emperor Nero, between 54 and 67* CE. *Michelangelo depicts him at the moment he was raised on the Cross by the Roman soldiers. All around him, people are distressed, but Peter shows great courage.*

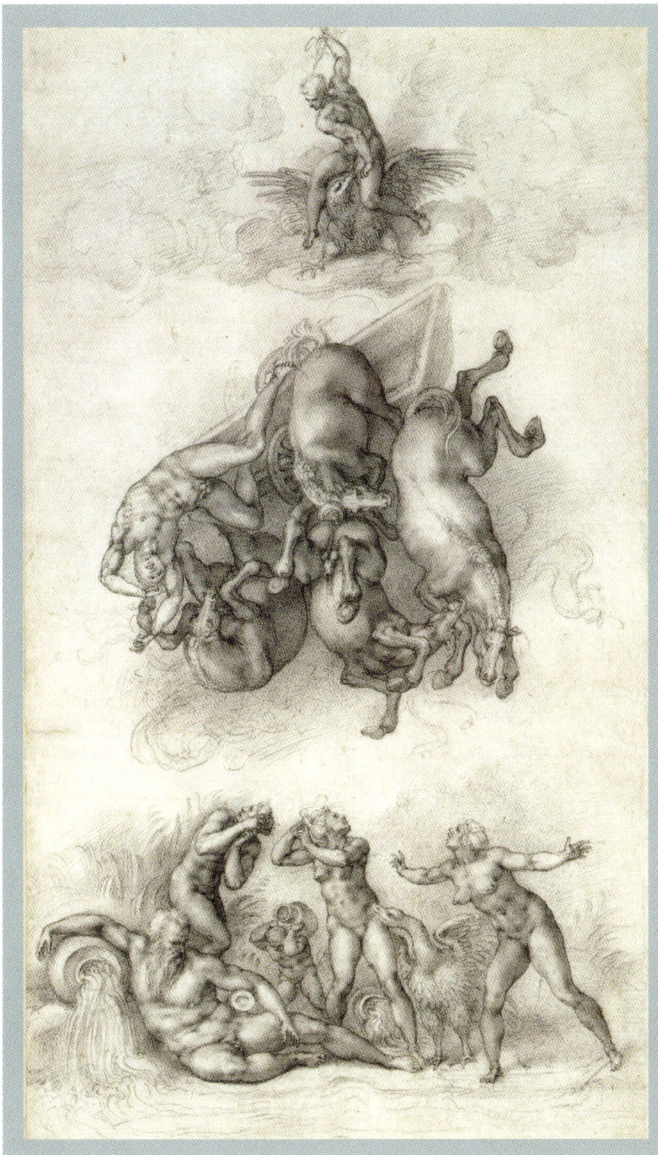

MICHELANGELO'S RELATIONSHIPS

Although his sexuality is alluded to in some of his poetry, and all his nude figures, whether men or women, are based on the male form, it is not clear whether Michelangelo had physical relationships. His biographer Condivi described his 'monk-like chastity', though he appears to have had several romantic friendships, such as with Tommaso dei Cavalieri (*c.* 1509–87): he was 23 years old when they met in 1532, while Michelangelo was 57. His poetry on the death of Cecchino dei Bracci also suggests romantic connections. Some of the young men he became close to, such as the models Gherardo Perini and Febo di Poggio, took advantage of him, either stealing from him or asking him for money and gifts. Later, Michelangelo referred to di Poggio as 'that little blackmailer'. It seems that he was close to only one woman: the widow Vittoria Colonna, whom he met in Rome in 1534. They wrote sonnets for each other and were in regular contact until she died. Condivi recalls Michelangelo saying that his sole regret in life was that he did not kiss her face in the same manner as he had kissed her hand.

The Fall of Phaeton, *1533. Michelangelo made this drawing in Florence in the summer of 1533 for Tommaso dei Cavalieri, who loved it and showed it to the Pope, Cardinal de' Medici and others, who were all extremely impressed.*

ST PETER'S BASILICA

In 1546, Pope Paul III appointed the 71-year-old Michelangelo chief architect of St Peter's Basilica. Until then, various artists and architects had held the position, including Bramante, Raphael and Sangallo, but little progress had been made. Michelangelo was persuaded to take over the project and he retained the post for the next 17 years. A self-taught architect, he uniquely blended his fluid approach to sculpture with an understanding of engineering and proportion, and the result of his labours on St Peter's was an enduring influence on architecture. By the time Michelangelo was appointed, St Peter's had been under construction for 40 years, and there had been no cohesion between the various chief architects. Despite his repeated protests that he was not an architect, Michelangelo proved himself to be exceptionally pioneering and innovative. When he undertook the project, he substantially increased the scale of the four major piers at the crossing that supports the dome and enhanced the thickness of the perimeter of the church. The previous architects had followed the ancient rules of Vitruvius (*c.* 80/70–15 BCE), but Michelangelo broke away from that, instead following his artistic vision. He also returned to Bramante's original plan that focused on Pythagorean principles of harmony and proportion, and used the circle and the square. His main contribution to the building was the vast central dome that dominates the skyline of Rome, although it remained uncompleted at his death in 1564 and was eventually completed to his design in 1590 by Giacomo della Porta (1532–1602).

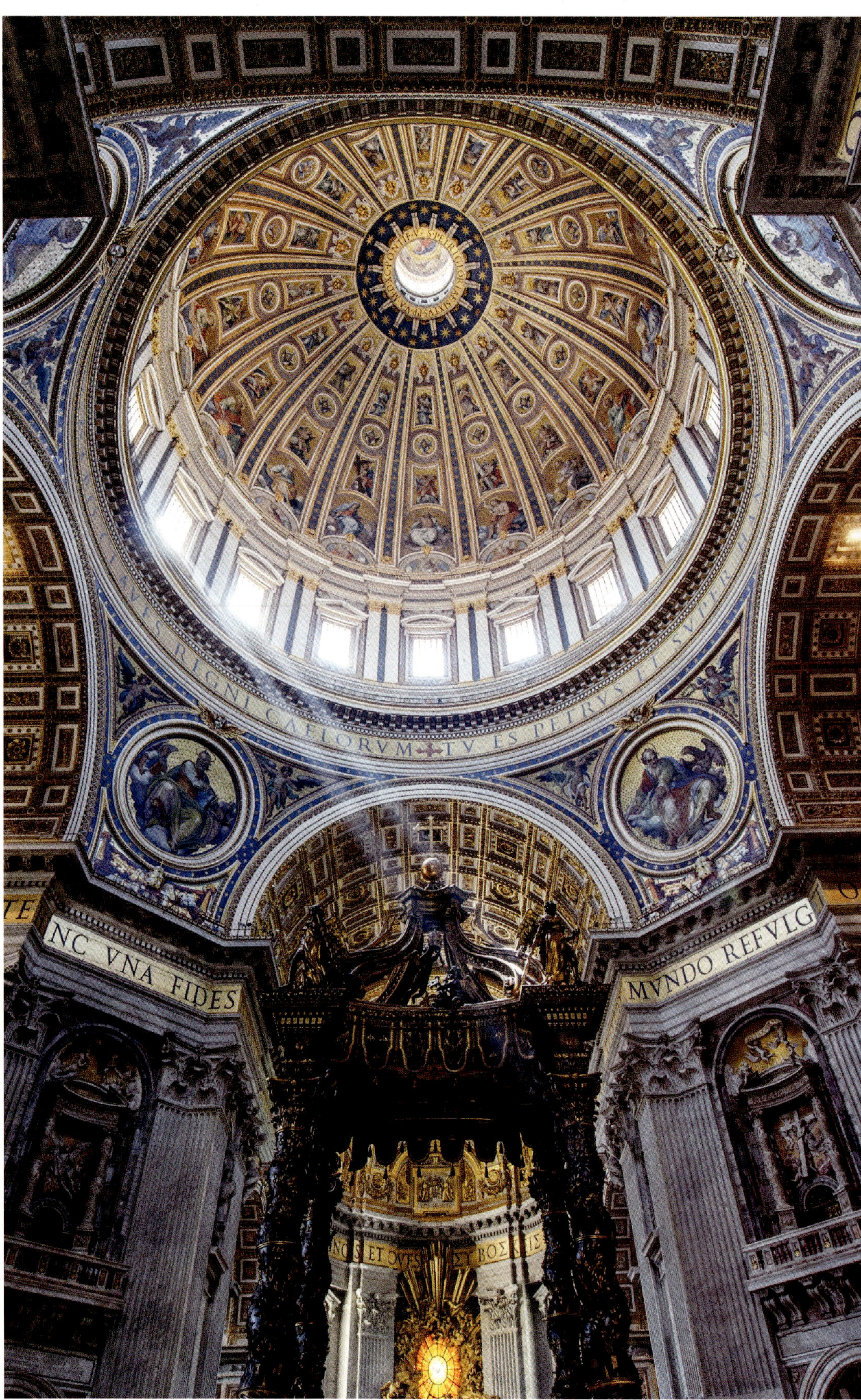

Interior view of Michelangelo's dome. From the floor of the basilica to the top of the external cross, the dome of St Peter's rises to a total height of 136.6 metres (448 ft). Its internal diameter is 41.5 metres (136 ft) and light floods in through the windows around the circumference.

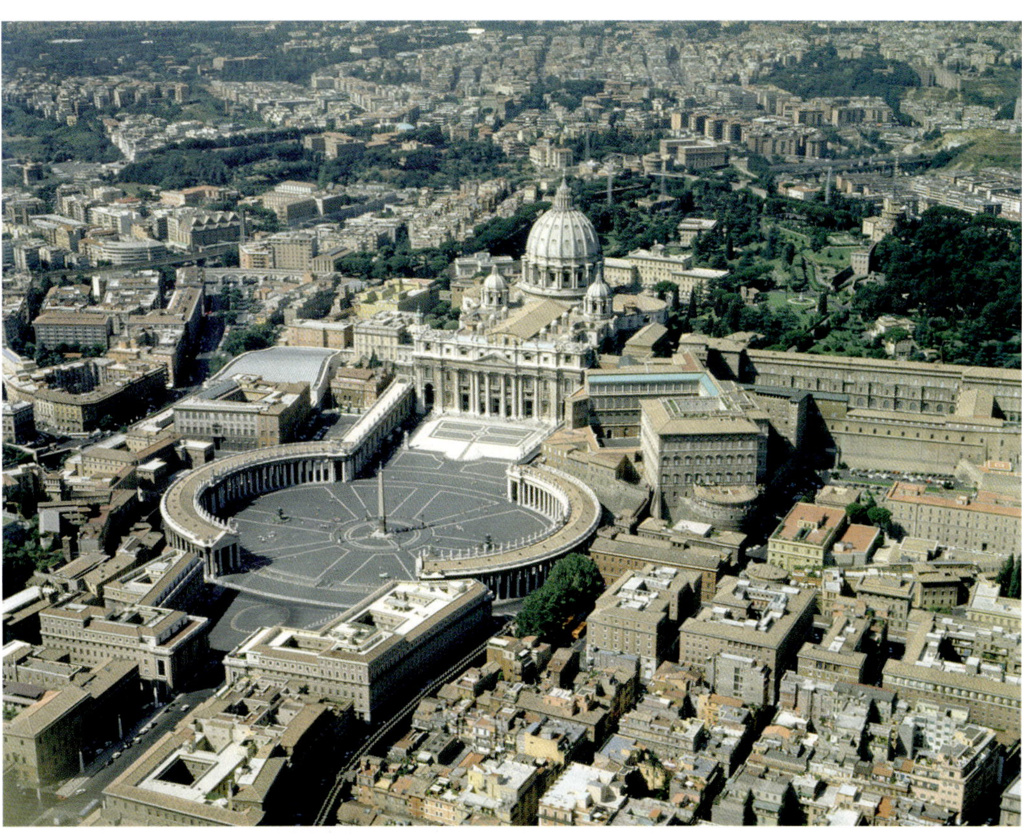

Aerial view of St Peter's Basilica, Vatican City, Rome, Italy. When Michelangelo took over the design of St Peter's Basilica, he inherited numerous schemes designed and redesigned by previous architects. Although each one was different, they all wanted a dome as breathtaking as Brunelleschi's in Florence. With his clarity of vision, Michelangelo did not simply dismiss the ideas of the previous architects, but drew on them, reverting to Bramante's Greek Cross but interpreting it in his own grand way.

St Peter's Basilica, Vatican City, Rome, Italy. Completed in 1590, the cupola of Michelangelo's dome dominates the skyline of Rome and meets the requirement of being as impressive as Brunelleschi's dome is in Florence.

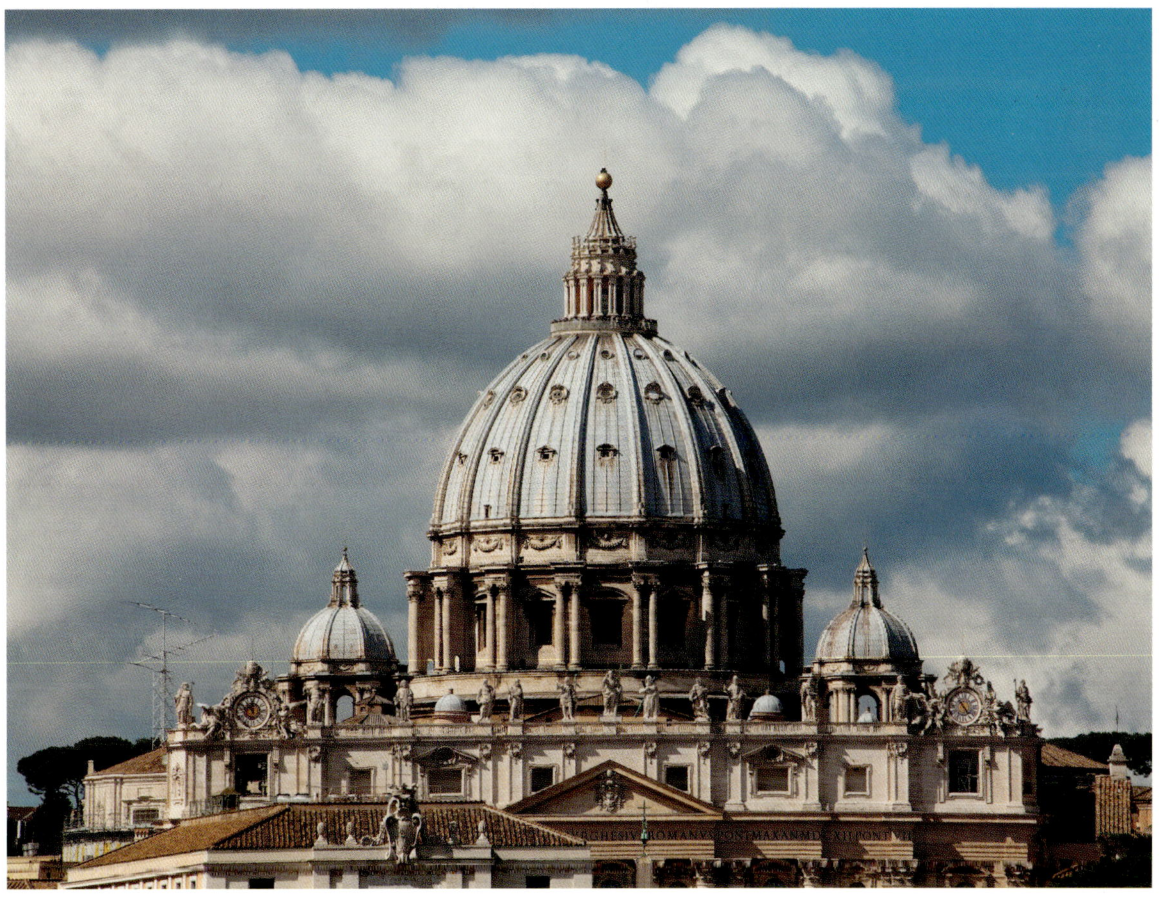

PIAZZA DEL CAMPIDOGLIO

With his understanding of engineering and sculpture, and his unique method of basing architectural proportions on the anatomy of the human body, Michelangelo undertook many successful architectural projects. Ultimately, he adapted the processes he used as a sculptor and painter, and his belief that buildings should be able to be viewed from any angle with no bad vantage point. Even his planning differed from other architects of the time. While most produced several sketches on different sheets of paper, Michelangelo layered detailed drawings on top of his first sketches. These layers helped him to

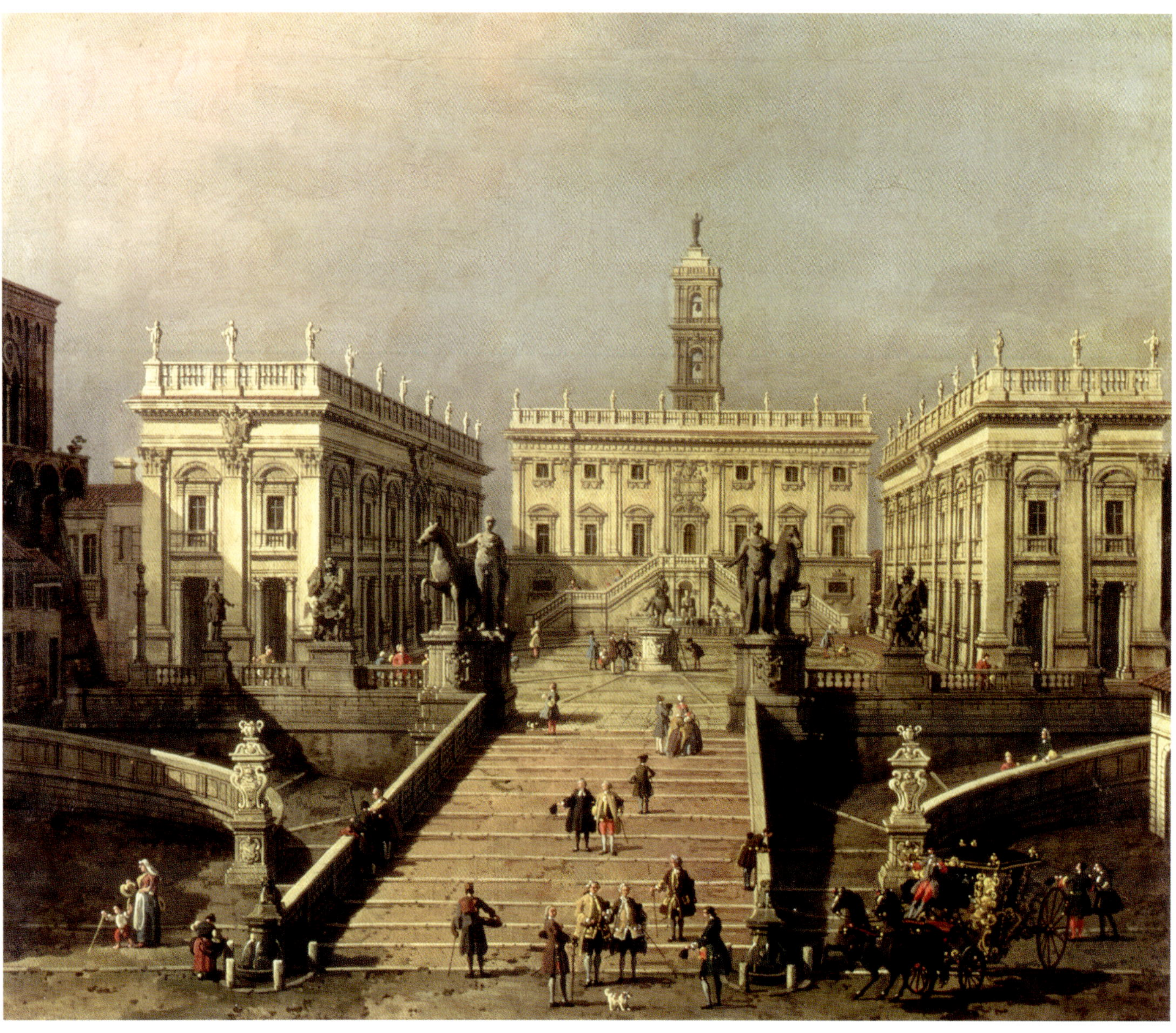

View of Rome: The Piazza del Campidoglio and the Cordonata, *Canaletto, c. 1740–5. Canaletto (1697–1768) became famous during the eighteenth century for his paintings of Venice, but he also painted in Rome and England. This is his view of Michelangelo's Piazza del Campidoglio, depicted from a raised viewpoint showing the Cordonata, which is flanked at the bottom by two Egyptian lions. At the centre of the Piazza is the equestrian statue of Marcus Aurelius. The building on the right is the Palazzo dei Conservatori and in the distance is the Palazzo Senatorio.*

envisage the designs in three dimensions. Next, he built either a wax or a clay model, and continued to develop and refine these until his designs met his vision. His interest in light, shadow and space meant that he viewed architecture differently from many of his contemporaries. His approach was free and unconstrained, and he was comfortable going against traditions, such as changing proportions and details. Among his many projects was the redesign of the Piazza del Campidoglio on Capitoline Hill. For this he created an original trapezoid-shaped space with a large ramp – the Cordonata, which complemented the surrounding buildings. To unify other structures around the square, he designed façades for the Palazzo dei Conservatori and the Palazzo Senatorio. The focal point of the piazza was a second-century bronze equestrian statue of Emperor Marcus Aurelius, which Michelangelo placed on a marble oval pedestal.

PALAZZO FARNESE

When Cardinal Alessandro Farnese became Pope Paul III in 1534, Antonio da Sangallo the Younger began designing him a grand palace, but Sangallo died in 1546 and the Pope asked Michelangelo to finish the building. This happened as Michelangelo was starting to work on St Peter's Basilica, so his time was extremely limited and he worked on the palazzo in stages – completing the façade, sides and rear of the building first, then adding a third floor. To create a grand impression, around the upper exterior, he added a huge, projecting cornice carved with lilies that were the Farnese family

Façade of the Palazzo Farnese, Rome, Italy. Initially designed in 1517 for the Farnese family, this building was expanded by Antonio da Sangallo the Younger when Alessandro Farnese became Pope Paul III in 1534. After Sangallo's death in 1546, Michelangelo took over the design, creating an impressive palace for the Pope and his descendants.

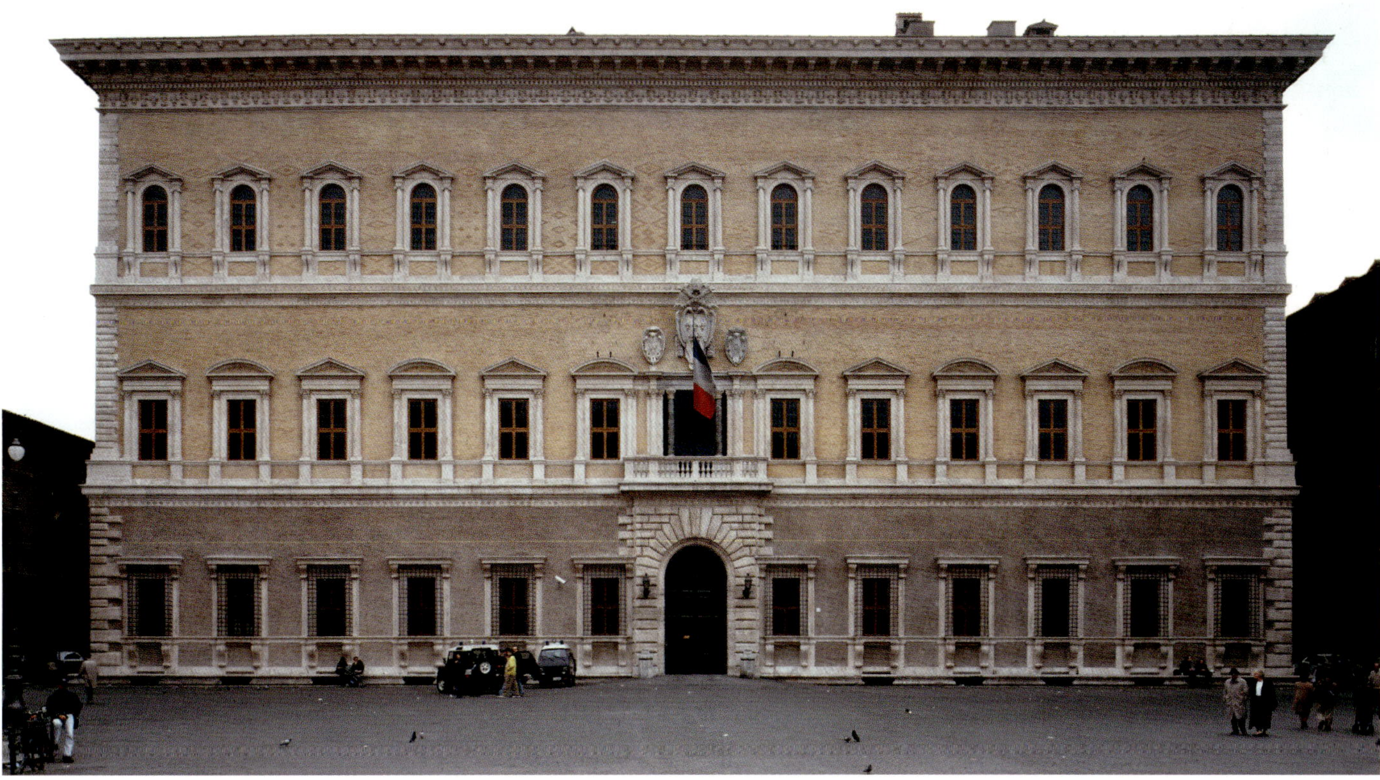

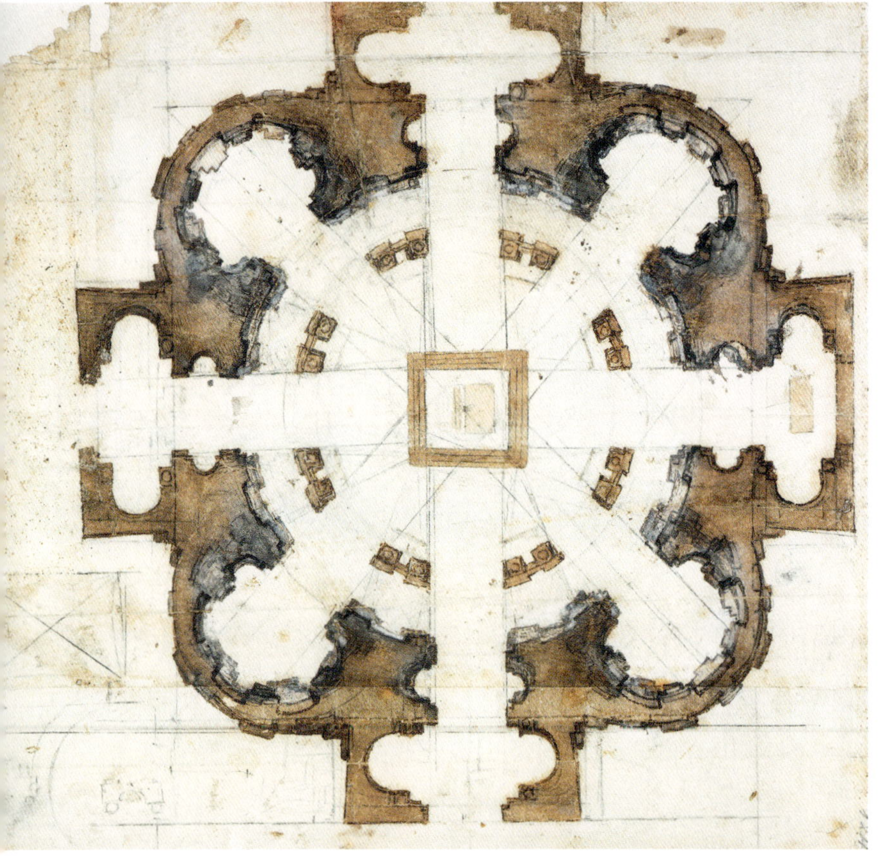

Drawing for San Giovanni dei Fiorentini, c. 1559. One of five designs created by Michelangelo for the construction of San Giovanni dei Fiorentini that were never realized.

symbol. The cornice emphasized the horizontality of the structure, and to compensate for its size, Michelangelo incorporated large windows on the upper storey, to match those on the lower two floors. This was completely unconventional; windows on top floors were traditionally smaller than those below. He also made a massive entrance in the lower centre of the palace, with a papal balcony directly above. Over that was a large projecting relief of the Farnese coat of arms, and in the inner courtyard were Doric, Ionic and Corinthian columns. Overall, he ensured that the design recalled grand buildings of ancient Rome.

HONORARY CITIZEN

Once Michelangelo had left Florence in 1534, he never returned. Florence was his first home and his loyalty to it remained, but as he began undertaking more commissions, especially architectural projects, he did not have time to go back. In addition, Rome was taking over from Florence as the hub of Renaissance activity, where new developments in art, architecture, literature and science occurred and many of the greatest contemporary minds gathered. Michelangelo was highly respected; advising on ancient Roman discoveries and continuing to prove his talents. On 10 December 1537, he was made an honorary citizen of Rome and given the official title 'Master Michelangelo, sculptor'. However, for the last decades of his life, rather than sculpture, his most considerable contribution to the city was in its architecture.

MORE ARCHITECTURE

Soon after his election, Pope Pius IV, born Giovanni Angelo Medici (1499–1565), ordered a number of civic improvements to the city of Rome. After improving and renaming some streets, in 1561, he commissioned Michelangelo to create a gatehouse within the Aurelian walls that encircled Rome. Replacing a previous gatehouse, this was to be a grand and monumental exit and entrance to the city. To complement the city walls and the medieval streets that still remained, Michelangelo designed a gatehouse that resembled a Roman triumphal arch. It was named Porta Pia after Pope Pius IV, but it was not completed during Michelangelo's lifetime and the final design differs from his original.

Two years after he had designed Porta Pia, Michelangelo was commissioned to convert the vast central hall of the ancient Baths of Diocletian (built

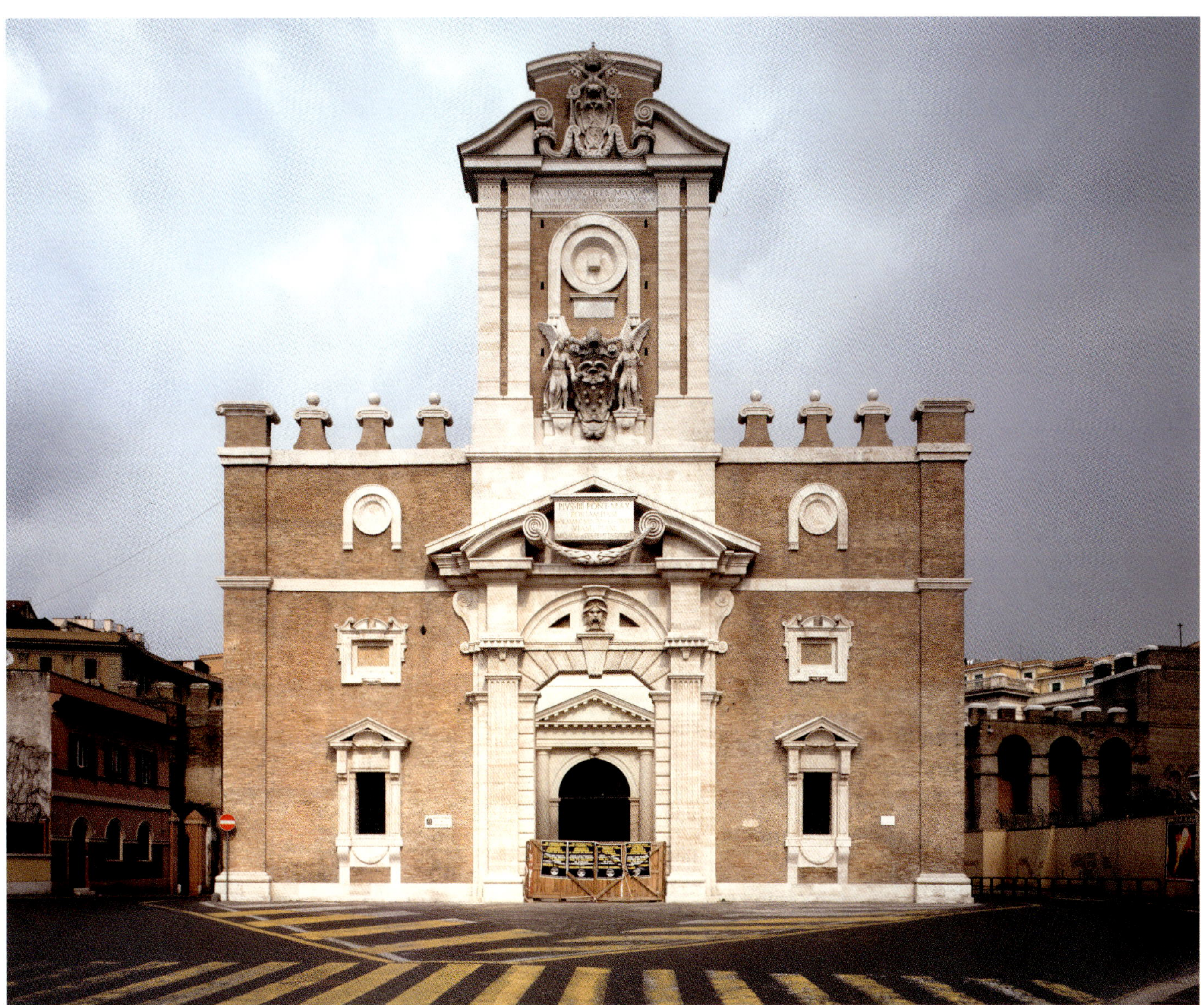

Porta Pia, 1561–5, Rome, Italy. Designed by Michelangelo to replace the Porta Nomentana, Porta Pia was one of Pope Pius IV's civic improvements to Rome and was named after him. Construction ended in 1565, after Michelangelo's death.

between 298–306 CE) that had been neglected, into a church for the Carthusian monastery. He transformed the site into a large charterhouse with an adjoining church, the Santa Maria degli Angeli e dei Martiri. Other architectural commissions included the interior of the Church of Santa Maria degli Angeli and the Sforza Chapel in the Basilica di Santa Maria Maggiore.

As well as the iconic dome of St Peter's, Michelangelo's most notable work is probably the Laurentian Library at San Lorenzo, with its extraordinary vestibule staircase in three parts, leading to a luminous reading room of harmonious proportions (see overleaf). All of his building designs demonstrate his imaginative use of the classical language of architecture to create innovative, more unconventional versions of his own.

Reading Room of the Laurentian Library, San Lorenzo, Florence, Italy. Built to emphasize the Medici family's intelligence and culture, the Laurentian Library is an example of early Mannerist architecture. The Reading Room, seen here, is light and harmonious. Each desk is lit by windows along the wall which form a series of bays.

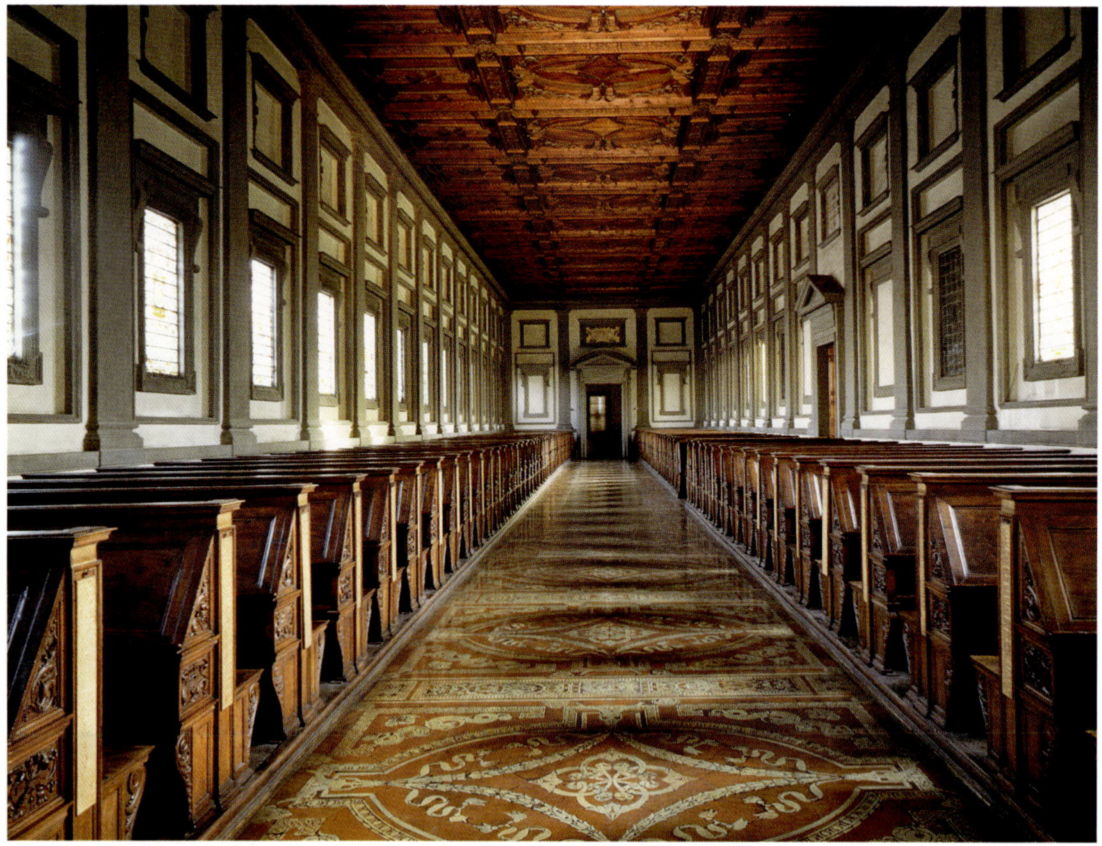

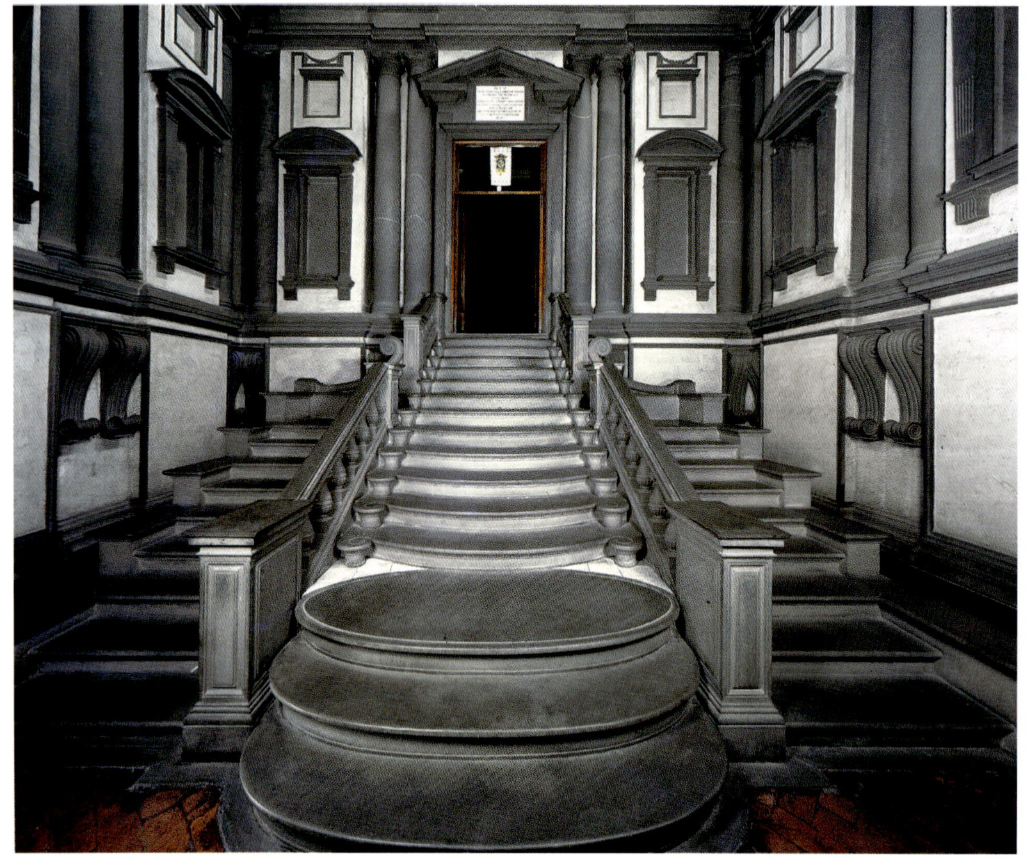

Staircase of the Laurentian Library, San Lorenzo, Florence, Italy. One of the greatest elements of the Laurentian Library is this free-standing marble staircase that leads up to the reading room and takes up half of the floor of the vestibule. The treads of the centre flights are convex and vary in width, while the outer flights are straight.

MICHELANGELO THE MAN

According to his biographer and apprentice Condivi, Michelangelo was restrained and self-controlled in his personal life. 'However rich I may have been, I have always lived like a poor man,' he once told Condivi. Condivi also wrote in his biography of Michelangelo that he often forgot to eat or drink and ate 'more out of necessity than pleasure'. Another of his biographers, Paolo Giovio (1483–1552) wrote of his 'rude and uncivilized' behaviour, that he lacked generosity and was unwilling to teach his art to others, and that 'his nature was so rough and uncouth that his domestic habits were incredibly squalid'.

Of medium height, Michelangelo had a strong, muscular body, and he followed his father's advice not to wash. His habits were unusual, even for the period, as he often slept in his clothes and wore buskins – open-toed boots – for months at a time. Indeed, he sometimes left them on for so long that when he did remove them his own skin came off with them. A keen horse rider, he remained in good health throughout his 88 years, apart from occasionally suffering from kidney stones, and he worked until the end of his life. He had several close friends, mainly men, and the only people to dislike him seem to have been other artists who were jealous of him. However, on the whole, he remained solitary; Condivi described him as a man who 'withdrew himself from the company of men'.

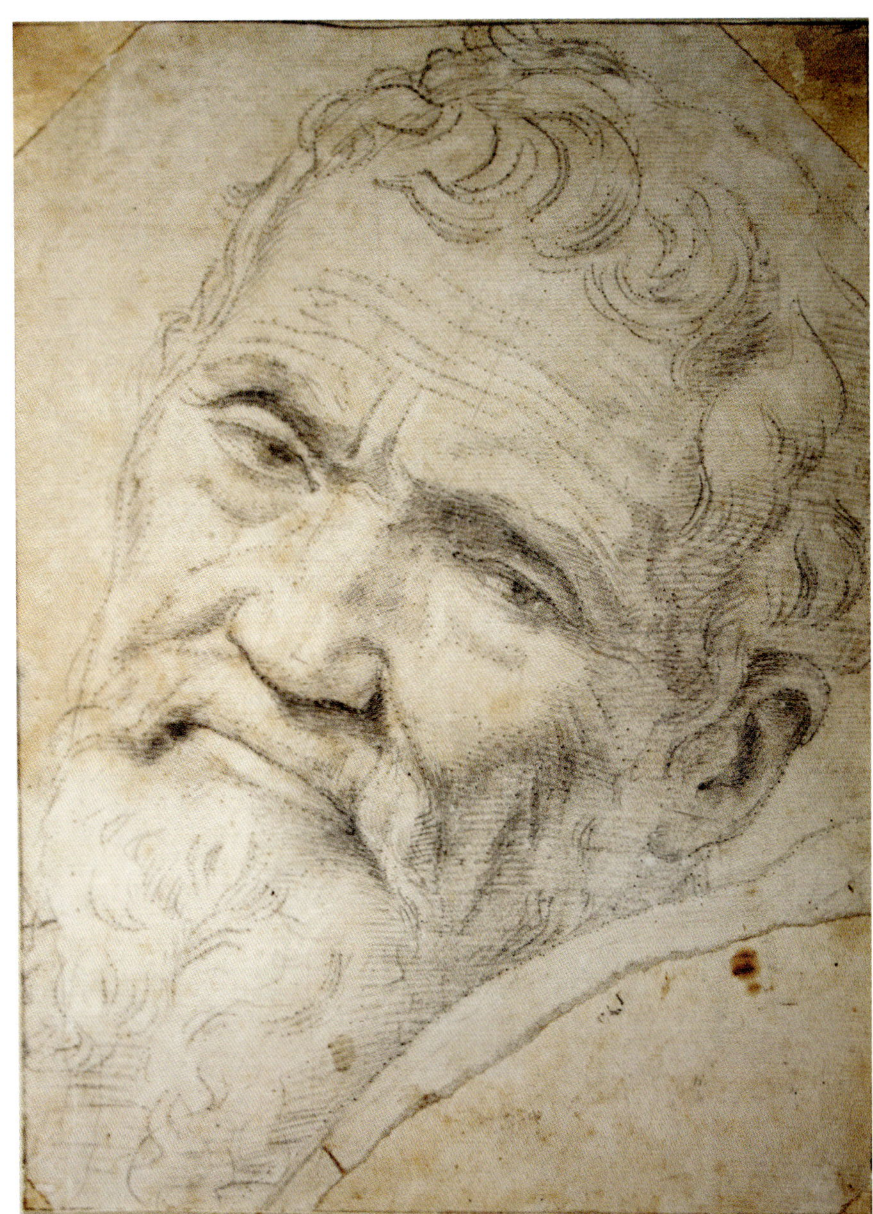

Portrait of Michelangelo, *Daniele da Volterra, 1548–53. Drawn by his pupil Daniele da Volterra when Michelangelo was about 73 years old, this conveys the deep affection felt by the young apprentice for his master and also reveals how well he had learned from Michelangelo.*

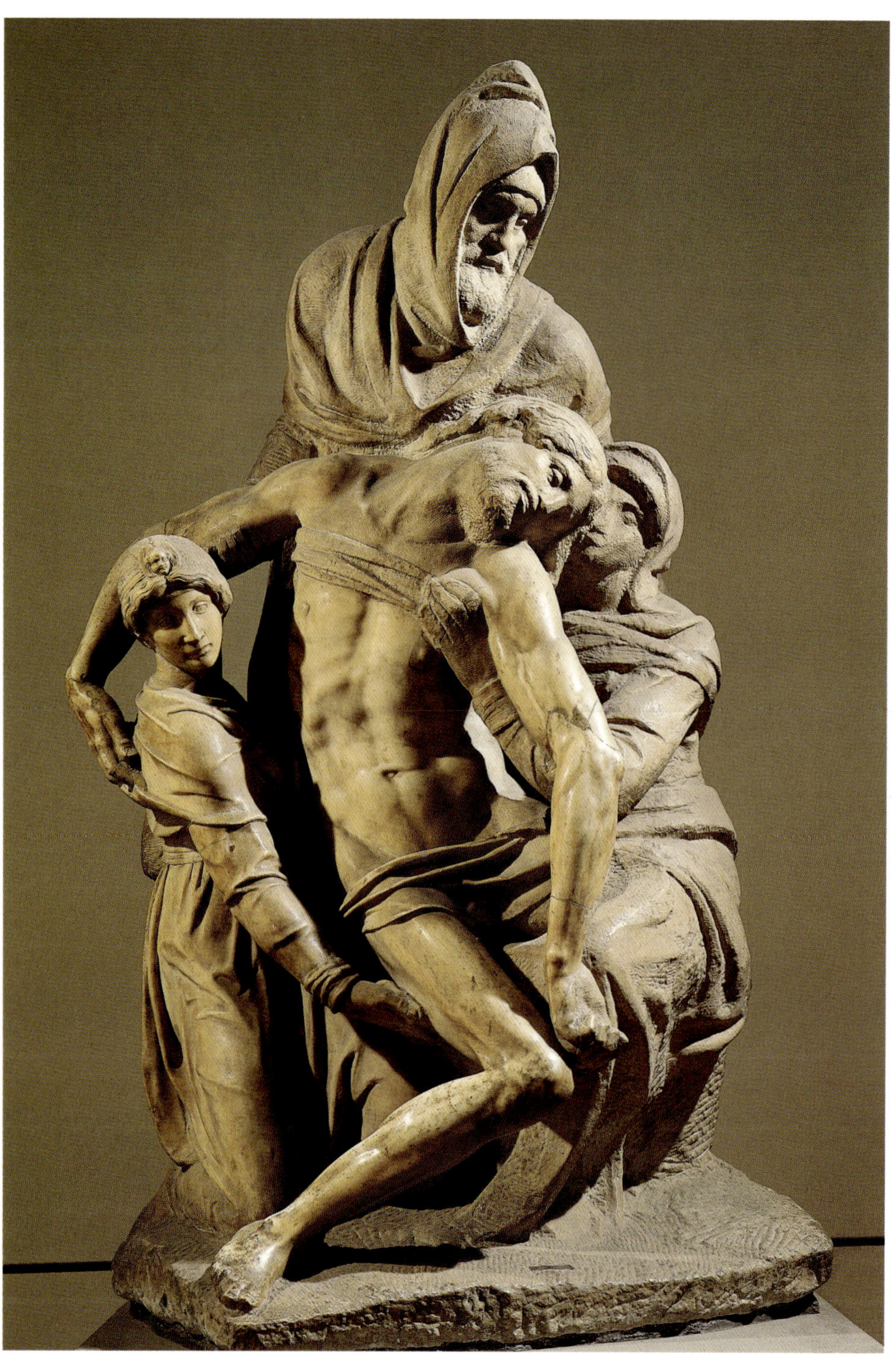

The Deposition, c. 1547–55. Also called
the Florentine Pietà, this sculpture depicts
four figures: the body of Christ, Mary
Magdalene, the Virgin Mary and Nicodemus
(or Joseph of Arimathea), which is also
a self-portrait. According to Vasari,
Michelangelo made the sculpture when he
was in his 70s to decorate his tomb in Santa
Maria Maggiore in Rome, but later sold it.

BURIAL FOR A GENIUS

Michelangelo remained working
and active until his death at the
age of 88. Towards the end of his
life, he produced more marble
sculptures. Especially known are
another *pietà* and *The Deposition*,
which is also sometimes called
the *Florentine Pietà*. In the latter,
Michelangelo created a self-
portrait as Nicodemus or Joseph
of Arimathea, who lowers Christ's
body into the arms of the Virgin
Mary and Mary Magdalene after
the Crucifixion. Six days before his
own death, Michelangelo was still
working on the *Rondanini Pietà*.
In January 1564, Michelangelo,
who was healthy at 88, contracted
a digestive ailment which caused
him problems with sleeping, but
he continued working. When
he became feverish, he stopped
working on his *pietà* and went
riding, hoping to tire himself out.
However, it seems that he suffered
a stroke, as his assistant Tiberio
Calgani (1532–65) later told his
nephew Lionardo Buonarroti
(1519–99) that he had been in the
rain, speaking incoherently. On
15 February 1564, Michelangelo
dictated a letter to Daniele da
Volterra, asking Lionardo to come
to Rome from Florence. He signed
the letter himself. Three days later,
in his home in Rome, he died,
surrounded by Tommaso de' Cavalieri, his friends
Diomede Leoni (1510/20–90) and Daniele da
Volterra, and his servant Antonio del Francese.
It was three weeks before his 89th birthday. His
wish was to be buried without fuss in his beloved
Florence, and Lionardo asked Duke Cosimo I

de' Medici for permission. This was granted, even though the Romans wanted him buried there. Lionardo managed to have his body taken quietly from Rome and to Florence, to the Basilica of Santa Croce. Although Michelangelo had wanted a private burial, the basilica was filled with weeping mourners. Next, and against the Buonarroti family's wishes, the coffin was opened. According to Vasari, Michelangelo's body showed no sign of decomposition even though he had been dead by then for 25 days. Eventually the coffin was closed and Michelangelo's body interred. Duke Cosimo I de' Medici had called for a funeral worthy of a prince.

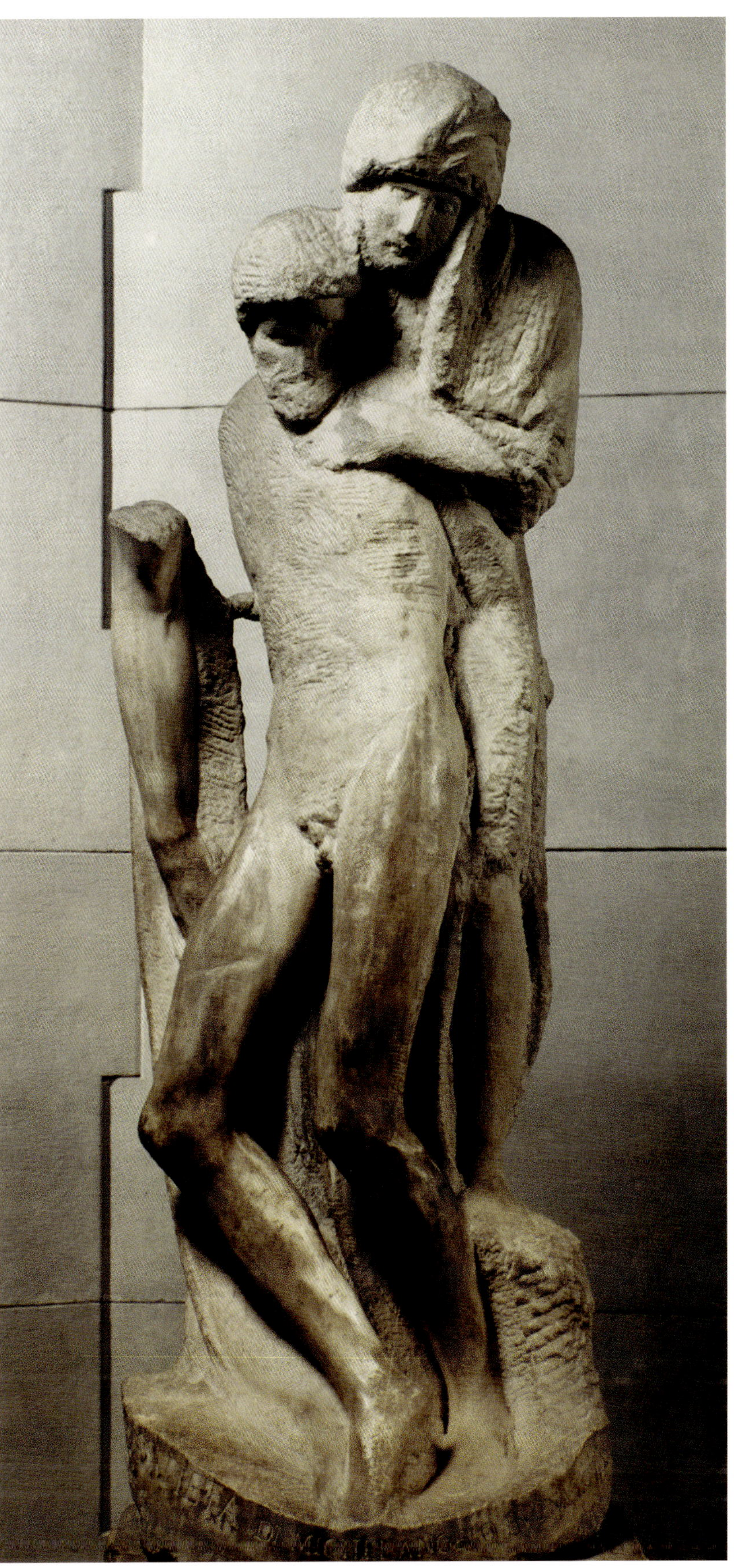

The Rondanini Pietà, 1552–64. Michelangelo worked on this statue from 1552 until six days before his death. Representing the Virgin Mary mourning her dead son, it contrasts with his Pietà of 1499. As he was feeling so ill, he hacked at the marble and the result became two slender, elongated figures that helped to inspire Mannerism.

EPILOGUE: MICHELANGELO'S LEGACY

A towering figure in the history of Western art and culture, Michelangelo is generally seen, along with Leonardo and Raphael, as one of the three giants of the High Renaissance, although he outlived them both by more than 40 years. He was devoted to his calling, and the art he produced, with its physical realism and psychological insight, was unprecedented. His influence has been profound, and his statues of *Pietà* and *David*, and his frescoes for the Sistine Chapel, are possibly the most famous works of art in the world. Several of his later works, including paintings, sculpture and architecture, initiated the Mannerist art and design movement. Among the most obvious artists who were influenced by him were Raphael, who closely followed his ideas after spying on Michelangelo's work in progress on the Sistine ceiling, while Pontormo (1494–1557), another contemporary, drew on the twisting figures of *The Last Judgement* and the frescoes of the Cappella Paolina. As well as the Mannerist movement, Baroque artists such as Peter Paul Rubens (1577–1640) and Gian Lorenzo Bernini (1598–1680) also developed their work from Michelangelo's ideas. Vasari wrote about Michelangelo's influence: '[His] work has proved a veritable beacon … of inestimable benefit to all painters, restoring light to a world that for centuries had been plunged into darkness. Indeed, painters no longer need to seek for new inventions, novel attitudes, clothed figures, fresh ways of expression, different arrangements, or sublime subjects.' In the nineteenth and twentieth centuries, the sculptures of Auguste Rodin (1840–1917), Camille Claudel (1864–1943) and Henry Moore (1898–1986) directly evolved from Michelangelo's examples. Meanwhile, in architecture, Michelangelo's foyer of the Laurentian Library was one of the first buildings to use classical forms in a dynamic way, while the dome of St Peter's inspired many other domes on churches and civic buildings across the world. Michelangelo first became a celebrity when he was in his early twenties, and his reputation as one of the greatest artists in history continues to this day.

The Kiss, *Auguste Rodin, 1888–98. During his first trip to Italy in 1875, Auguste Rodin studied the paintings and sculptures of Michelangelo intensely. On his return to Paris, his ensuing work was criticized for appearing too lifelike and he was accused of making a mould from a live model. The influence of Michelangelo remained with him throughout his life, especially the sense of natural movement and anatomical accuracy.*

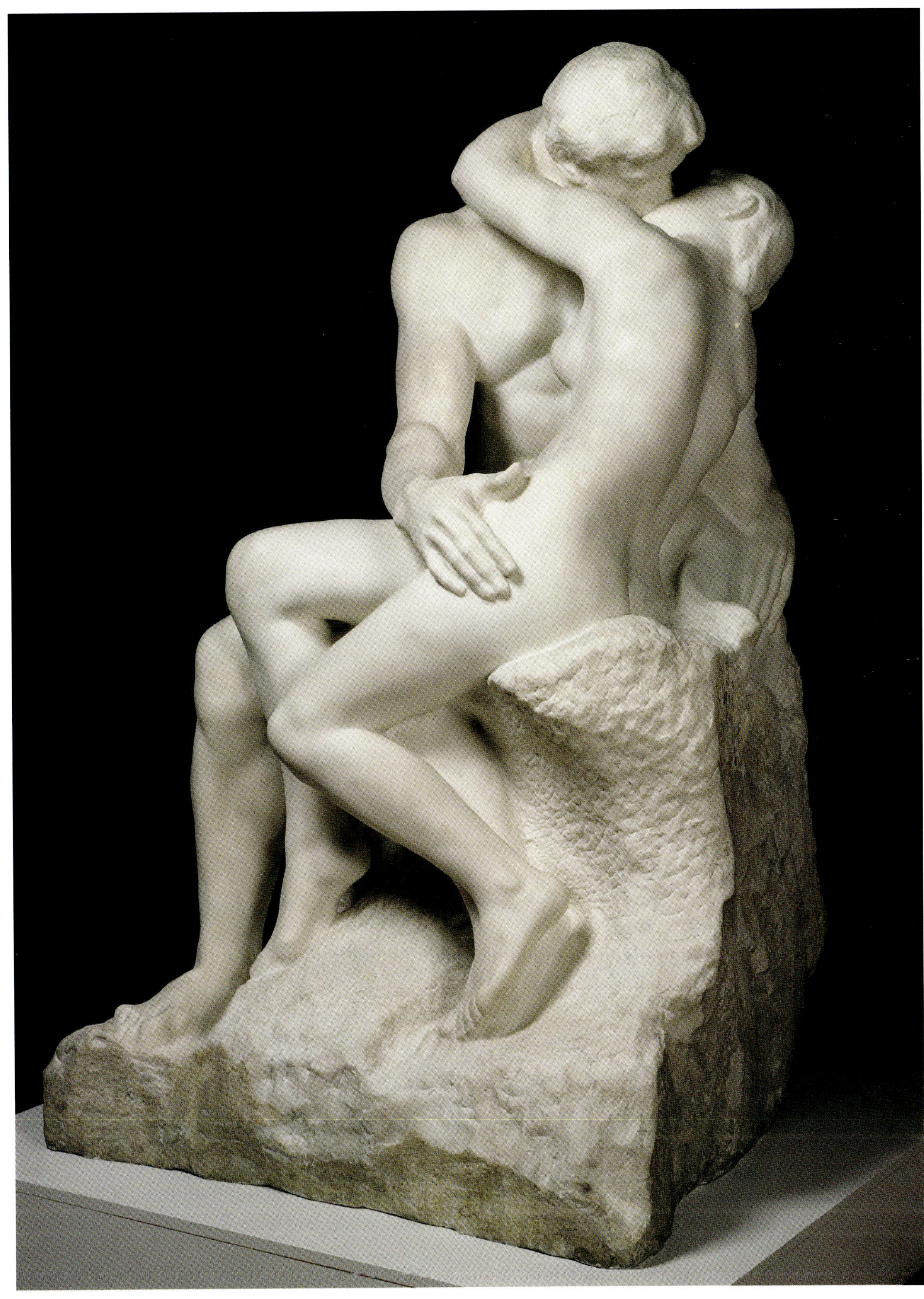

TIMELINE

1470s

1475–81 Michelangelo Buonarroti is born in Caprese on 6 March. His mother dies when he is six years old.

1480s

1485–8 At school, Michelangelo is taught by the Humanist Francesco da Urbino. His father remarries. He is apprenticed to the Ghirlandaio brothers in Florence.

1490s

1490–5 Michelangelo lives and works in the Medici household, but leaves when Lorenzo de' Medici dies. Lorenzo's son Piero asks him to return to the Medici court and create a snow statue, but through the rise of Savonarola, the Medici are expelled from Florence, and Michelangelo leaves for Bologna and Venice.

1497–9 Invited by Cardinal Raffaele Riario, Michelangelo moves to Rome. He visits the marble quarries of Carrara for the first time and creates the *Pietà* for the French cardinal Jean de Bilhères.

1500s

1502–4 On his return to Florence, Michelangelo is commissioned by the local authorities to produce a bronze David, now lost. He also creates a monumental marble statue of *David*, which is hugely admired and placed in front of the Palazzo della Signoria. He is commissioned to paint *The Battle of Cascina* in the Hall of the Great Council, near to another battle scene to be painted by Leonardo da Vinci.

1500s continued

'05 Michelangelo paints the *Doni Tondo*, and he sculpts a Madonna with the Christ Child (the *Bruges Madonna*) before he is summoned to Rome to build a tomb for Pope Julius. He spends eight months in Carrara selecting marble for the tomb.

'06 Furious that the Pope has given up his tomb project, Michelangelo returns to Florence in April, but in November, he reconciles with the Pope who orders a colossal bronze statue of himself for the city of Bologna. This takes Michelangelo over a year to execute.

1508–12 Pope Julius II commissions Michelangelo to paint his uncle's Sistine Chapel ceiling. Despite protests that he is a sculptor, not a painter, the Pope insists. The work takes Michelangelo four arduous years.

1510s

'13 Pope Julius II dies, but Michelangelo signs a new contract for his tomb with Julius's heirs. He carves marble statues of two slaves and Moses for the modified tomb.

'16 Michelangelo signs another contract for the Julius tomb. The new pope, Leo X, commissions him to design a façade for the Medici family church of San Lorenzo in Florence.

1517–20 Michelangelo spends most of the following three years in Carrara and Pietrasanta, quarrying marble for the façade of San Lorenzo and the Julius tomb. Suddenly, and with no explanation, Pope Leo X halts the making of the San Lorenzo façade.

1520s

'24 Still working on the Julius tomb when he can, Michelangelo begins work on a new Medici Chapel and the Laurentian Library in Florence, travelling to and from Carrara to select marble for the projects.

1527–30 During the Sack of Rome, the Florentine government appoints Michelangelo Governor and Procurator General of the city's fortifications. He is then sent to strengthen defences in Pisa, Livorno, Venice and Ferrara, and soon after he returns, Florence is taken by imperial forces. A death warrant is issued for him and he goes into hiding.

1530s

'32 After being pardoned by the Pope, Michelangelo moves to Rome. He signs a new contract with Julius's heirs for a smaller tomb, but falls out with them. He meets Tommaso de' Cavalieri, to whom he dedicates many poems and drawings.

1533–41 Michelangelo develops a close friendship with Vittoria Colonna and dedicates poems and drawings to her. Pope Clement commissions him to paint *The Last Judgement* on the Sistine Chapel altar wall. When Clement dies, the new Pope Paul III orders him to stop working on the Julius tomb and continue with *The Last Judgement*.

1540s–1550s

'42 Michelangelo starts painting *The Conversion of St Paul* in the Pauline Chapel.

1545–50 The Julius tomb is finally set up in San Pietro in Vincoli, Rome. Most of it is executed by other sculptors according to Michelangelo's plan, but he is unsatisfied with it. On finishing *The Conversion of St Paul*, he begins *The Crucifixion of St Peter*. In 1547, he begins *The Deposition* for his own tomb. Pope Paul III appoints him official architect of St Peter's Basilica and his close friend Vittoria Colonna dies.

1560s

'64 Still working hard, Michelangelo contracts a digestive ailment, and while feverish, he goes for a walk in the cold night air. He dies on 18 February. The Pope wants to have him buried in St Peter's Basilica, but Michelangelo's nephew and heir takes his body back to Florence where it is buried in Santa Croce.

FURTHER INFORMATION

Life, Letters and Poetry, G. Bull and P. Porter (translators) and Michelangelo, OUP Oxford, 2008
Lives of the Most Eminent Painters, Sculptors and Architects, G. du C. de Vere (translator) and Giorgio Vasari, Modern Library, 2007
Michelangelo (Basic Art Series), G. Néret, Taschen, 2007
Michelangelo: A Portrait of the Greatest Artist of the Italian Renaissance, W. E. Wallace, André Deutsch Ltd, 2018
Michelangelo and the Pope's Ceiling, R. King, Pimlico, 2006
Michelangelo: His Epic Life, M. Gayford, Fig Tree, Penguin Random House UK, 2013
Michelangelo, The Complete Paintings, Sculptures and Architecture, F. Zöllner, C. Thoenes and T. Pöpper, Taschen, 2017
Michelangelo, The Graphic Work, Taschen, 2017.

LIST OF ILLUSTRATIONS

Page 28
View of the City of Rome, in the *Nuremberg Chronicle*, Hartmann Schedel (author), Michael Wolgemut (illustrator), Wilhelm Pleydenwurff (illustrator), 1493, woodcut. Wikimedia Commons.

Page 29
Bacchus, 1496–7, marble, 203 cm (80 in), Museo Nazionale del Bargello, Florence, Italy. Bridgeman Images.

Detail of satyr from above sculpture. akg-images/ Rabatti&Domingie.

Page 31
The Madonna and Child with St John and Angels (The Manchester Madonna), *c.* 1497, possibly as early as 1494, tempera on wood, 104.5 × 77 cm (41⅛ × 30⅓ in), The National Gallery, London, UK. akg-images/World History Archive.

Pages 32–3
Pietà, 1498–9, marble, 174 × 195 × 69 cm (68½ × 76¾ × 27⅛ in), St Peter's Basilica, Rome, Italy. Photo © Luisa Ricciarini/Bridgeman Images.

Page 32: Detail of the above. Bridgeman Images.

Page 34
The Entombment, 1500–1, tempera on panel, 161.7 × 149.9 cm (63⅔ × 59 in), The National Gallery, London, UK. Bridgeman Images.

Page 35
Photograph of the Carrara quarries in Tuscany. Shutterstock Images.

Page 36
St Paul, 1501–4, marble, 127 cm (50 in), Piccolomini altarpiece, Duomo, Siena, Italy. Photo © Raffaello Bencini/Bridgeman Images.

St Peter, 1501–4, marble, height: 127 cm (50 in), Piccolomini Altarpiece, Duomo, Siena, Italy. Photo © Nicolò Orsi Battaglini/ Bridgeman Images.

Page 37
Study for David with his Sling, 1503–4, pen and ink on paper,

37 cm × 19.5 cm (14½ × 7⅔ in), Department of Prints and Drawings, Musée du Louvre, Paris, France. Bridgeman Images.

Page 38
David, 1501–4, marble, 5.17 m (17 ft), Galleria dell'Accademia, Florence, Italy. akg-images/Andrea Jemolo.

Page 40
David's head, detail of above sculpture. Bridgeman Images.

David's hand, detail of above sculpture. Photo © Luisa Ricciarini/Bridgeman Images.

Page 41
Madonna of Bruges, *c.* 1504–5, marble, height 128 cm (50⅓ in), Church of Our Lady, Bruges, Belgium. Photo © Paul Maeyaert/ Bridgeman Images.

Page 42
Study for the Battle of Anghiari, Leonardo da Vinci, 1503–4, pen and ink on paper, 16.5 × 15.3 cm (6½ × 6 in), Gallerie dell'Accademia, Venice, Italy. Bridgeman Images.

The Battle of Cascina or *The Bathers*, after Michelangelo, Aristotile da Sangallo, 1542, 77 × 130 cm (30⅓ × 51 in), Holkham Hall, Leicester, UK. Bridgeman Images.

Page 43
A seated male nude twisting around, 1504–5, pen and brown ink with brown and grey wash and lead white, 41.9 × 28.6 cm (16½ × 11¼ in), The British Museum, London, UK. Bridgeman Images.

Page 44
Nude studies of a forward- and a right-facing man, *c.* 1504, pen and brown ink over preliminary drawing in black chalk, 27 × 19.6 cm (10⅔ × 7¾ in), Graphic Collection Albertina, Vienna, Austria. akg-images.

Page 45
Holy Family with the Infant St John the Baptist (Doni Tondo), 1505–6, tempera grassa on wood, diameter 120 cm (47¼ in),

Galleria degli Uffizi, Florence, Italy. Bridgeman Images.

Page 46
Portrait of Pope Julius II, Raphael, *c.* 1511, oil on panel, 108.7 × 81 cm (42¾ × 31⅞ in), National Gallery, London, UK. Bridgeman Images.

Page 47
Design for the Tomb of Pope Julius II, *c.* 1505–6, pen and brown ink, brush and brown wash over stylus ruling and lead-point, 51 × 31.9 cm (20 × 12½ in), Metropolitan Museum of Art, New York, USA. Rogers Fund, 1962.

Page 48
St Matthew, 1505–6, marble, 216 cm (85 in), Galleria dell'Accademia, Florence, Italy. akg-images/Rabatti&Domingie.

Page 49
A letter written from Rome by Michelangelo in 1509 to his father in Florence, The British Museum, London, UK. Granger/Bridgeman Images.

Page 50
Scheme for the Sistine Chapel ceiling, *c.* 1508, pen and brown ink over a sketch in lead point and stylus (vault study); black chalk (arms and hands) on paper, 27.4 × 38.6 cm (10¾ × 15⅛ in), British Museum, London, UK. Bridgeman Images.

Page 51
Study for the Libyan Sibyl, *c.* 1510–11, red chalk on paper, 28.9 × 21.4 cm (11⅜ × 8½ in), The Metropolitan Museum of Art, New York, USA. Purchase, Joseph Pulitzer Bequest, 1924.

Pages 52–3
The Sistine Chapel ceiling, 1508–12, fresco, 40 m × 14 m (131 ft 3 in × 45 ft 11 in), Vatican Museums and Galleries, Vatican City, Rome, Italy. akg-images/Erich Lessing.

Page 54
Detail of an *ignudi*, 1509, fresco, Sistine Chapel ceiling, Vatican Museums and Galleries, Vatican City, Rome, Italy. Bridgeman Images.

Study for Adam, 1511, dark red chalk over stylus underdrawing on paper, 19.3 × 25.9 cm (7½ × 10 ⅛ in), The British Museum, London, UK. akg-images.

Page 55
Judith and Holofernes, 1509, fresco, Sistine Chapel ceiling, Vatican Museums and Galleries, Vatican City, Rome, Italy. akg-images/Erich Lessing.

Page 56
The Creation of the Sun, Moon and Plants, 1511, fresco, Sistine Chapel ceiling, Vatican Museums and Galleries, Vatican City, Rome, Italy. akg-images/Erich Lessing.

Page 57
The Fall of Man and *The Expulsion from Paradise*, fresco, 1508–12, Sistine Chapel ceiling, Vatican Museums and Galleries, Vatican City, Rome, Italy. Bridgeman Images.

The Creation of Eve, 1508–10, fresco, Sistine Chapel ceiling, Vatican Museums and Galleries, Vatican City, Rome, Italy. akg-images/Erich Lessing.

Page 58
The Prophet Jeremiah, *c.* 1508–12, fresco, Sistine Chapel ceiling, Vatican Museums and Galleries, Vatican City, Rome, Italy. © Mondadori Electa/Bridgeman Images.

Page 59
The Cumaean Sibyl, 1510, fresco, Sistine Chapel ceiling, Vatican Museums and Galleries, Vatican City, Rome, Italy. Bridgeman Images.

Page 60
The Delphic Sibyl, 1509, fresco, Sistine Chapel ceiling, Vatican Museums and Galleries, Vatican City, Rome, Italy. © Mondadori Portfolio/ Bridgeman Images.

Pages 60–1
The Flood, 1508–12, fresco, Sistine Chapel ceiling, Vatican Museums and Galleries, Vatican, Rome, Italy. akg-images/Erich Lessing.

INDEX